Mutiny in the

Civil War

By
Webb Garrison

WHITE MANE BOOKS
SHIPPENSBURG, PENNSYLVANIA

Unless otherwise noted, illustrations are from the author's collection.

This White Mane Books publication
was printed by
Beidel Printing House, Inc.
63 West Burd Street
Shippensburg, PA 17257-0152 USA

In respect for the scholarship contained herein, the acid-free paper used in this book meets the guidelines for permanence and durability of the Committee on Production Guidelines for Book Longevity of the Council on Library Resources.

For a complete list of available publications
please write
White Mane Books
Division of White Mane Publishing Company, Inc.
P.O. Box 152
Shippensburg, PA 17257-0152 USA

Library of Congress Cataloging-in-Publication Data

Garrison, Webb B.
   Mutiny in the Civil War / by Webb Garrison.
      p. cm.
   Includes bibliographical references (p.) and index.
   ISBN 1-57249-215-5 (alk. paper)
   1. United States. Army--History--Civil War, 1861-1865. 2. Confederate States of America. Army--History. 3. Mutiny--United States--History--19th century. 4. Military discipline--United States--History--19th century. 5. United States--History--Civil War, 1861-1865--Social aspects. 6. Soldiers--United States--Social conditions--19th century. 7. Social classes--United States--History--19th century. I. Title.

E491 .G37 2001
973.7'13--dc21
                                                                                    00-051253

Contents

Introduction

This study was triggered by a single sentence penned by a distinguished scholar. In his volume entitled *They Fought for the Union*, Francis A. Lord, Ph.D., devoted a single column to mutiny. It begins with the statement that "Mutiny in the Federal army was rare after 1861."

Having years ago launched a personal filing system that deals almost exclusively with topics rather than battles and generals, upon coming across Lord's comment I looked into my mutiny file and found references to several dozen incidents. Most of them occurred in ranks of fighting men in blue—not because they were less respectful of authority than their foes in gray, but because immense quantities of Confederate records have been destroyed or lost.

Lord's too-hasty verdict suggested that mutiny deserved a detailed look. It has taken more than twenty years to bring that inquiry to conclusion, of sorts. Any statement concerning the number and nature of mutinies that took place during four years of war must be qualified. Despite the Articles of War and Acts of Congress, commanders used their own judgment in deciding whether or not to treat an incident as a mutiny. Some commanders were lenient, while others were tough. Many a general officer tried to avoid the risk of having his own leadership questioned in the aftermath of a mutiny, so used soft words in describing resistance to his authority. Others seem almost to have been eager for an opportunity to engage in very public washing of dirty military linen.

It's an oversimplification to suggest that "an act of mutiny was anything that a commander treated as such." Yet that comes very close to the truth. The issue is also complicated by the fact that physical action such as stacking arms without orders could signal that a mutiny was in progress, whether or not the term was applied to it. Numerous clearly mutinous actions were treated, not as mutinies, but as "disaffections" or "refusals to obey orders." Yet some military and naval officers used "mutiny" to label a disturbance such as a revolt of coal miners against foremen and mine owners.

Outbreak of the American Revolution forced the Continental Congress to establish a military force and to frame standards of discipline. As one important aspect of this move, Articles of War borrowed from Britain with little change were adopted. These initially consisted of "101 rules and articles" that stipulated in detail the government of armies.

During the reign of King Richard II in the fourteenth century, *Statutes, Ordinances and Customs* of the armed forces constituted one of the earliest published English-language codes of its sort. Three centuries later it was supplanted by the *Laws and Ordinances of Warre,* but the Articles of War were not formulated until much later. On July 30, 1775, American lawmakers adopted the English Mutiny Act with no significant changes. This dated from the reign of William and Mary, and was enacted by Parliament in 1689 as a reaction to a serious mutiny in England's armed forces.

At Morristown, New Jersey, two thousand soldiers of the Pennsylvania Line joined in mutiny on January 1, 1781. Before the month ended, men of the New Jersey Line also revolted. Though covered by the Mutiny Act that carried the death penalty, these uprisings were so clearly caused by scarcities of food and other essentials that Congress took a direct hand in dealing with them.

Commissioners met with Pennsylvania Line mutineers very early in 1781. They tried to meet reasonable demands and disbanded numerous units. Revolt against authority among soldiers of the New Jersey Line was quickly quelled and two mutineers were executed. Lawmakers subsequently wrestled on numerous occasions with what constitutes mutiny and how it should be punished.

Though mutiny was dreaded by ships' masters at least as much as a slave uprising was feared by plantation owners, it wasn't until 1806 that Congress decreed that "if any person in the navy shall make, or attempt to make any mutinous assembly, he shall, on conviction thereof by a court martial, suffer death."

Six years earlier, Congress has taken another hard look at mutiny in military forces. Legislation passed on April 23, 1800, stipulated:

> any officer or soldier who shall begin, excite, cause or join in any
> mutiny or sedition, in any troop or company in the service of the
> United States, or in any party, post, detachment or guard, shall
> suffer death, or such other punishment as by a court martial shall
> be inflicted.

A number of significant deviations from the principles and procedures established by the U.S. Congress will be noted in the accounts included herewith. In practice, a double standard prevailed. Officers who refused to obey orders or engaged in other acts of rebellion were treated quite differently from enlisted men who committed the same offense.

Again, courts-martial considered evidence and rendered punishments for mutiny only occasionally. A group of officers often considered evidence and meted out punishment without benefit of a formal inquiry. In some cases, men considered to be mutineers were shot immediately after their offense upon orders of a commander. Other commanders quickly quelled mutineers and put men back into the ranks without having consulted their superiors.

During the second session of the Second Confederate Congress, detailed legislation concerning mutiny was passed. Under its terms, the death penalty was eliminated and a fine plus imprisonment was substituted. In theory, even these punishments could not be imposed upon Rebel soldiers without trial by a military court or court-martial. In practice, commanders continued to arrive at quick verdicts and to mete out justice as they saw fit.

Among Federal forces, a commanding general in the field was given authority previously reserved to the President. Under terms of a March, 1863, statute a commander was authorized to approve or disapprove of sentences imposed upon mutineers by courts-martial. Reading of a small number of cases described in these cases will show that many punishments were carried out without having consulted the commander of an army.

The vast majority of mutinous incidents described here are documented in the Official Records (OR). Sources of a handful that do not appear in the OR are indicated. Many names here listed in full appear in abbreviated form in the text, but have been found in indices to individual volumes of the OR the massive volume cumulated index.

Abbreviations

ACW	*America's Civil War* magazine
ALE	Neely, *The Abraham Lincoln Encyclopedia*
AMB	McHenry, *Webster's American Military Biographies*
B	Boatner, *The Civil War Dictionary*
B&G	*Blue & Gray* magazine
B&L	*Battles and Leaders of the Civil War*
CMH	*Confederate Military History*
CV	*Confederate Veteran*
CW	Basler, ed., *The Collected Works of Abraham Lincoln*
CWT	*Civil War Times*
D	Dyer, *Compendium*
DxD	Long, *The Civil War Day by Day*
E	Faust, ed., *Encyclopedia*
EC	Current, ed., *Encyclopedia of the Confederacy*
GB	Warner, *Generals in Blue*
GG	Warner, *Generals in Gray*
JSHS	*Southern Historical Society Papers*
LDD	Miers, ed., *Lincoln Day by Day*
Lee's	Freeman, *Lee's Lieutenants*
LL	*Lincoln Lore*
MOLLUS	Military Order of the Loyal Legion of the United States
NOR	*Official Records of the Union and Confederate Navies*, 30 volumes, are cited with a series number (expressed in roman numerals), followed by a volume number, and page number(s).
OR	*The War of the Rebellion: Official Records of the Union and Confederate Armies,* 127 volumes, are cited with a series number (expressed in roman numerals), followed by a volume number, part number (if applicable), and page number(s).
PCM	Proceedings, Court-martial Sgt. William Walker
REL	Freeman, *Robert E. Lee*
RR	Moore, ed., *The Rebellion Record* (d = diary; doc = documents; p = poetry and incidents)
WWW	Sifakis, *Who Was Who in the Civil War*

Part I

Pay–Low, Slow, or None

1

Wrong Color Skin–William Walker, January 11, 1863

Findings and Sentence of General Court-Martial
Hdqrs. Department of the South

HILTON HEAD, *S.C., JANUARY 11, 1864*

I. At the general court-martial which convened at Hilton Head, S.C., Sgt. William Walker, Co. A., [PCM] South Carolina Volunteers, was arraigned and tried.

CHARGE — Mutiny

Specifications: 1st—On August 23, 1863, he did join in a mutiny at Seabrook Wharf when on detail, and did not go to camp when ordered to do so by 1st Lt. Geo. W. Wood.

2nd—On August 23, 1863, he did use threatening language to 1st Lt. Geo. W. Wood, saying that "I will shoot him."

[PCM]—On November 19, 1863, he did unlawfully take command of his Company A, and did march the same with others of the regiment in front of his commanding officer's tent and there ordered them to stack arms and when his Comdg. Officer Lt. Col. A. G. Bennett inquired of the Regiment what all this meant, he, the said Sgt. William Walker replied: "We will not do duty any longer for ($7) seven dollars per month." When they were remonstrated with and ordered to take up their arms and return to duty, he, the said William Walker, did order his Co. A. to let their arms alone and go to their quarters, which they did, thereby exciting and joining in a general mutiny.

II   FINDING OF THE COURT

The court having maturely considered the evidence adduced, finds the accused as follows:

OF ALL CHARGES, "Guilty"

3

III   SENTENCE

And the court does, therefore, sentence him, the said William Walker, Co. A, [PCM] S.C. Regiment (two thirds of the members concurring) to be shot to death with musketry at such time and place as the Commanding General may direct. [PCM]

This record does not appear in the OR, but a 28-page handwritten transcript of the court-martial is held by the National Archives. The abbreviated segment of it here has been set in type widely used for such documents that do appear in the OR. At least nine men named William Walker appear in the OR: a bushwhacker, a major in the 13th Iowa; a major in the 27th Massachusetts; a Rebel sea captain; a captain in the C.S. 1st Artillery, Army of Alabama; a civilian living in Van Buren, Arkansas; and a Unionist guerrilla branded by his foes as "notorious." Five William Walkers are found in naval records, but none is the subject of the military trial. [NOR, 1-27; NOR, 2, 1-3]

It is impossible to determine whether the omission of the William Walker who was convicted and executed for mutiny was omitted from the OR deliberately or by chance. Had he not rebelled over pay, the sergeant would have been another obscure ex-slave who was willing to put his life on the line for the Union.

As best he could tell, Walker was born about 1841 near Hilton Head or near Savannah, Georgia. As a youngster, he became familiar with coastal waters of Georgia and South Carolina. It is all but certain that he served as a pilot for vessels of the U.S. Navy during the winter of 1862-63. His name does not appear in the record in this connection, however. That was typical, rather than unusual. Hundreds of American Indians are cited in the OR by name. Though great numbers of ex-slaves aided Federal forces by giving information and serving as guides and pilots, such a person is normally cited only as "a black," or "a contraband" and is nowhere identified by name.

Cmdr. John F. Worden of the USS *Montauk* filed a February 2, 1863, report concerning actions of his vessel from January 24 through that date. Under date of January 28 he wrote:

> I learned through the medium of a contraband, who has been employed upon these waters as a pilot, the position of the obstructions below the fort [McAllister] and the location of the torpedoes placed upon the spiling (*spelling as in original))* in the channel way. This information, with the aid of the contraband, whom I took on board, enabled me to take up a position nearer the fort in the next attack upon it. [NOR, 13, 627-28]

That next attack took place on February 28, after the *Montauk* had been joined by the *Daffodil, Dawn, Seneca, Wissahickon,* and

Dawn. Meanwhile the *Seneca* had discovered the Rebel blockade runner *Nashville* (also known as the *Rattlesnake*) stranded in Georgia's Big Ogeechee River not far from the fort. [NOR, 1, 13, 628]

In the fight that lasted for much of the day, Fort McAllister did not suffer major damage. However, the 1,221-ton *Nashville* was destroyed by fire from the Federal warships. Worden rejoiced that he had been able to take part in "final disposition of a vessel which has so long been in the minds of the public as a troublesome pest." Rear Adm. Samuel F. DuPont quickly congratulated Worden, saying that he, too, felt "extremely gratified at being rid of the *Nashville*." During the engagement the *Montauk*

Cmdr. John L. Worden of the USS *Montauk*
Harper's History of the Great Rebellion

was hit under her bottom and suffered significant damage. [NOR, 696–98, 701–11; NOR, 2, 1, 261]

During his court-martial, Walker testified with pride that he had served the U.S. Navy as a pilot. He was aboard the *Montauk* on the day she and her fellow warships engaged the *Nashville*, he said. According to the man accused of mutiny, it made his heart glad to see the blockade runner so badly damaged that her powder magazine caught fire and she went down after a tremendous explosion. [PCM]

A few months earlier, during the preceding August, Gen. Rufus Saxton had been given the go-ahead to recruit five thousand black soldiers. It's unlikely that he bothered to keep up with what was being done by the U.S. Congress; few commanders had the time or the inclination to keep a watch upon the capital.

On July 16, Congress passed its Second Confiscation Act. It labeled all slaves who fled from their masters into Union lines as "captives of war" who were to be treated as freedmen. This bill was then and is now seen as the first specific step toward emancipation. It included a provision concerning one of Abraham Lincoln's most cherished notions—that any ex-slave who agreed to go to an overseas colony should receive free transportation.

Language of the act included a direct warning to slave holders. Any of them who did not surrender to Federal forces by September 15 would be penalized by having their slaves set free. Provisions of the Fugitive Slave Act, under which all runaways were required to be returned to their owners, remained in force so far as the border states of Kentucky, Missouri, Maryland, and Delaware were concerned.

Military commanders who read newspaper accounts or received brief summaries of the Confiscation Act took it to mean that they were free to put some ex-slaves into uniform. Those who received a digest of the Militia Act passed late in July were reasonably well informed on the subject. Under terms of the second Congressional edict, the President was authorized to receive blacks "into the service of the United States" so that they could perform "any military or naval service" for which they were found competent.

At Hilton Head, Saxton's August authorization to bring a substantial number of ex-slaves into the volunteer military services was based upon Congressional actions taken during the previous month. Saxton and some of his officers were ready to act. There is a widespread notion according to which no South Carolina unit entered Federal service. This view overlooks what took place at the enormous Federal base deep inside the Confederacy.

Beaufort was the county seat located at the edge of Port Royal, scene of the November, 1861, Federal naval victory widely known as Hilton Head. Just 15 months after that spectacular victory, on January 31, 1863, the 1st South Carolina Volunteers (African descent) was organized at Beaufort. Early in 1864 the unit's name was changed to the 33rd U.S. Colored Troops.

In May, 1861, the 2nd South Carolina Volunteers (African descent) was organized at Beaufort and Hilton Head. It became the 34th U.S. Colored Troops on February 8, 1864. Sparse and sometimes inaccurate records make it impossible to know precisely how many men were included in these two black regiments. Neither is it possible to determine what percent of these troops were willing

After its capture, Port Royal became a huge Federal supply depot.
Library of Congress

volunteers and how many had been forcibly impressed. Like all units of their sort, they had white officers. Many if not most of these officers moved into black regiments for the sake of the promotions that they received in the process. [D, 3, 1636]

As a riverboat pilot, Walker was exempt from any form of duress that could have been exerted to put him into uniform. He seems to have talked over the matter of his future with his wife, Rebecca, several times. They came to agreement on the fact that service in Federal forces seemed to offer him the best chance for a decent life. Thousands of their fellow blacks who had been slaves on the coastal islands were now without homes, without jobs, without food and without hope for the future.

One month after the 2nd South Carolina Volunteers was formally organized, the third regiment of this sort came into existence at Hilton Head and Beaufort. History of the unit is difficult to follow because it became the 21st U.S. Colored Troops in March, 1864. One thing about this regiment is certain, however. On April 24 Walker signed up for a three-year hitch in the new regiment before it was given a number or officers. Possibly because of his experience as a pilot he entered military life, not as a private, but as a sergeant in Company A. [D, 3, 1636; PCM]

It is equally possible that his rank, high for a black volunteer, stemmed from the fact that he was about 5'7" tall, extremely muscular, and showed no evidence of mixed racial ancestry. He was illiterate, unable even to scrawl a portion of his name, but to white officers he looked like "better fighting material" than the average black South Carolina volunteer.

At the time he made his mark in order to become a Federal soldier, Walker was probably told about pay and benefits. Under terms of the Militia Act, he was entitled to $10 per month in cash minus $3 per month for clothing. Saxton and officers who were moving into black units clearly knew exactly what the black volunteers—non-commissioned officers included—could expect from the government that was happy to get their services.

Walker had not been wearing the insignia of a sergeant for more than two months before he got word that agitated him so badly he could not sleep. White soldiers at Beaufort, Hilton Head, and everywhere else in the Union, were paid $10 per month in cash plus a $3.50 cash clothing allowance. They could use the latter as they pleased. Skilled and knowledgeable pilots, black or white, were in great demand. Civilian ships' captains and naval commanders were in desperate need of such men. There is no record of what Walker had been paid as a river pilot, but it is virtually certain that he received more than 50 cents per day.

This matter, plus the rank of which he was proud and keenly conscious, probably caused him soon to begin to exhibit what white officers called "an insubordinate disposition." Four months after he began a new chapter in the story of his life, Walker had a dispute with 1st Lt. George W. Wood. For reasons unknown he and some of his comrades were ordered by Wood to remain on detail after they believed they had served their time. The coal-black sergeant muttered that he believed he'd go back to camp instead of remaining on duty. Wood gave him a peremptory order to stay where he was, and later charged that Walker grumbled that he'd like to shoot his lieutenant.

Sgt. William Walker. Many Federal commanders didn't want black soldiers, of whom this man was typical.

National Archives

There is no record that the incident resulted in an official inquiry. Yet when Walker was on trial for his life, Lt. Adolf Bessy testified at length about the incident. His recollection was not sufficiently clear for members of the court to decide whether the quarrel was started by Walker or by Wood, however. In spite of his fuzzy memory concerning details, Bessy stressed that the sergeant had a gun in his hand at one time and repeatedly threatened to shoot Wood.

Though this fracas did not result in disciplinary action, it made Walker a marked man whom officers felt should be watched closely. A few days before or after this incident, the sergeant and his fellow volunteers each received from the paymaster their $7 per month for time served.

By then it would have been all but impossible for them to be unaware that they were getting a trifle more than half as much cash as white volunteers. Many men of the 3rd, still stationed at Hilton Head, probably muttered to themselves and grumbled to their comrades and relatives about the gross inequity. Walker almost certainly heard such talk, and probably initiated it at times. No man to take an injustice lying down, he began making plans about dealing with it. To make matters worse, no paymaster made his appearance during a period of more than three months.

On November 19, Walker decided that he'd had enough. He apparently did not stage a protest about not having received his pay for 90 days. Instead, in action somewhat like that of black militants more than a century later, he created a furor over inequities in the pay scales of blacks and whites. At a point close to the headquarters tent of Lt. Col. Augustus Bennett, he created a great commotion over the fact that he and his comrades were being treated little if any better than during their slavery years.

Angry words were exchanged between the black sergeant, speaking for a file of men who stood behind him, and his commanding officer. Bennett may or may not have known that the unequal pay scale had been adopted by Congress. He clearly felt that he could not and would not put up with another instance of insubordination on the part of a troublemaker. Both men shouted; Bennett turned his back and returned to his quarters, and Walker reputedly gave a signal to the men who had accompanied him. At the signal, all of them stacked their arms and the sergeant was said to have led them, weaponless, back to their camp. [PCM]

To Bennett, Walker was guilty of having incited a mutiny. He quickly put his views on the record, consulted with superiors, and placed the unruly sergeant under arrest. The sergeant remained in custody for the two months that intervened before a formal court-martial was convened at Hilton Head.

Seven white officers made up the jury whose responsibility it was to determine the guilt or innocence of William Walker. Lt. Samuel L. Alford of the 8th Maine served as judge advocate and Lt. J. A. Smith of the 47th New York was appointed to defend the accused. During examinations and cross-examinations, the sergeant expressed fervent patriotism. He and his fellow members of the 3rd South Carolina didn't know hardly anything at all about military rules, he explained. According to him, officers gave black volunteers some instructions and lots of orders, but "didn't say much else about anything at all."

Given an opportunity to speak in his defense, Walker held his head high with pride as he briefly summarized his career as a pilot for the U.S. Navy. "For sure," he said, "I didn't give Colonel Bennett no back talk. I did just like he said. I picked up my arms and went back to the Company A street." [PCM]

There is no record that any other member of the regiment was charged. Some of them gave fuzzy testimony about events that took place on the momentous day in November. None of them had a clear memory about the first and second specifications, which grew out of charges leveled by Wood. Though the proceedings were lengthy, it took the panel of judges only a short while to reach their verdict.

Reduced to the rank of private, Walker went along when his regiment was ordered to Jacksonville, Florida, shortly after the trial. They went as soldiers who would receive $7 per month in cash; he went in irons. As part of the verdict of the court-martial, it was noted that the sergeant was owed $21 in back pay. This did not go to his widow, however, for his record said that he was responsible for the loss of "a Prussian musket complete with bayonet" plus a cartridge belt and 40 rounds of ammunition. In addition, he was in debt to the United States in the amount of $59.06—the value of clothing issued to him. [PCM]

On January 11, 1864, the former pilot who had incited mutiny over low pay and no pay was shot to death by musketry. A few white officers had joined black regiments because they sincerely believed that military service would help to lift former slaves out of poverty and misery. Col. Thomas Wentworth Higginson of the 1st South Carolina (Colored) was an ordained Unitarian minister who had for a time served as a captain in the 51st Massachusetts. He registered his personal indignation at the way "the Walker mutiny" was handled. During postwar years he told friends that the sergeant's real offense was having the "wrong color skin."

Col. Robert Gould Shaw of the 54th Massachusetts—first black regiment recruited in the North—was much more vocal than Higginson. He, too, was ignored at Hilton Head and in Washington. Gov. John A. Andrew of Massachusetts was usually heard clearly and loudly in the capital. This time, his commentary upon military

Men executed by a firing squad often sat upon their own coffins.
Library of Congress

life had no effect. Having learned from Shaw and Higginson what had transpired in the state where secession began, Andrew became furious about William Walker's one-man mutiny over pay. Of it he wrote that "The Government which found no law to pay him except as a nondescript and a contraband, nevertheless found law enough to shoot him as a soldier." [Berlin, 394-95]

Col. Robert G. Shaw led the famous 54th Massachusetts.
Harper's History of the Great Rebellion

Col. Thomas W. Higginson, commander of the 1st South Carolina—a regiment made up entirely of ex-slaves

The assault of the 54th Massachusetts upon Fort Wagner, near Charleston, was featured in the motion picture *Glory*.

2

Princely Paymaster–John Charles Fremont, Summer, 1861

HEADQUARTERS WESTERN DEPARTMENT
Saint Louis, July 30, 1861
The President of the United States:

My Dear Sir: You were kind enough to say that if occasions of sufficient gravity arose I might send you a private note.

I have found this command in disorder, nearly every county in an insurrectionary condition, and the enemy advancing in force by different points of the southern frontier. . . .

Our troops have not been paid, and some regiments are in a state of mutiny, and the men whose terms of service have expired generally refuse to enlist. I lost a fine regiment last night from inability to pay them a portion of the money due. This regiment had been intended to move on a critical post last night. The Treasurer of the United States has here $300,000 entirely unappropriated. I applied yesterday to him for $100,000 for my paymaster, General [T. P.] Andrews, but was refused. We have not an hour for delay. . . . This morning I will order the treasurer to deliver the money in his possession to General Andrews, and will send a force to the treasury to take the money . . . I trust to you for support.

With respect and regard, I am, yours, truly,

J. C. FREMONT
Major-General, Commanding

[OR I, 3, 416–17; Greeley, 1, 584; Foley, MOLLUS, 5, 487]

There is no record that the President responded to this report concerning unlawful action by a major general. He probably reasoned that no reply was necessary; in the two or more days it would have

13

taken for a message to reach Fremont from the capital, money seized by force would have been handed out to troops and spent by them. Years later, the general who had raided the U.S. Treasury pretended to believe that failure to hear from Lincoln meant that his actions were given tacit approval. [B&L, 1, 280]

Sent to serve as a battlefield general, the one-time candidate for the presidency had become a paymaster on a big scale. No action comparable to his was taken later during the conflict, despite the fact that pay was often a source of major problems in Federal and Confederate forces alike. Fremont's subsequent conduct suggests that Lincoln's failure sternly to rebuke him or to take severe disciplinary measures may have caused the ego of the self-appointed paymaster to swell even larger.

Barely five years earlier, the man famous as The Pathfinder was far more widely known than was attorney Lincoln of Springfield, Illinois. Fremont won the Republican nomination in 1856 and became the party's first candidate for the presidency. Lincoln, who at that time had not held an elective office for seven years after serving one term in the House of Representatives, was an ardent backer of Fremont. His enthusiasm is clearly indicated by the fact that he made an estimated 50 speeches on behalf of the candidate. [ALE, 118]

It was one thing to campaign for the loser in 1856 as a citizen holding no office. It was quite a different matter to deal with the famous and fiery Pathfinder as the 16th President who by virtue of office was commander in chief of Federal armed forces. Very early in his administration, Lincoln began wondering what to do with Fremont. His prominence plus his military experience meant that he could not be ignored. Lincoln would have sent him to France as minister to that nation had not William H. Seward, secretary of state, opposed such a plan. On July 3, 1861, Fremont became commander of the military Department of the West, with headquarters in St. Louis. [CW, 4, 420]

The same day, Adj. Gen. Lorenzo Thomas issued General Order No. 40. It stipulated that the State of Illinois plus all states and territories west of the Mississippi River and east of the Rocky Mountains would be included in the new department. This edict put Fremont in control of a region of enormous size. Writing about his vast responsibility years later, he claimed:

> For reasons not wholly military, the President reserved the State of Kentucky, but assured me that so soon as I had succeeded in raising and organizing an army for the descent of the Mississippi river, he would extend my command over that State and the left bank of the Mississippi. [B&L, 1, 278]

Evidence by which to know positively whether this was wishful thinking or an accurate interpretation of Lincoln's long-range plan does not exist.

Less than a week after assuming command at St. Louis he raided U.S. Treasury offices in the city in the name of soldiers' pay. Years earlier, he had shown disdain for accepted rules of military conduct. During the conflict with Mexico over California he played a significant role in forming the short-lived Bear Flag Republic. Its Anglo inhabitants were eager to make it a part of the United States. Both Com. Robert F. Stockton and Gen. Stephen W. Kearny wanted control of the region. [OR I, 3, 390]

Stockton named Fremont as governor, but after two months in that office he was arrested by Kearny. According to the general, Major Fremont was guilty of mutiny, disobedience, and conduct prejudicial to military order. A lengthy court-martial that stretched from late 1847 into early 1848 ended with a verdict adverse to Fremont and a sentence that the military jury judged appropriate. Though President James K. Polk suspended the sentence, the man who was widely revered as "father of California" resigned from the army in protest.

He held huge estates in the region taken from Mexico, whose gold made him extremely wealthy. Having gained international fame as an explorer much earlier, it was natural that in 1856 the fledgling Republican Party should choose him as its first presidential candidate. [AMB, 131]

Fremont's loss to Franklin Buchanan had not diminished his national stature—or his enormous ego. Five days before reaching St. Louis, he ignored regulations and named Richard M. Corwine as his judge advocate general. Though Corwine served for about six months, he never received a commission. In January, 1862, the President requested the secretary of war to inquire into irregular commissions issued to Corwine and others and try to arrange for "meritorious ones" to be paid. [CW, 5, 107]

The commander of the Department of the West arrived at his headquarters post in St. Louis on July 25, 1861. In the Missouri city and in Washington it was widely known that he faced enormous problems. He was expected to organize an army in a state where slavery was legal and widespread, hence was full of secessionists. Guerrilla warfare was already under way on the border. He had a limited number of untrained volunteers for his military force, but did not have enough money or weapons or supplies to keep these men in the field. Yet had an officer of less personal influence seized U.S. Treasury funds with which to pay soldiers, a court-martial would almost certainly have followed.

On August 14 Fremont declared martial law in St. Louis County, in which the city was located. Simultaneously he named Maj. Justus McKinstry of the U.S. Army as his provost marshal. McKinstry later became the most notorious supplier to the military of inferior or "shoddy" goods, by means of which he made a small fortune. Two weeks later the general extended martial law to the entire state. By this time, he had organized a personal bodyguard of about three hundred men, probably the largest such body that functioned during the war. In many respects, he seemed to think of himself as a medieval prince instead of a commander of volunteers in a bitterly divided state. [OR I, 3, 442, 466]

In conjunction with his extension of martial law, Fremont took a step that he knew would give Lincoln sleepless nights. During his inaugural address the new chief executive had stressed that his consuming goal was to re-establish the Union by bringing back into it "so-called seceded states." It was widely acknowledged that he was not opposed to slavery where it existed and that he personally sanctioned Fugitive Slave Laws. In this climate, the man who had gained fame as The Pathfinder issued the first emancipation proclamation of the war. All slaves of persons shown to be enemies of the Federal military force were declared to be freedmen. When the edict was published in newspapers on the following day a bold headline noted: "Slaves of Rebels Declared Free." [OR I, 3, 467; St. Louis *Dispatch*, August 31, 1861; Hoerner, 242; Greeley, 1, 585]

Lincoln biographers Nicolay and Hay later wrote that the one-state move toward emancipation was taken in a bid to boost Fremont's popularity in the North. Whether that was a significant motivating factor or not, he knew that he was taking a step contrary to the expressed views of his commander in chief, who wanted nothing done that might lead border states to secede. Lincoln took no action until September 2, when he penned a "private and confidential" letter he said was written "in a spirit of caution and not of censure" despite being sent by special messenger.

The commander in chief courteously—almost respectfully—requested that the emancipation edict be modified to conform with the Congressional Confiscation Act of August 6, which carefully bypassed the slavery issue. Lincoln's stance was partly based upon a factor with which Fremont was familiar; the President wanted nothing done that might tip Kentucky into the Confederacy. [OR I, 3, 469–70; CW, 4, 351–52, 506]

In his lengthy September 8 reply to his chief, the commander of the Department of the West characterized his edict as having been "as much a movement in the war as a battle." He then refused to retract it without receiving from the President a direct order to do so. Before his message reached the capital, Lincoln had requested Gen. David Hunter to go to Missouri as an advisor to Fremont. [OR, 3, 477–78; CW, 4, 513]

While Hunter was going from east to west, Mrs. Fremont, the beautiful former Jesse Benton who was a daughter of powerful Sen. Thomas Hart Benton, was traveling in the opposite direction. As soon as she reached the capital she asked to see the President. He responded that she could come—at midnight, if necessary. For once, a wife who gained the ear of the chief executive did not change his mind. Three days after listening to her appeal Lincoln "very cheerfully" ordered that her husband's emancipation clause be modified to conform with the Con-

Gen. David Hunter, subordinate to Fremont in Missouri

Buttre Engraving

fiscation Act. [CW, 4, 519; OR I, 3, 485–86; Nicolay and Hay, 4, 420]

On the next day, September 12, he took pains to notify Jesse Fremont that he had not acted in a spirit of hostility toward her husband. His conciliatory message to her was sent in full awareness that a corporal who defied the expressed wishes of his colonel or a colonel who took such a stance with respect to his commanding general would be considered guilty of mutiny. [LDD, 3, 66; CW, 4, 515, 517–18, 519]

In Missouri, Col. Francis P. Blair, Jr., of the 1st Missouri Light Artillery had begun openly criticizing Fremont. A member of a politically powerful family, Blair and his relatives were staunch supporters of Lincoln and had worked for his election. He was arrested in September and threatened with court-martial for having disregarded the expressed wishes of his commanding officer. [LE, 119]

By then it was clear that the man who gained fame as The Pathfinder was completely out of control. On October 7, Lincoln requested Gen. Samuel R. Curtis to give his confidential opinion concerning a difficult question. "Ought Gen. Fremont to be relieved from, or retained in his present command?" That night, General in Chief Winfield Scott drafted an order for Fremont's removal. [CW, 4, 549]

Meanwhile, Blair had been busy in St. Louis. Newspapers as far away as Baltimore reported on October 11 that Blair had preferred

Mrs. Jesse Benton Fremont, whose   Frank Blair, Jr., an influential politician
father was a powerful senator   who became a general
        Missouri Historical Society   O'Neill Engraving

charges against his commander. Fremont, said the politician/soldier, was guilty of "neglect of duty and unofficer-like conduct, disobedience of orders, conduct unbecoming an officer and a gentleman, extravagance and waste of the public moneys, and despotic and tyrannical conduct." [RR, 3, d43]

Blair's charges did not result in a trial; it was not necessary because of documents that were drawn up on October 24. Special messenger Leonard Swett was selected to deliver them at St. Louis. Scott sent what seems except for the date to have been a duplicate of his earlier order authorizing Hunter to relieve Fremont from command.

Lincoln's letter to Curtis was among the most curious he ever wrote. He authorized delivery of the Scott order unless Fremont had fought and won a battle or was then engaged in battle. Swett knew that it would be difficult to get Scott's order into the hands of Fremont, who was in camp. He picked an officer known to have "legitimate business inside Gen'l Fremont's lines" and entrusted the message to him. [OR I, 3, 553; CW, 4, 562; 5, 7]

Capt. Thomas J. McKinney reached Fremont's camp at 5:00 A.M. on November 1, after having ridden hell-for-leather for 36 hours. He talked his way inside and managed to put Scott's order into the general's hand. Initially refused permission to leave, by a subterfuge he got out about 11:00 P.M. and reached Hunter the following day.

Corpulent Gen. Winfield Scott, standing, at the last cabinet meeting he attended

Writing from Springfield on November 2, Fremont formally relinquished "command of the Western Department and of this Army in the field" to Hunter. [OR I, 3, 559]

Fremont had delivered a farewell address to his men early that day. He then reputedly "left without giving any information about the Gov. property." According to Swett, the deposed general who had rebelled against the authority of his commander in chief took with him "his body guard, 50 Indians and a paymaster with between 200,000 & 300,000$." The paymaster was arrested the following day and some of the money was recovered. [CW, 4, 562–63]

Gen. Henry W. Halleck, who eventually became Lincoln's chief military advisor and aide, was soon sent to take command of the Department of the West. Hunter, who had been a central figure in the drama by which Fremont was relieved of command, had by then been ordered to Fort Leavenworth. From his new post he dispatched a December 23 letter whose tone was fully as mutinous as anything Fremont had said to Lincoln.

Gen. Henry W. Halleck, who opposed "negro stealing" by soldiers while in Missouri

Library of Congress

He angrily told his commander in chief that he was "very deeply mortified, humiliated, insulted and disgraced" at having been "sent here into banishment." His only sin, he tartly informed the President, was "carrying out your views" concerning a military move in Missouri.

Not yet having fully recovered from effects of his dealings with another insubordinate general, Lincoln drafted a reply but waited for about a month to send it. In words that can be read as half jocular or as extremely angry, he told Hunter that he found it "difficult to answer so ugly a letter in good temper." He then chided his general in a fashion never used with Fremont, warning him that he was "adopting the best possible way to ruin" himself. [CW, 5, 84-85]

Upon arrival at St. Louis, Halleck found the city and the state to be in excited chaos. German troops were on the brink of mutiny, he said. They believed that if they made enough trouble, Fremont would be sent back. Earlier, Germans had staged organized protests on behalf of the ousted general in cities as far away as Cincinnati. [OR I, 7, 532-33; OR I, 8, 490, 828-29; RR, 3, d18; Nevins, 1, 384]

Evidence concerning Fremont's role in stirring up trouble after being relieved of command is contradictory. He could have been deeply involved—or he could have been watching events unfold from a distance. Whatever the case, scars from wounds inflicted upon Lincoln by the man lauded as "Princely Paymaster" by some of his Missouri subordinates were slow to heal.

A small minority of vocal national leaders applauded Lincoln's decision to rescind the emancipation clause of the Fremont proclamation. Joshua Speed of Kentucky stressed that citizens of that state "have great fear of [a slave insurrection]." Hence he didn't like the idea of making concessions to abolitionists. Joseph Holt, Federal judge advocate general, openly denounced the attempt at emancipation. [ALE, 150]

Most abolitionists and some middle-of-the-road leaders castigated the President who tolerated insubordination for not supporting his insurgent general. Gov. James W. Grimes of Iowa called the
Fremont clause "the only noble and true thing done during this war."
Senator Charles Sumner said of Lincoln that the Fremont incident
revealed "how vain [it was] to have the power of a god and not use it
godlike." Sen. Benjamin Wade said that the President's action "could
only come of one, born of 'poor white trash' and educated in a slave
State." Sen. Orville Browning, a close friend of the chief executive,
decried his actions with respect to the clause concerning emancipation in Missouri. [ALE, 38, 253, 293]

Abolitionist Simon Cameron used the Missouri incident as a
springboard from which to launch a campaign of his own. His annual
report of December, 1861, advocated immediate freedom for Southern slaves and induction of them into the Union army. Lincoln had
most copies of the report recalled and maintained superficial cordi-
ality with his secretary of war. Early in January, however, without
having consulted Cameron the President notified him that he was about
to become U.S. Minister to Russia.

Mark E. Neely, Jr., assessed the Fremont affair from the distance of more than a century. He pointed out that Lincoln's action

Sen. Benjamin F. Wade led a strong   Simon Cameron, Lincoln's first
anti-Lincoln movement in Congress.   secretary of war
National Archives

clearly did not lead a majority of Missouri citizens to rally to the Union. "The most unpopular measure taken by President Lincoln in the first year of the war was his revocation of Fremont's emancipation proclamation for Missouri," the Lincoln scholar concluded. [Neely, 49]

Despite his severe setback in public opinion, Lincoln weathered the storm that crashed upon Missouri in the aftermath of the great Treasury raid. John Charles Fremont did not despite the fact that his popularity soared momentarily. In 1864 he accepted another nomination for the presidency, this time from a group of anti-Lincoln radical Republicans. Almost immediately realizing that he was likely to come in last in the November balloting, he withdrew from the political contest. That effectively ended the power struggle between an aspiring major general and his commander in chief.

3
New Yorkers–2,400 Angry Men, August, 1861

Maj. Gen. Benjamin F. Butler, commander of the military Department of Virginia, stared from a window of Fort Monroe with surprise. He had dealt with a mutiny on the previous day, August 15, by having men whom he considered ringleaders placed under arrest. These having been sent to Fort Calhoun where they would face formal charges, remaining members of the 9th New York had grimly obeyed his order to return to duty. That seemed to him to indicate that trouble from the fact that pay for these men was long overdue had come to an end.

Signals given by aides on the following morning made it clear that he was urgently needed outside the fortress. He didn't think it possible that a new outburst had occurred among members of the 9th, but sensed that he faced fresh trouble. He was right. This time, members of the 2nd New York had stacked their arms and refused to do duty. By the time Butler reached their encampment, mutiny had spread into ranks of the 10th New York. Like most members of the 9th and the 2nd, these men were fighting mad over nonpayment of money they had earned the hard way.

Butler did his best to calm the agitated men in blue, but while he was starting to tell them what he planned to do word arrived that a company of volunteers from Massachusetts had also rebelled. They, too, were so furious at not being paid that they were willing to face a court-martial—or, at least, thought they were. Most incipient mutineers were raw volunteers who had received barely enough training to learn a few simple maneuvers. Some of them knew a little about ways in which the Empire State dealt with members of its militia units.

Hardly a man in an affected unit had the vaguest idea about consequences of disobedience to a Federal commander. Most of them knew what was meant by a firing squad, but they thought the only culprits who went before such executioners had been convicted of treason.

At Butler's order, recalcitrant New Yorkers plus nearly one hundred comrades from Massachusetts slowly and sullenly fell into line. Their commander delivered a full-scale tongue-lashing, complete with an imaginative description of convicted mutineers facing a firing squad.

Having been a highly successful criminal attorney before donning a uniform, Butler had never seen a military execution—and had no desire to have some take place in his command now. Hence he tried to ignore restless movements by men who were supposed to be rigidly at attention while he spoke to them.

Massed soldiers formed so large a body that those at the rear plus right and left flanks could not understand a word their commander said. Keenly conscious of this factor as a result of long experience in large courtrooms, Butler was sure that men close to him would tell their comrades what they heard. After having finished scolding and warning his troops he turned to the immediate future.

"You men know the office of the Adams Express Company," he said loudly. "This office has $26,000 belonging to the government. I intend to take charge of it. I will have every cent distributed among you. You'll get one month's pay. You can send some home. But keep enough to tide you over for a few days. Then the rest will come from Washington.

"My brother is headed for the capital," he continued. "He'll get the balance due you. Some of you have not been paid for three months. You are due $33 plus your cash clothing allowance. Every dollar will be paid. My brother will be back within 72 hours.

"When I dismiss you, go to the express company. You'll have to sign a receipt. Then an officer will hand out the money. Don't hang around; go back to your camps. Quit complaining. Show what kind of soldiers you are. You'll have every penny soon."

The general took a deep breath, then shouted: "Company . . . dismissed!"

To his gratification, men fell out and only a few grumbled audibly. Butler congratulated himself at having broken a mutiny without a shot being fired.

A lengthy report about the necessity of paying men promptly and in full, drafted that night, went to General in Chief Winfield Scott. He had taken care of the pay issue for the present, Butler explained. Then he wrote that Washington must send clothing immediately. Two months earlier he had requisitioned enough for 10,000 men

Benjamin F. Butler was satirized as playing Sancho Panza to Lincoln as Don Quixote.

and had watched as his papers were endorsed by officers of the quartermaster's department. Clearly as angry with Washington as his men had been about their pay, he continued:

> That clothing has not yet arrived in suits of uniforms. Large numbers of coats are here and no trousers; large numbers of shoes are here, but no hats; there are large numbers of shirts, but no flannel sacks. It would seem as if there was an ingenuity exercised to prevent the receipt of full uniforms, but I suppose it is simply the coincidence of mistake. [OR I, 51, I supp., 446-47]

Butler was not guileless; he knew that failure to properly supply his men was far from an isolated case. War had come with such sudden fury that even the industrial North was far from ready for it. Many outfits had been issued clumsy and dangerous Belgian muskets; most of the troops under his command at least had Harpers Ferry weapons.

Born in New Hampshire, the commandant of Fort Monroe became an orphan very early. His mother ran a boardinghouse in Lowell, Massachusetts, so it was natural for him to think of himself as a native of the Bay State. An ardent Democrat very early, he became one the most successful criminal lawyers in his adopted state.

He went to the Democratic national convention of 1860 with his mind made up. During the Charleston, S.C. conclave he voted 57 times for the same man—former U.S. Secretary of War Jefferson Davis. When Democrats split into two factions, Butler switched his allegiance to the most diehard states' rights candidate of the Democratic pack—John C. Breckinridge of Kentucky. He didn't then dream that he'd soon have to treat both Davis and Breckinridge as enemies. [GB, 60-61]

As a brigadier general of militia, he led the 8th Massachusetts to Washington on the heels of Lincoln's April, 1861, call for 75,000 men. By the time he reached the capital, it was under a secessionist blockade. Virginians not yet calling themselves Confederates had taken control of rivers with such skill that ships couldn't get into or out of Washington.

John C. Breckinridge resigned as Vice President in order to become a Rebel general.

Dictionary of American Portraits

Office of the Adams Express at Fort Monroe

Butler briefly breached the blockade by successfully taking his 8th Massachusetts to Washington from Philadelphia. After having been in uniform for less than a month, as commander of the military Department of Annapolis, the Democrat secured strategic points and trains resumed running between the capital and the North.

Maryland, a border state in which slavery was legal, held thousands of Southern sympathizers. So many lived in Baltimore that after an April riot Washington was terrified at the idea the big port city might push the state into secession. Butler, who seldom waited for official sanction in order to act, seized Fort Hill and took control of Baltimore.

Aging Gen. Winfield Scott, titular head of the U.S. Army, was incensed that he had not been not consulted in advance of this move. To Gen. Robert Patterson in Philadelphia, Scott fumed that the attorney from Massachusetts "occupied Baltimore without my knowledge." To make matters worse, he had requested troops from Pennsylvania and Scott was forced to explain things to Patterson. [OR I, 2, 637-38]

Last-minute preparations for an execution

Though Scott was highly displeased at what Butler had done, the President was inordinately grateful. Hence Lincoln—who often neglected to consult anyone before acting—took a step that was regarded askance by many of his aides. On May 16 the man from Illinois named the Democrat whose body was small but whose influence was very large as the first of his major generals. [WWW, 96]

The chief executive was keenly aware that his action did not please some members of his cabinet. He didn't bother to point out to them that he had accomplished two goals by means of one appointment. Butler seemed to him to have the makings of a splendid commander, so he was likely to be a major military asset. Simultaneously, he was removed from his home state and in Massachusetts its powerful Democratic Party was significantly weakened.

Probably because Scott still wielded great power, a May 15 order directed Gen. George Cadwalader to relieve Butler at Annapolis. That day, he was directed to proceed to Fort Monroe at the tip of the Virginia peninsula and take command of the military Department of Virginia. [OR I, 2, 639]

Butler turned livid when he received this order and immediately directed an appeal to Simon Cameron, secretary of war. He'd be satisfied to be relieved altogether if his services were no longer needed, he wrote, but he refused to be disgraced. Hence he requested that the matter be referred to Lincoln. "To be relieved of a command of a department and sent to command a fort, without a word of comment, is something unusual at least," he argued. Then he added that "I am so poor a soldier as not to understand it otherwise than in the light of a reproof." He requested but never got a personal interview with Cameron and Lincoln. Obediently turning his back upon Annapolis, on May 21 he made his way to Fort Monroe—cursing for the entire journey.

Though the man from the East didn't know it when he was ordered there, the installation to which he was sent was among the largest and strongest on the continent. Work was started a few years after the War of 1812 in a move designed to block enemy warships from America's inland waterways. Named in honor of President James Monroe and built at a cost of $2,500,000, it had granite walls that were 35 feet thick. As additional precautions, a deep moat was constructed and there was but one entry way. Widely lauded as "the Gibraltar of Chesapeake Bay," Monroe was designed to dominate many waters of Virginia, Maryland, and North Carolina.

Butler reached his new command at 8:00 A.M. on May 22. His anger at the top brass in the Federal military establishment was still smouldering long afterward. This factor may account in part for the lenient way in which he dealt with insurgent troops. The crisis over pay didn't erupt until he had been at Monroe for two months. He was confronted with an entirely different but equally important issue before the end of his first full day at the fort.

As reported to Scott on May 25, his investigation of Monroe's water supply was interrupted by a visit from a Rebel. He introduced himself as Major Cary of the Virginia volunteers and said he had urgent business. Two days earlier "three negroes, field hands, belonging to Col. Charles Mallory, now in command of the secession forces in this district," had fled to Monroe as a place of refuge. Detained by the picket guard, they were individually interviewed by Butler the following morning. All told the same story. They believed they were about to be shipped to Carolina "for the purposes of aiding the secession forces there."

When Major Cary appeared at the fort, he demanded to know what would be done with the runaways. Butler knew the position of the Lincoln administration. In his inaugural address the new chief executive had said he intended to see the Fugitive Slave Law enforced everywhere. As a result, numerous military commanders had already returned runaways to their owners. Drawing upon his long experience as an attorney, the new commander of the fort decided to adopt a different course of action.

He was badly in need of laborers, and the three fugitives appeared to be strong and healthy. So Butler drafted a receipt for Colonel Mallory. Along with it, he explained that he had taken the slaves for military purposes "as I would any other property of a private citizen when the exigencies of the service seemed to require." He knew that Mallory was aware that soldiers on both sides commonly seized, or impressed, property of citizens when it was needed for their operations. In the present case, Butler pointed out, he planned to make use of "property [in the form of three slaves] that was designed, adapted, and about to be used against the United States [by the enemy]."

Carey protested that the Union general was proposing a violation of the Fugitive Slave Law. To his consternation, Butler pointed out that this statute "did not affect a foreign country, which Virginia affected to be." In Maryland, a state that he categorized as loyal, runaways were regularly returned to their owners. Emphasizing the fact that he was bending over backward to accommodate Mallory, he made an offer. If the owner of the slaves would "take the oath of allegiance to the Constitution of the United States," he said, he'd "deliver the men up to him and endeavor to hire their services of him if he desired to part with them."

The attorney/general probably made that offer tongue-in-cheek. He got about what he expected from Major Cary, who lamely told him that Mallory was "absent from the region." [OR I, 2, 648–51]

Butler didn't realize for several weeks how much he had accomplished by developing a radical new interpretation and treating runaway slaves as contraband of war. That put them in the same category as gunpowder, cotton, and ammunition. His usage was picked up almost instantly because it neatly solved the vexatious question of how to deal with the Fugitive Slave Law. The contraband category was in virtually universal use among Federal officers within months. Once adopted as standard, it was widely used for the duration. [OR I, 3, 255; OR I, 5, 129; OR I, 6, 186; OR I, 7, 499]

There is no record that Lincoln ever sent a dispatch expressing his thanks to the Democrat from Massachusetts, but he could not have failed to be deeply grateful. As commander in chief of Federal armed forces, he sometimes elevated the spirit of a regulation above its literal meaning. Had he been in charge at Fort Monroe when 2,400 angry New Yorkers began making threats, he probably would have taken about the same steps that Butler did.

Eager to be strictly correct, the attorney in uniform soon noted that he had made one mistake. He found the 2nd New York camped nearby when he reached his command post and initially listed it as being made up of 782 three-year volunteers. Within days, he noted that these men had enlisted for only two years.

Two months before they ran the risk of court-martial, members of this regiment had been in the first real battle of the war at Big Bethel, Virginia. They saw the epic clash between the CSS *Virginia*,

Contrabands on their way to work on fortifications at Fort Monroe

aka *Merrimack*, and the USS *Monitor*. During the world's first battle between ironclads, numerous rifle shots originated on shore; some of them may have come from men of the 2nd.

Soldiers who formed this regiment were mustered into Federal forces at Troy, New York, on May 14, 1861, by Col. Joseph B. Carr. They had their fill of combat long before their enlistments expired. They fought at White Oak Swamp, Malvern Hill, Harrison's Landing, Bristoe Station, Munson's Hill, Fredericksburg, and Chancellorsville as well at numerous spots less well known. [D, 3, 1406]

Their comrades who made up the 9th New York, led by Col. C. Rush Hawkins, were popularly known as Hawkins' Zouaves. They were also at Big Bethel, and spent only two months at Fort Monroe before going with Butler to Hatteras Inlet, North Carolina. During about a year in Rebel territory, they went deep into it at Camden and Port Royal, South Carolina. Having been ordered back to the North, they spent only a week near Washington before being sent into regions where fighting was heavy. These once-recalcitrant New Yorkers were at South Mountain, Antietam, and Fredericksburg before taking part in the siege of Suffolk, Virginia. [D, 3, 1408-9]

Col. Justin Dimmick organized the third regiment whose members became rebellious in August, 1861. Made up almost entirely of men from New York City, the unit went directly from there to Fort Monroe and was waiting for its new commandant when Butler arrived. Some of the many battles in which these men took part were: Second Bull Run, Antietam, Chancellorsville, Gettysburg, Mine Run, Morton's Ford, the Wilderness, Spotsylvania, North Anna River, and Cold Harbor. They were at Petersburg on the day the biggest explosion of the war created The Crater. Later they were at Appomattox Court House when the Army of Northern Virginia was surrendered. Many of the men in this Zouave regiment remained in uniform for 50 months. [D, 3, 1409]

At the time of the mutiny, Benjamin F. Butler could have taken a hard line similar to that adopted by other commanders who faced similar situations. His ingenuity in finding a less than regulation way to cool tempers instead of asking for a court-martial saved three splendid regiments for the Union. What's more, as soon as he saw that rebellion in the ranks was over, he sent orders to Fort Calhoun. Imprisoned members of the "committee" of ringleaders that presented grievances and spoke for more than two thousand angry comrades were released and restored to ranks of the 9th without censure on their records.

4

Mexicans, Kentuckians, New Yorkers, and Blacks

Col. Edward S. Canby of the 19th regiment, U.S. Army infantry, had been in uniform for 31 years. He had fought in the Seminole War and the Mexican War, spending most of the rest of the time in frontier garrisons. A raw beginner such as one of Lincoln's "political generals" who had no experience couldn't possibly have handled the vast Department of New Mexico.

No man easily to become disturbed at what might take place in the immediate future, Canby was greatly agitated early in 1862. Writing to the adjutant general of the army on January 13 he laid it on the line, warning:

> The last mail from the east brought information from private sources that the paymster who was understood to be on his way to this country with funds for the payment of the troops has been detained at Fort Leavenworth and that no funds would be sent out until spring. Whether this report be true or not, the effect of this circulation through the country at this time will be exceedingly unfortunate, and it is greatly to be apprehended that the volunteer forces already organized will melt away by desertion, and the people of New Mexico will be rendered still more apathetic than they now are . . .
>
> The Mexican people . . . have a strong but hitherto restrained hatred for the Americans as a race . . . The long deferred payment of the volunteers [has led to] dissatisfaction, the consequence of which will be in the highest degree injurious to the interests of the Government. [OR I, 4, 84-85]

The paymaster did not arrive, and news that he would not come until spring fanned out into every corner of New Mexico. On January

20, Canby informed Washington that it was "communicated to the Mexican population and volunteers with almost telegraphic rapidity." Impact of this news was even more serious than he had anticipated. Summarizing a lightning-fast series of events he reported:

> the first result was a revolt in one of the companies of volunteers (militia) at Fort Union, and in two companies of the Second Regiment Volunteers at Camp Connelly, points 200 miles distant, but occurring within very short periods of each other and from the same alleged cause--the failing to pay and clothe them as they had been promised.
>
> The first of these was suppressed by the prompt and energetic action and the excitement allayed by the prompt and judicious conduct of Colonel [Gabriel R.] Paul. The second was not so easily managed, and about 30 of the mutineers made their escape and fled to the mountains. [OR I, 4, 86–87]

Destined eventually to become a major general in the U.S. Army, Canby hoped to capture the mutineers but did not. Most of his remaining men were Mexicans who continued to be restless and sullen, though they did not stage an open revolt because of lack of pay. Thirty men lost was a major blow to the tiny U.S. force in the vast territory.

Col. E. S. Canby, a longtime veteran of the U.S. Army, later became a general.

Leslie's *Illustrated Weekly*

Money soon became a thorny issue far to the east. Kentucky had a big and diverse population, with Unionist and secessionist views leading to clashes at many points. Lawmakers tried to take a neutral position in the sectional conflict. As was the case in Kansas earlier, each opposing force did all it could to bring the state into its column. Large numbers of weapons, believed to have been provided by Washington, were smuggled to known Unionists. Internal strife was never at so high a level as in "bleeding Kansas," but small conflicts broke out everywhere. These made travel uncertain and dangerous.

The state that Lincoln desperately wanted to keep in the Union was soon invaded by Confederates. Late in 1861, C.S. Gen.

Felix Zollicoffer led his men through Cumberland Gap and planned to strike at the heart of the state. His troops clashed with the enemy at Mill Springs, where he was killed under circumstances often described simply as "unusual." Since the ball that felled him may have come from his own ranks, it is possible that it was fired by a Unionist who had penetrated his force.

In August an estimated 10,000 Rebels led by Gen. Edmund Kirby Smith moved into the state in a fresh attempt to give meaning to its star on the Confederate battle flag. More than six thousand Federal volunteers who made up the garrison at Richmond were forced to surrender to the invaders.

There was grave danger that Confederates would establish positions on the Ohio River and close it to traffic. In this critical situation Gov. J. F. Robinson, who was loyal to the Union, believed that

C.S. Gen. Felix Zollicoffer died at Mill Springs under somewhat mysterious circumstances.

The Soldier in Our Civil War

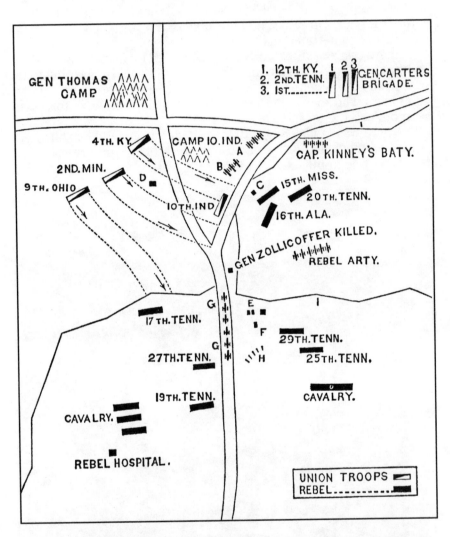

Plan of the battle at Mill Springs, Kentucky

The Rebellion Record

quick and drastic action was essential in order to rapidly get volunteers into blue uniforms. A brief telegram of September 2, 1862, to Gen. Henry W. Halleck put the matter bluntly:

> The order to muster only at residential rendezvous is destroying our regiments. They cannot be moved from points where recruited, and unarmed, without danger of capture. The camps at Russelville and Henderson have 600 men each of the same regiment. They were promised pay and bounty. The failure to fulfill is demoralizing them, and I am advised that they are on the verge of mutiny. If you will order your mustering officer to muster them, I will advance the money. [OR III, 2, 505]

Halleck's September 3 reply to the governor is a classic example of rigid adherence to rules regardless of consequences. Clearly without having consulted the President, he condensed views of top War Department officials in just three sentences. Kentucky's governor, ready and willing to provide the money to satisfy men on the verge of mutiny and put them into the field to help hold the state in the Union, was told:

> The War Department declines to change the regulation in regard to mustering. Nearly every State is making the same application, and it would be impossible to supply mustering officers for separate detachments. If soldiers are ready to mutiny before they reach the rendezvous for mustering, they would be of little use afterward. [OR III, 2, 505]

Robinson's actions designed to deal with this dilemma took part on the state level and hence are not detailed in Federal records. Earlier, he seems to have made tentative plans to attend a conclave of loyal governors that was held late in September. He didn't make it to the meeting in Altoona, Pennsylvania, because urgent business required his presence in Kentucky. It is possible that he went to camps of disaffected unpaid men not yet mustered into Federal service. At Russelville and other centers where Federal promises of pay were not being met, the governor may have doled out enough cash to keep most of his volunteers from going over to the enemy.

Another crisis over pay erupted on the heels of the great Union victory at Gettysburg. Pennsylvania authorities who believed the Army of the Potomac was headed toward their state were frantic. One desperate appeal for help went to New York State, where several units of militia were dispatched to Harrisburg in June, 1863. One such body was the 68th regiment of the National Guard, under command of Col. David S. Forbes. He and his men at Fredonia were ordered on June 16 to take the field for three months of active service. In accordance with information previously given to him, Forbes' Special Regimental

Order No. 2, stipulated that "uniforms and equipments" would be provided in Harrisburg. They reached the Pennsylvania capital about midnight on June 26 and were forced to spend the night in the depot. Two days later they were mustered into Federal service for 30 days. [OR I, 27, II, 258-60]

Following orders, on the afternoon of June 30 the New Yorkers marched eight miles to Stinson's Ferry in order to guard it against "any attempt at crossing." New orders were received just 72 hours later. In accordance with them, Forbes and his men returned to Harrisburg and from the capital moved to Carlisle by train.

There they found that the bridge had been burned and the track had been torn up. After fording the river the following morning they marched 10 miles in intense heat. Ordered the next day to go to Newman's Gap, their only food consisted of "two boxes of wet, damaged hard-tack." They managed to supplement it, however, with "2 small pigs and 4 sheep" seized along the line of march. Bivouacked on a mountain, they were subjected to drenching rain that began about midnight.

On July 7 this unit of fighting men marched about 27 miles "through mud, with clothes and blankets wet and heavy." They expected to join the forces of Pennsylvania Gen. Jesse C. Smith, but upon reaching their destination found that he and his men had been gone for four days. During the long march their food had consisted of an occasional loaf of bread and canteen of milk, purchased from civilians. A scouting party found a settlement about four miles ahead, where arrangements were made to buy 150 biscuits and five loaves of bread.

Rain pelted down all night and was still descending in torrents on the morning of July 8. They marched through rain much of the day, then tried to dry their blankets at camp fires. After a 17-mile march the following day they made contact with musicians of the 49th New York, who guided them to the hill on which the regiment was camped. No rations were on hand; it was not until 4:00 P.M. on July 10 that Forbes secured four boxes of hardtack. [OR, 44, 261-64]

Though the battle of Gettysburg had ended a week earlier and Rebel forces were retreating into Virginia, the New Yorkers knew nothing about what had transpired. Ordered to move forward, they reached the Little Antietam River and found it out of its banks due to heavy rains. Since the bridge had been destroyed, National Guardsmen forded the river and moved through heavy mud about two miles into Maryland. When camped near Hagerstown that night, they were under "one of the most terrific thunder-storms ever known in this country."

Forbes, who became sick earlier, was now so weak that he relinquished command to Lt. Col. O. Lee Swift. After another hard day's march, men of the 69th were issued 40 rounds of cartridges and warned to expect an engagement at any moment. When nothing happened, they moved forward another 10 miles, and at this camp learned that "General Lee's army was retreating." Having recovered sufficiently to sit in his saddle when accompanied by a surgeon, Forbes was disappointed that men of the New York National Guard had not been given a chance to show their "discipline, courage, and ability" in combat. July 15 brought an order to proceed seven miles to Frederick City, Maryland, in order there to entrain for New York.

En route, the New Yorkers marched over the South Mountain battlefield during weather so oppressively hot that many became exhausted and fell out. No transportation being available at Frederick City, they marched four more miles and spent the night in woods near Monocacy Junction. Forbes tried to get transportation to Harrisburg, but failed. On July 17 he and his men were ordered to proceed to the Pennsylvania capital by way of Baltimore. They arrived at Elmira, New York, on Wednesday, July 22, after having traveled much of the way in open cattle cars. To their chagrin, they were told that it would be two or three days before pay and muster rolls could be brought up to date so they could go home. [OR I, 27, II reports, 265–67]

While waiting to be mustered out, men of the regiment learned that cost of their uniforms would be deducted from their pay. Forbes protested this ruling, pointing out that uniforms plus blankets issued by a Federal quartermaster were now ragged. They had been slept in on wet and muddy ground, he pointed out. Some were probably torn from "snapping them to get the water out when ordered to march." All had been "unavoidably roughly used in dirty coal and cattle cars" where his men had to sleep. A protest to the secretary of war brought a message that men would not be required to pay for uniforms and blankets, after all.

This news evoked a loud cheer, but the mood of men turned ugly when a telegram arrived saying that Maj. C. W. Campbell, the U.S. paymaster in the district, couldn't be at Elmira until late the following week. In his lengthy and detailed report, Forbes stressed that "This news caused the regiment to almost mutiny." [OR I, 27, II reports, 268–69]

Though he had no combat experience, Forbes was level-headed and clear-thinking when facing a crisis. He might have told his men that nothing could be done. Instead, he hurried to the quarters of U.S. mustering and disbursing officer Capt. La Rhett L. Livingston. He told Livingston that the 69th was ready to rebel after having been held nine days in Elmira, but that he "had no arms to enforce discipline." In this explosive situation, he requested that transportation be provided to Fredonia and that men be paid off there.

Livingston's initial response was negative. Realizing, however, that he might soon be faced with full-scale mutiny, the Federal officer relented. Forbes then contacted Supt. Charles Minot of the Erie Railway, who quickly agreed to provide a special train. Weary and disgruntled men of the 69th left Elmira at 3:40 A.M., arrived at Dunkirk six hours later, and marched to Fredonia. Campbell paid them off on August 10, nearly two months after they were mustered for 30 days of service. [OR I, 27, II reports, 270]

They heard the terrific cannonade of July 3 at Gettysburg, but had no way to determine what it meant. Gen. George G. Meade and his Army of the Potomac won the biggest battle ever fought in North America without the aid of the New Yorkers. They fought hunger, heat, rain, and sickness without ever catching a glimpse of a Rebel except a deserter or two whom they accidentally encountered and picked up. Not a shot had been fired at an enemy by any member of the regiment. Men who made it up might, however, have had their names permanently blackened by records of a mutiny—had it not been for their determined and resourceful commander.

Nearly two years later one of the Federal generals who had been at Gettysburg faced an explosive situation near Charleston. Gen. Alexander Schimmelfennig, then stationed on Folly Island just south of the city, reported "a spirit of mutiny" in April, 1864. It prevailed, he said, among men who made up "some of the colored regiments recently arrived in this district." These soldiers, among whom members of the 55th Massachusetts were numbered, had not been paid in more than a year. As a result, said Schimmelfennig, "A spirit of mutiny has developed." [OR I, 35, II corr., 66, 68–69]

Chances are good that the Federal commander of troops at Charleston would have faced much more than a mutinous spirit, had black fighting men not been aware of what happened to William Walker when he dared to complain (chapter 1). His old regiment, the 3rd S.C. (African descent) was now the 21st U.S. Colored Troops. Its surviving members had not seen a paymaster for months, but no man in it was willing to follow the example of Walker and risk a firing squad by protesting to white officers. [D, 3, 1636]

On Big Bay Island, Lt. F. L. Morrill of the 3rd New Hampshire, was decidedly unhappy with conduct of men from the 55th Massachusetts. He complained that during a period of six weeks, he often found pickets from this regiment asleep at their posts. That was probably as close as black soldiers dared come to action that could be labeled as mutiny by white officers. [OR I, 28, I reports, 46, 55]

Their comrades in the 54th Massachusetts were described as having been "mowed down like ripe wheat" at Fort Wagner in July, 1863. These black soldiers who were led by Col. Robert Gould Shaw had earlier been offered pay, but refused to accept it. Not a man in the regiment would take a dollar until the U.S. Congress changed the law and ordered that black soldiers be paid the same as whites. [E, 480]

Mexican volunteers in New Mexico, Kentucky Unionists eager to fight, members of a regiment of New York National Guards, and black soldiers in blue uniform were a diverse lot. They had one significant thing in common, though. All of them, and their commanders as well, struggled with low pay, slow pay, or no pay that led them to welcome the idea of mutiny.

Part II

Trouble with a Capital "T"

5

"A Strange Anomaly"–Fort Jackson, April 27, 1862

Located on the west bank of the Mississippi River about 75 miles south of New Orleans, Fort Jackson was built to take terrific punishment. The installation received a full measure of it, and more, from Federal mortar schooners and gunboats. Yet structurally it remained sound and surprisingly little damaged when inspected after being surrendered.

Capitulation of the Confederate bastion was a direct result of a mutiny on the part of many or most of its seven hundred men during the night of April 27, 1862. C.S. Gen. Mansfield Lovell had been ordered to New Orleans on October 7, 1861. There he took command of military Department No. 1. His strongest installations, Fort Jackson plus Fort St. Philip across the Mississippi on its east bank, had been erected for the defense of New Orleans.

Men inside a fortress that had been hammered for days revolted and turned upon their officers, rendering it helpless. Lovell professed incredulity when he learned of what had taken place. Reporting about the affair to Gen. Samuel Cooper he said that "The battle for the defense of New Orleans was fought and lost at Forts Jackson and St. Philip." He then amplified that summary by indicating that:

> The extraordinary and remarkable conduct of the garrisons of these forts, in breaking out in open mutiny after covering themselves with glory by their heroic defense, is one of those strange anomalies for which I do not pretend to account. [OR I, 6, 517-18, 648; NOR I, 18, 259]

Federal plans to engage the forts and to capture the largest city in the Confederacy began with selection of naval officers. Capt. David D. Farragut had been prize master of a vessel captured by his foster father at age 12. In January he was picked by the secretary of the navy to head the naval move upon New Orleans in the role of commander of the newly created West Gulf Blockading Squadron. [NOR I, 18, 5]

The choice made by Gideon Welles came as a surprise to many U.S. Navy veterans. Upon the outbreak of hostilities, Farragut had been viewed with outright suspicion. His New Orleans background plus his marriage to a Southern woman led to doubts about his loyalty to the Union. In the opinion of some Washington insiders, a man with a less questionable background should have been put in command of the all-important naval phase of the planned strike against the city of Farragut's birth.

U.S. Secretary of the Navy Gideon Welles, who had no prior experience on the sea

Pictorial Field Book

Farragut picked David Dixon Porter as his second-in-command. A foster brother of Farragut more than a decade his junior, Porter went to sea at age 11 and was a midshipman just three years later. On April 22, 1861, he was promoted to the rank of commander and was told to operate his mortar fleet in conjunction with Farragut's warships. A military force led by Gen. Benjamin F. Butler was to be poised to occupy the immense port city. That couldn't be done until the battle to which Lovell referred—anticipated by Federal forces weeks in advance—rendered New Orleans defenseless.

Confederates, who knew from the beginning of the war that the city would be attacked, had made elaborate plans. A line of hulks, chained together, was moored across the river. They were placed in such fashion that when attacking vessels were stopped, they would be in direct line of fire from the heaviest guns of Forts Jackson and St. Philip. A fleet of eight vessels was moored close to the city. Two of these, the *Louisiana* and the *Manassas*, were ironclads that could be expected to give Federal warships a rough time.

As an additional precaution, numerous little boats were heavily loaded with "fat pine." This common product of Southern forests included a great deal of hardened pine tar, so was highly inflammable. By use of these "fire-rafts" Rebels expected to be able to illuminate the river. They hoped that any attempt by Federal vessels to

Thomas Nast depicted U.S. Gen. Benjamin Butler as "Fishing for the big ones" in New Orleans.

Stormy Ben Butler

pass the forts at night would be thwarted by the line of hulks plus guns of the forts directed upon targets clearly revealed by fire-rafts.

By late February, the West Gulf Blockading Squadron included 34 vessels. Some of these were needed at Galveston and Mobile. Two were at Key West taking on coal. Based at Ship Island, Farragut selected 24 for the move against New Orleans. His flagship, the USS *Hartford*, was a 2900-ton first-class screw steamer—without a protective layer of iron. One of his best-known vessels, the comparatively small USS *Harriet Lane*, was named for the niece of President

Guns of the former revenue cutter *Harriet Lane* were bigger than most field artillery used on land.

The Soldier in Our Civil War

James Buchanan who served as his White House hostess. With Porter's 19 mortar schooners included, the attacking force was believed to have slightly more guns than the 116 or so in the pair of Rebel forts. [NOR I, 18, 40; NOR II, 1, 98–99]

Farragut and Porter were in complete agreement that it would be futile to attempt to run past the Confederate installations until they had been softened up. On April 18, Porter's 13-inch mortars began lobbing two hundred-pound shells at and into Fort Jackson. Capt. William L. Robertson of the 1st Louisiana Artillery was in the fort when the shooting started. He later wrote a detailed account of experiences during nearly a week in which about 13,500 shells were directed against Jackson. Much of the time, some of the guns inside the fortification were speaking their responses to Federal fire. [B&L, 2, 99–100]

Porter developed and presented a detailed plan of attack that did not include an attempt to run past the forts. A demand for surrender should be made, he proposed, and if it was not accepted his mortars could "open deliberate fire; keeping two shells in the air all

David E. Farragut, whose Southern ties did not interfere with his service for the Union

H. Wright Smith Engraving

the time." Since Jackson was casemated and St. Philip was not, he urged that most fire should be directed at the stronger of the two fortifications. Three or four warships could fire frequently, he suggested. Their gunners could "coolly and conveniently load" and aim because his howitzers would keep Rebels busy. [NOR I, 18, 145–46]

Farragut rejected Porter's plan, reasoning that Confederate guns had been designed and put into place in order to deal with wooden warships. Seventeen of his vessels had steam engines, so he was confident they could move fast enough to get past Fort Jackson during darkness. Led by Cmdr. Henry M. Bell, the gunboats *Pinola* and *Itasca* had earlier demolished the relatively flimsy barrier—sometimes called a chain—that had thrown across the river. This meant that Farragut and his subordinates could proceed at full speed. [NOR I, 18, 367]

He weighed anchor at 2:00 A.M. on April 24 and launched his hazardous move. The Federal fleet was detected before it reached Jackson, and Rebel gunners there and at St. Philip prepared to give it everything they had. Soon, however, many of them found that they couldn't depress their pieces sufficiently to hit enemy vessels. Despite this factor, they fired as rapidly as they could in the direction of "several black, shapeless masses, barely distinguishable from the surrounding darkness, moving silently, but steadily, up the river."

According to Robertson, "The flashes of the guns, from both sides, lit up the river with a lurid light." This, he reported, was simply a prelude to "the great artillery duel which then followed." Describing the exchange of gunfire between ships and both shores, he wrote:

> The mortar-shells shot upward from the mortar-boats, rushed to the apexes of their flight, flashing the lights of their fuses as they revolved, paused an instant, and then descended upon our works like hundreds of meteors, or burst in mid-air, hurling their jagged fragments in every direction. The guns on both sides kept up a continual roar for nearly an hour, without a moment's

interruption, and produced a shimmering illumination, which, though beautiful and grand, was illusive in its effect upon the eye and made it impossible to judge distance accurately. [B&L, 2, 100]

Fire directed at Jackson continued until past 4:50 A.M., when the last of Farragut's vessels passed the fort. Porter later discovered that many of his "bombshells descended 18 or 20 feet" into the wet ground before exploding. These did little damage, but he considered them to have been demoralizing, producing an effect much like that of an earthquake. "When the bombshell hit the ramparts, they did their work effectually," he reported. [NOR I, 18, 360–61, 365]

Three of Farragut's gunboats didn't get through, but the rest of them and all of his warships did. Reporting to Porter before the day ended, his foster brother told him:

> We had a rough time of it . . . but thank God the number of killed and wounded was very small considering. This ship [the Hartford] had only 2 killed and 8 wounded. . . . We have destroyed all but two of the [Rebel] gunboats, and those will have to surrender with the forts; so you hold them in statu quo until I get back. I think if you send a flag of truce and demand their surrender, they will do it, for their intercourse with the city is cut off. . . . You supported us most nobly. [NOR I, 18, 142]

Men on both sides realized that slow-moving troop transports could not duplicate the feat of Farragut's fast warships. That meant military occupation of New Orleans could not take place until the guns of Jackson and St. Philip were silenced. There was an additional urgent factor in the complex equation. Farragut's ships were now "cut off from coal, provisions, and ammunition."

Porter was under the impression, mistaken as he soon found out, that "fire from the ships must have been very destructive to life" in Fort Jackson. Hence he sent Lt. John Guest to the Rebel position under a flag of truce. When a demand for surrender was made, he was told simply that "The demand is inadmissible." [NOR I, 18, 368]

Porter soon discovered that only a few casualties had been inflicted, so strongly disagreed with the view that men in the two forts were ready to give up. In a dispatch from the Federal mortar-flotilla on April 25 he warned Farragut that "You will find the forts harder to take now than before unless their ammunition gives out."

His judgment was based on the fact that his men had "thrown bombs at them all day" and had "tantalized them with rifle shots." Enemies never fired a gun, he reported. To him this meant they were saving their ammunition and would be ready to use it if an attempt was made to carry the forts by assault. [NOR I, 18, 143, 357]

Despite his misgivings, Porter sent another surrender demand to Jackson under a flag of truce. Again led by Guest, members of the mission this time stressed that terms offered were generous. Officers would be permitted to keep their side arms on only one condition. They would have to give their paroles of honor "not to serve against the United States during the rebellion until regularly exchanged." Though the second overture was also rejected, Porter held out hope that Rebel leaders in New Orleans would soon order the surrender of both forts. [NOR I, 18, 369]

Inside Jackson, C.S. Gen. J. K. Duncan had been present for much of the action. As commander of Cost Defenses, the fortification plus St. Philip and a body of sharpshooters on the riverbank were under his control. He issued a congratulatory order on April 27, saying to men in both forts:

> You have nobly, gallantly, and heroically sustained with courage and fortitude the terrible ordeals of fire, water, and a hail of shot and shell wholly unsurpassed during the present war. But more remains to be done. . . . Your officers have every confidence in your courage and patriotism, and feel every assurance that you will cheerfully and with alacrity obey all orders and do your whole duty . . . Be vigilant, therefore, and stand by your guns, and all will yet be well. [OR I, 6, 544]

Inside beleaguered Fort Jackson, its commandant knew that a substantial amount of damage had been done. Reports he had received led Capt. Edward Higgins to believe that most structures of wood were in shambles. At least one of them, he knew, had been set on fire by an enemy shell and had burned. Water ranging from about eight to 15 inches in depth covered all horizontal exterior surfaces and sloshed about in most of the casemates. Casualties had been incredibly low, however. A detailed Rebel list, naming each casualty and his condition, showed that nine men had been killed and 33 had been wounded. This compared with the Federal loss of one hundred men aboard just one of Farragut's vessels. [NOR I, 18, 284, 369, 372]

Only a few of Jackson's guns had been disabled, and its magazines were far from empty. Damage to the exterior was extensive, but superficial; thick granite walls of the fort were as stout as ever. Unless the enemy found a new source of firepower or an unexpected change should take place in the situation, Higgins had every reason to believe he could hold out until Porter's howitzers used up their ammunition.

Two or three hours after dark on April 27 some of his officers heard what seemed to be musket or rifle shots inside the fortress. When they ran to investigate, they came under fire from their own men. Extensive investigations later suggested that about 250 members of the garrison, or slightly more than one-third, had secured weapons before staging a full-scale mutiny. These men and their unarmed comrades not only quit servicing their pieces, they spiked many of them. Then they set out to try to kill their officers. All efforts to bring the situation under control failed. A Catholic priest, Father Nachon, added his pleas to those of officers but he failed to persuade men to begin obeying orders again.

Well before midnight, matters were out of control. Even had men been willing to serve guns, so many had been disabled by men who made up their crews that the fort was virtually defenseless. Officers took shelter wherever they could; though many a shot rattled in the darkness, not one of them was seriously injured by fire from mutineers. Some of them saw an exchange of signals between members of their garrison and men in Fort St. Philip. They guessed, correctly as events proved, that many or most enlisted men in the east-bank fortress knew that the mutiny had been planned and expected to take advantage of it.

As the first dim light of pre-dawn broke on April 28, men from both forts began taking to small boats. Rowing strenuously, hundreds of them sprang to the nearest point of land out of range of the forts. These mutineers now added desertion to their offenses, taking to the bayous in order to avoid capture. Though Porter had no details, he knew that he now had Rebel officers where he wanted them. A renewed demand for surrender on the same relatively generous terms that had been rejected earlier was now eagerly accepted.

Porter's description of the members of the garrison who remained at Fort Jackson, though far from unbiased, is of significant interest. The Stars and Stripes having gone up over the surrendered bastion, he wrote of Rebels in it:

> The sun never shone on a more contented and happy looking set of faces than those of the prisoners in and about the forts. Many of them had not seen their families for months, and a large portion had been pressed into service distasteful to them, subject to the rigor of a discipline severe beyond measure.... Instead of the downcast countenances of conquered people they emerged from the fort (going home on their parole) like a parcel of happy schoolboys in holiday times. [NOR I, 18, 371]

Confederate officials later concluded that of the estimated 1,400 men in the two forts, only the members of the Saint Mary's Cannoneers remained faithful. [CMH, 13, 42–44; OR I, 6, 518, 640; NOR I, 18, 531–49]

During the entire war, no other mutiny had so profound an effect upon public opinion. A formal investigation into the revolt and its causes led to a report that was intended to soothe the frightened public in seceded states. During lengthy testimony, witnesses who admitted they were guessing named at least seven factors that could have affected members of Fort Jackson's garrison. (1) Many foreigners were included in the body. (2) The constant barrage of federal shells had a demoralizing effect. (3) Bickering between officers of the army and the navy fostered discontent. (4) The terms of surrender offered by Porter were remarkably generous. (5) News that New Orleans had surrendered made men think it would be useless to hold the forts. (6) There were very few Louisiana natives in the garrisons. (7) An unduly great number of men charged with defending the forts were of German extraction. [OR I, 6, 555-646]

In its "Report of Facts," the Rebel court of inquiry presented a theory much like that of Lovell. Its most remarkable finding was to the effect that "for this strange revolt no cause could be ascertained." [OR I, 6, 640]

6

Volunteers vs. Generals—The Anderson Cavalry, December 24, 1862

Lt. Col. William Spencer didn't attempt to conceal his annoyance. On Christmas Day he had spent half the afternoon trying to answer questions and satisfy complaints from his men. Now a delegation was back before dark, wanting to waste more of his time. He told its members to speak up, but to make it short and snappy.

A spokesman for the group nodded assent. "We are less than satisfied with the answers you gave us," he began. "Rumor has it that marching orders are on the way here. If they come before our grievances are fully addressed, the Anderson Cavalry will stack arms."

Spencer was not surprised; he hadn't been able to answer questions because he didn't know their answers. He had made it clear that someone with more rank and more information would have to be consulted. Personally frustrated and more than a little angry the commander of the regiment said nothing. He simply waved both hands in a sweeping motion that signaled "Get out!"

Orders arrived the following morning. Spencer and a handful of subordinate officers directed men to prepare to march. No destination was indicated, but everyone in camp knew that a major battle was in the offing. In what they described as "a quiet and orderly manner," men of the regiment stacked their arms and refused to budge.

One month earlier, Gen. David S. Stanley had been put in command of all cavalry in the Department of the Cumberland. Gen. William S. Rosecrans had previously notified him and other commanders that he expected momentarily to meet and to crush forces under C.S. Gen. Braxton Bragg at or close to Murfreesboro, Tennessee.

Stanley knew earlier that men of the Anderson Cavalry were making trouble. If the battle that was in the offing turned out to be

As commander of cavalry in the Department of the Cumberland, U.S. Gen. David S. Stanley had oversight of the Anderson Cavalry.

National Archives

as big as expected, every man would be needed. Hence he sent an officer to the recalcitrant regiment with a conciliatory offer. The Anderson Cavalry would be held in reserve, he promised. Soon Maj. A. G. Rosengarten arrived with fresh news. Federal forces had experienced a momentary setback but expected quickly to win a glorious victory at Stones River.

That persuaded officers of the cavalry unit to shout their readiness to fight. Some privates indicated willingness to go with them, but the majority refused. They told Rosengarten that they "firmly adhered to their original design until their wrongs were righted, and until they were properly officered." [OR I, 20, II, 354, 370]

From his headquarters post at Nashville, Rosecrans issued Special Order No. 20 on December 28. Under its terms, 33 members of the Anderson were named to act as temporary officers "until appointments are made." This extraordinary measure clearly indicated that the regiment was not properly officered, a major source of complaint.

Six of the men selected by Rosecrans refused his order to serve as temporary officers. Five other "temporary officers" proved to be absent on parole or from sickness. Commissioned officers already present with the Anderson included 1st Lts. Henry O. Tinstman and James B. Curtin; both of them became temporary captains. Second Lt. Allison McDowell, also on duty, was made temporary first lieutenant of Company B. [OR I, 20, II, 356–57]

Rosecrans gave Gen. R. B. Mitchell temporary authority to deal with the disobedient regiment. These men had disgraced themselves, he said, and he didn't intend to submit to their whims. If they didn't go to the front at once, he told Mitchell, he planned to disgrace them "as well as make them otherwise bitterly regret their folly." [OR I, 20, II, 357]

By the following day, December 30, heavy fighting was under way at Stones River. Mitchell apparently delegated the Anderson matter to Gen. James D. Morgan, who promptly took what he regarded as decisive action. In company with Lt. Col. M. F. Wood and his 10th Illinois regiment, he followed the Murfreesboro-Lebanon Pike to the camp of the Anderson Cavalry. Its men followed his order to form two ranks facing the Illinois regiment.

Morgan informed members of the Anderson that he had brought troops with him to compel their obedience to an order to go to the front. After he gave some assurances, about 170 men followed Wood toward the field of battle. They soon encountered retreating men in blue who had no weapons, having been captured and paroled by a force under C.S. Gen. Joseph Wheeler. Wood selected a spot that could be used as a camp for the night and told men to be ready to march at 1:00 A.M.

He then returned to the larger segment of the Anderson Cavalry but these men stubbornly "refused all orders or attempts to induce them to go forward." The situation was reported by him to Morgan in Nashville as soon as he reached the city. From the general, Wood got instructions "to arrest and confine all who refuse to obey orders or do duty."

Only 70 men in the regiment that had numbered about one thousand at its formation "avowed their willingness to do duty." Following Morgan's instructions, Wood had the remainder of the Anderson "arrested and confined in the city work-house." He did not make a count of the prisoners, but estimated that there more than two hundred of them.

On the following day, it was found that the work-house was not large enough to hold all of the men under arrest. In addition to 309 held there, 101 more members of the Anderson had been put into the yard of the county jail. Many records are chaotic and not all of them agree. According to a January 26 report by Capt. H. C. Austin, inspector of military prisons in Nashville, he took office on January 4. He said that on that day he found 88 members of the Anderson in the city jail and 315 in the work-house. [OR I, 20, II, 354, 360, 363]

On December 31, five men who acted for the entire regiment drafted a statement that was directed to Edwin M. Stanton in Washington. According to it, most men still in the Anderson had requested to be placed under arrest so that their complaints could be fully investigated. A detailed petition was attached to the explanatory document addressed to the U.S. secretary of war. The petition read:

> We, the undersigned, members of the Anderson Troop, believing that we have been enlisted into the service of the United States under false pretenses, do hereby request, in consideration of the following reasons, a proper investigation, whether or not we are now held, or can be held, under any other terms than those of our enlistment:
>
> 1st. That we were enlisted for a body guard and special service at the headquarters of Maj. Gen. D. C. Buell, then commanding the

Members of the "special body" were badly needed when heavy fighting broke out at Stones River, or Murfreesboro.

The Soldier in Our Civil War

Army of the Ohio, and promises were made by the recruiting officer in charge that should we not be assigned to the service for which we enlisted, we should at once receive our discharge, and be provided with transportation to our respective homes.

2nd. Without our knowledge or consent as members, said battalion was increased to a regiment, and, even as such, we were deprived of the privilege of selecting our own officers.

3rd. Orders were issued and promises made that we should be engaged in no other service than that for which we were enlisted.

4th. That we have now been in the United States service over four months, with not more than 15 commissioned officers, some companies not having even one, and with our arms, equipments, &c, in such imperfect condition as to render the regiment partially unfit for service. [OR I, 20, II, 367]

Early in the day on which this petition was drafted, an unidentified officer had returned to the camp. With the regiment formed in line, he directed "all who were willing to obey all orders emanating from superior officers" to step forward two paces. Only a few moved, so the rest of the men in the regiment's camp who had not earlier displayed obedience were placed under arrest at this time. [OR I, 20, II, 356]

Members of the troop who kept careful records noted that about two hundred of their number who earlier went into combat remained in camp. Keenly aware that these totals left 350 or more of their comrades unaccounted for, they wrote that some were "quietly sleeping the sleep that knows no waking." Others who were sick or wounded were believed to have found "temporary refuge in humane institutions." The vast majority of the 350 were described simply as missing. Most of these were presumably deserters. [OR I, 20, II, 371]

Capt. H. Atkinson was placed in temporary command of the regiment on January 3. He ordered that the camp be moved the following day, and when this was done he sent a few others who refused to obey orders to jail. Members who were judged to be loyal were put to work as scouts and pickets in the vicinity of their new camp. [OR I, 20, II, 362]

Numerous civilians from Philadelphia began arriving at Nashville soon after Stones River came to an end. Since his force remained on the field after the enemy withdrew, Rosecrans triumphantly labeled the bloody conflict as a Union victory. Many analysts later challenged that verdict, holding that the battle was virtually a draw. According to this point of view, little if anything had changed except that Federal forces had suffered more than 12,000 casualties and among Rebels more than 10,000 men were dead, wounded, or missing. (E, 1096)

Gen. William S. Rosecrans, standing, told aides that he considered Stones River to be a great Federal victory.

Harper's History of the Great Rebellion

Visitors from the City of Brotherly Love showed little or no interest in statistics from Stones River; they were there on behalf of Pennsylvanians they felt had been wronged. On January 16 another lengthy statement went to Washington. This time, it was signed by W. H. Stokes, Robert Thomas, James M. Stewart, and Samuel Murphy, M.D.

Having interviewed as many of the confined men as possible and having talked with officers willing to give them time, the self-appointed committee aimed at brevity but did not achieve it. To the secretary of war, they reported that the "present suffering and disgrace" of the Anderson Cavalry was a direct result of "false representation made to them in advertisements in the public newspapers of Philadelphia, and by persons by

Gen. Don Carolos Buell, at whose headquarters the Anderson Cavalry expected to be stationed

Buttre Engraving

whom they were enlisted." Men signed up for service in the regiment, they said, because they were told that it would enter "special service." That is, the unit would be attached to the headquarters of Buell and its members "were not to be employed as ordinary cavalry."

These false representations were blamed for the impasse that had developed near the capital of Tennessee. Six separate findings were enumerated by members of the self-appointed committee, obviously made up of men who were accustomed to being heard with respect if not deference. Crucial aspects of the matter, as they saw it, were: (1) the War Department never authorized formation of a cavalry regiment "for special service"; (2) deception was practiced at the time of their enlistment; (3) by the time the regiment reached strength of almost one thousand men it had only 13 commissioned officers; (4) men of the Anderson were not given the privilege extended to other Pennsylvania regiments of electing their officers; (5) no pay had ever been issued to the Anderson, and up to and including the recent battle it had not been attached to any department or division of Federal forces; and (6) false representations plus arrival at Nashville with "but 10 commissioned and non-commissioned officers" had greatly demoralized the regiment. [OR I, 20, II, 372]

Since the second long message to the secretary of war originated in Washington, most or all civilians who framed it must have gone to the capital in person. One day after the document was written, Adj. Gen. Lorenzo Thomas took action in the name of the secretary of war. Maj. N. H. Davis, an assistant inspector general of the U.S. Army, was ordered to Nashville. Thomas directed him to "inquire minutely into the circumstances" concerning the arrest and treatment of confined men and "everything connected" with the case of the Anderson Cavalry. In addition, Davis was specifically required to report to Washington the names of men who fought at Stones River and were subsequently imprisoned. [OR I, 20, II, 373]

Rebellious actions labeled as mutiny were much more common than had been realized until the present study was made, and many of them were of major significance. In preparing his two-volume *Rise and Fall of the Confederate Government,* Jefferson Davis felt that the mutiny at Fort Jackson (chapter 5) merited space. Yet it took place with such speed that it would have been impossible to involve the War Department of the Richmond government even if participants had wished to take such action. In the case of mutiny among Federal units, commanders in the field habitually took whatever action they considered necessary without asking for or receiving guidance from Washington. Direct action by Edwin M. Stanton in the case of the Pennsylvanians under arrest for mutiny had no close counterpart, making the case unique in the annals of the war.

At his Nashville headquarters Rosecrans on January 19 authorized Mitchell to release all confined members of the Anderson who were willing to go on duty. He also sent word to the regiment that he'd permit men of each company to select six of its members, from whom he would nominate "the most suitable for appointment as commissioned officers."

Deliberate reference to the nominating process by the commanding general indicated his willingness to accept prevailing customs concerning choice of officers up to and including the rank of colonel. The governor of the state from which a unit was organized was normally responsible for choosing or approving these officers. Men making up dozens of Pennsylvania regiments had earlier elected their own officers, most or all of whom were approved by the governor.

On the day after the new offer was made, the number of men from the Anderson who were in confinement dropped to 208 according to one report. Subsequently, four more of them were jailed after having refused to do picket duty. There was some evidence that visiting civilians had influenced the 208 men who decided not to accept their commanding general's terms. [OR I, 20, II, 349–50, 363]

Less than 24 hours after a compromise of sorts had been effected, Mitchell took still another step. Terms of the deal were put into the record by means of his Special Order No. 20. Yet there was no written reference to "the crime of mutiny" until January 25. Reporting to the inspector general who was sent by the secretary of war, Provost Marshal John A. Martin, colonel of the 8th Kansas, used the term as though everyone involved knew precisely why men of the Anderson had been placed in confinement. [OR I, 20, II, 362]

Following instructions given to Davis by Stanton, Capt. Alfred Vein of the rebellious regiment compiled a list of its members who "were engaged in the battle of Murfreesborough, who have since been confined or are now in confinement." Nine of these men, he said, were in combat for four consecutive days. Two sergeants and seven corporals were on the Vein list, which ran to 75 names. [OR I, 20, II, 365–66]

All signs point to the probability that Stanton was getting a great deal of heat from Pennsylvania. Two days after having instructed Davis to examine all circumstances of the Anderson Cavalry affair, he bypassed aides and personally told Mitchell that he wanted a telegraphic report stating:

> 1st What number of the Anderson Cavalry are imprisoned.
>
> 2nd. On what charges, and by whose order, they are imprisoned.
>
> 3rd. The description of building in which they are imprisoned, and the number in each prison.
>
> 4th. Whether the prisoners are humanely treated, and have proper conveniences for cleanliness and health.

5th. When they are to be tried, and whether you have made
any threats or expressed any ill-will against them.

The telegram from Washington ended with the terse directive that "The
names of the prisoners you will send by mail." [OR I, 20, II, 373–74]

Mitchell, who was furious at the turn of events, sent a long telegram to Stanton on the day after having received the secretary's directive. He said that the men in question had been treated like "all other
soldiers placed in confinement for high crimes." Then he stressed
that he had personally made it clear to them "that mutiny in the face
of an enemy was punishable by death, and unless they reconsidered
their action some of them would be made examples of."

They had heard from his own mouth that he considered their
actions to be "cowardly in the extreme, a disgrace to themselves and
their State." Civilians from Philadelphia had been a source of great
annoyance, he noted. One of them had warned that half a million
dollars would be spent before they budged from the stance they had
taken.

"If these men [of the Anderson] are sustained in their present
course," Mitchell fumed, "we might just as well abandon the cause
for which we are fighting. Other men will take advantage of any clemency shown to them." Almost as though he were taunting the secretary of war, he informed him that by order of Rosecrans a
court-martial was already in session. According to Mitchell, 350 Pennsylvanians were still in custody—96 in the jail-yard and 254 in the
work-house. [OR I, 20, II, 374]

One week later, Davis used telegraph lines to file a preliminary
report concerning his investigation. In his opinion, some members of
the regiment were "leading spirits in this mutinous course," but he
did not know their identities. Rosecrans apparently did, since he had
a number of them on trial "for mutiny and disobedience of orders."

Reliable sources had informed him, Davis said, that "hundreds
of the troops are closely watching this matter, and their future action will be shaped by the result in this case." His lengthy dispatch
ended by stressing his judgment that the case was "a very important
one to the service." [OR I, 20, II, 374–75]

On February 4 Davis filed a much longer and more detailed
final report of his investigation. He devoted most of it to a summary
of what he had learned from officers. They told him that the troop
was originally assigned to Buell's headquarters, where it did such
valuable service that the general requested and got authority to raise
three more regiments in order to form a full battalion.

Organization was not completed, he told the secretary of war,
but the regiment took to the field in Pennsylvania and Maryland at the
time the latter state was invaded by the Army of Northern Virginia.

No horses were issued until after the Anderson Cavalry reached Louisville about November 9. Formal statements of grievance seem to have been issued both at Carlisle, Pennsylvania, and at Louisville.

Officers vowed that no deception had been practiced in enlisting these men. They were told that their duties would consist of "scouting, secret expeditions, escorts, guards" plus "service of a daring and dashing character." Men of the regiment were well armed and mounted, according to officers. During their march (astride their horses) from Louisville to Nashville they seem to have been influenced by contacts with "disloyal families." As a result, they began voicing grievances and refusing to do duty. Warned that they would be arrested and punished, officers told Davis, "They dared any general to interfere with their rights; they had money and influence."

Stanton's agent then summarized in detail their mutinous conduct after having arrived at Nashville. His conclusion, identified as such, indicated that he felt some men had been deceived concerning their enlistment "but not to the extent claimed." Insufficient officers had been appointed, he conceded, but added that "interference and influence of friends at home" had contributed largely to "demoralization and want of discipline." Rebellious men magnified their grievances and looked for pretexts, in the opinion of Davis.

He stressed his judgment that there was "no good excuse for their mutinous and disobedient conduct." Then he echoed the views of Mitchell by saying that hundreds or thousands of troops were watching the case. In his opinion, "the good of the service" demanded that "an example be made of a portion of this regiment." [OR I, 20, II, 345–50]

Four days after the extremely detailed Davis report went to Washington, Rosecrans authorized Col. William J. Palmer of the Anderson to proceed to Nashville in order to reorganize the regiment into 11 companies, made up of men who had fought. He was asked at the same time to nominate enough commissioned officers to fill voids. [OR I, 20, II, 376]

Soon after his arrival at the camp, Palmer reported the condition of the regiment to be "just about as bad as it was possible to be." He decried meddling by citizens and "the unfortunate encouragement given to the mutineers" by committees from Philadelphia. Fifteen mutineers having been selected by Rosecrans to stand trial, he queried their comrades who were still confined and found them ready to return to duty. As a result he "released them from the smokehouse" and put them into barracks in Nashville.

Rosecrans, he noted in his report to Col. J. B. Fry, had given them the privilege of electing their own officers but had subsequently rescinded it. The regiment had only 15 horses plus about 250 carbines and sabers. It had no wagons and very few tents. Reorganization was "rather worse than beginning fresh" in Palmer's opinion, but he was undertaking it. Almost as a postscript he noted that several mutineers had been discharged by order of the War Department and labeled this as having a very bad effect on their comrades. [OR I, 20, II, 376–77]

Two weeks later, Rosecrans—who apparently did not know that members of the Anderson claimed never to have received any pay—ordered that pay due to mutineers should be withheld. A few days later Special Orders from the War Department demanded the release of mutineers Charles De Ward, Samuel Hildeburn, Charles H. Warner, and Lewis G. Reed. Rosecrans pointed out that two mutineers had earlier been discharged upon orders from Washington and gave it as his opinion that "It would have an excellent effect upon the discipline of the regiment if these discharges be revoked." There is no record that a reply was made to his suggestion. [OR I, 20, II, 377]

Rosecrans' staff must have been in chaos nearly as great as that of the Anderson Cavalry. He apparently knew nothing of attrition in its ranks and thought it held one thousand men instead of the approximately seven hundred who were still accounted for. On March 18 he notified Washington that three hundred members of the regiment fought in the battle of Stones River and that the remaining seven hundred "were under guard at Nashville for mutiny." [OR I, 20, II, 375]

Following a directive from the secretary of war, "remaining members of the old Anderson Troop"—whatever their number may have been—were mustered out of service. One week later Rosecrans consented to release the men who had been tried and convicted of mutiny and the sentence of the court-martial was suspended by his order. On May 20, Gov. Andrew G. Curtin of Pennsylvania approved a list of officers for the newly constituted regiment, no longer a cavalry unit and now designated as the 60th Pennsylvania. [OR I, 20, II, 351, 379]

On May 23 the long-drawn drama came to a quiet end. Rosecrans notified Washington of the successful reorganization of the regiment and said that "The new officers are commissioned." There is no certainty that any members of the original regiment remained in uniform. According to Dyer, who found evidence that it was organized in Carlisle rather in Philadelphia, the Anderson Troop Cavalry was mustered out at Murfreesboro on March 24, 1863. [OR I, 20, II, 380; D, 3, 1569]

No one in Nashville or in Washington ever publicly acknowledged that the outcome of this long-drawn case was influenced by high-placed civilians. Neither is there any record concerning how many of its former members continued in uniform when it ceased to exist. A few comrades of mutineers—possibly men who had fought at Stones River—may have joined other units and fought to the end. By the time the Army of Northern Virginia surrendered, former mutineers had been back in Philadelphia for nearly two years. There they presumably resumed their pre-war careers as merchants and tradesmen, attorneys, teachers, artisans—and ultimate inheritors of family fortunes.

7

Armed Mutiny by Eight Hundred Men— The 79th New York, August 13–14, 1861

At least six components went into a mixture that exploded violently on the morning of August 14, 1861. First, many members of the Union's Highlander Regiment, officially designated as the 79th New York, had heard a rumor according to which their kilts would be taken from them. Second, at least one man in four was violently angry with the commander of their brigade. Col. William T. Sherman of the U.S. Army drilled his men constantly despite the searing heat. His lack of mercy fueled the circulation of ugly tales about how he took better care of his horses than his men during the Federal retreat from Bull Run in late July.

A third factor contributing to willingness to mutiny overshadowed the first two. One of the British army veterans in the ranks of the 79th may have been responsible. He or a comrade started a rumor that raced through their camp like lightning. They were about to return to New York! Men had enlisted "for three years or the duration of the war," but in April everyone thought the sectional struggle would be over by July. That meant they'd been tricked about their enlistment terms. Believing that they had been duped, many of them later admitted, "It didn't take much more to get the ball rolling" toward defiance of orders.

On May 24 the regiment had proudly paraded in uniform. Col. W. B. Franklin of the 12th Infantry, U.S. Army, reported to Hamilton Fish of the Union Defense Committee that men were ready to leave in six hours. They did go to Washington immediately, but few if any in the regiment knew on May 14 it was formally accepted from Gov. E. D. Morgan for three years of service. [Lord, 203; OR III, 1, 122, 202]

Hamilton Fish, who headed Union recruitment efforts in New York
Dictionary of American Portraits

Fourth, many discontented officers had addressed a petition to the War Department that pointed out the regiment's heavy losses at Bull Run. Col. James Cameron—earlier commander of the New York State Militia—had died on the field, and despised Lt. Col. Samuel M. Elliott had taken command. Every company had suffered casualties, and green soldiers told one another that they'd already done more than their share for the war effort.

The U.S. War Department initially voiced what seemed to be approval of the petition to go home and reorganize. This stance probably resulted from the fact that Simon Cameron, secretary of war, was a brother of the dead commander of the 79th. Soon the attitude in the War Department was reversed and the petition to go home and reorganize was denied. This

Federal forces retreating from Bull Run were partly covered by Gen. Louis Blenker and his brigade.

Library of Congress

led one officer after another to announce that he'd turn in his commission and go back to civilian life. [Woodruff, 97]

Enlisted men didn't have the privilege of deciding whether or not to stay in uniform, but they jealously guarded what they and hundreds of other regiments considered a near-sacred privilege that became a fifth source of grievance. They were convinced that it was their right to choose their commanding officer, and they intended to do so. Election of officers was linked with the strong states' rights mood that prevailed in the North as well as the South.

All plans had been made to elect a new colonel on the afternoon of August 13. Three days before the time set for the election, Isaac Stevens arrived and produced his papers. He made it clear that he was now in command of the 79th, and no election would be held. A West Pointer, Stevens lost an arm in the Mexican War. Service in Algiers and with the French army in Italy had made him tough as nails. He knew that discontent was rumbling in the camp before taking command, but intended to pay no attention to it. [Commager, 189; E, 718a]

This turn of events triggered more resignations by officers. When the ripple effect ended, the 79th held only one captain and a few lieutenants who had been with it since it was mustered. Every other officer was dead, in a hospital, or on the way to New York. Before Elliott plus Maj. David McClellan and Capt. Thomas Barclay had been gone an hour, a new rumor took off like a rocket and became a fifth contributor to boiling rage. Elliott's real reason for leaving was fear that his past activities would become public, the story alleged. According to it the greedy egg-sucking bookkeeper who didn't have a drop of Scottish blood in his veins had been paid $10,000 to entice men into uniform! [Todd, 203]

Difficult as it would have been to deal with multiple sources of discontent, there's a chance that Stevens could have doused the flames had not a potent sixth factor entered into the equation. Enlisted men were forbidden to have alcohol, but there was no way to keep it out of a regiment camped within sight of the unfinished dome of the Capitol. Whisky dealers abounded in the District of Columbia, and they were veterans at circumventing military regulations. By the evening of August 13, an estimated one man in four was drunk and most sober members of the 79th had a nip or two under their skin. [Commager, 487–89]

The Washington correspondent of the *Philadelphia Press,* an eyewitness to events of Wednesday, August 14, described them in detail for his readers. Apparently having heard rumors that news was likely to be made, he went to Meridian Hill early that morning. In the camp of the 79th he found its eight hundred or so members to

Gen. William T. Sherman *(center left)* was accused of taking better care of his horses than his fighting men.

Artist Thule Thulstrup

be "more like a mob than a regiment of soldiers." To him it seemed clear that "those who had drunk the most were the most turbulent." [OR, 124, 749; *Philadelphia Press*, August 1861]

Until he had been in the camp a few minutes, he did not realize what had happened earlier. At a dress parade the previous evening Stevens had notified his men that they were to march out at 6:00 on August 14. Their destination may have been Maryland, but many men in the ranks thought they were being ordered into strife-torn Virginia. A member of the regiment wrote that "the mutiny commenced by the men's refusing to strike their tents as commanded. There were to be struck at 5 A.M., and the Regiment was to move at 6 o'clock." [Commager, 487-89]

When his order was ignored, Stevens repeated it. Men of the regiment stood sullenly in line to signify that they didn't intend to obey any more orders. Their new commander tried persuasion, but he had no effect upon them. Hence he "sent to each company singly and read the articles of war," warning them of the consequences of disobedience.

Lt. William Lusk wrote that the camp where hundreds of angry men were assembled became "a scene of the wildest confusion." To one of the few officers still in the regiment, the mutiny seemed to be "more trying by far than the musketry or cannonading of Bull Run." [Commager, 487-89]

When Stevens saw that men in the ranks had no intention of striking their tents, he directed the handful of officers to perform this chore. They obeyed, wrote Lusk, "amid the jeers, the taunts, and the insults of an infuriated mob." While tents were being struck, one man showed Lusk that his gun was ready to be fired. He told the lieutenant that "it was intended for one officer at least to die." Once the tents were down, defiant men pitched them again to symbolize their refusal to go on the march.

Probably as a result of receiving a dispatch asking for his help, Gen. Daniel Sickles came to the camp. Momentarily, it looked as though he might be mobbed as an angry mob formed a cordon around his horse. Sickles, however, "coolly rode through the mutineers, and though unarmed, his demeanor prevented them from assaulting him." Acting as though he was ignoring the belligerents, he casually puffed upon a cigar. [*Philadelphia Press*, August 1861]

Early in the afternoon Sickles managed to disarm most members of the regiment. Once this was done, he selected men who appeared to be trustworthy and formed them into a guard. "No persuasion could induce the men to return to their duty," the newspaper correspondent wrote.

All other measures having failed, the new commander of the Army of the Potomac took action. Unaware of what Sickles had already done, Gen. George B. McClellan sent a dispatch to Gen. Andrew Porter, provost marshal of the capital, in which he said:

> The brigade commander [Sherman] of the Seventy-ninth Regiment New York Volunteers having reported that the regiment is in a state of open mutiny, you are directed to proceed with a battery, the two companies of the Second Cavalry [U.S. Army], and as many companies of regular infantry as you may deem proper, to the encampment of that regiment. On your arrival there you will order such as are willing to move to march out of camp, leaving the disaffected portion of the regiment by themselves. You will then order the latter portion to lay down their arms, and will put them under a strong guard. The ringleaders you will put in double irons.
>
> You are authorized, if necessary, to use force to accomplish the object. Report the result as soon as possible. [OR I, 5, 561]

By this time, Lusk and the other lieutenants who remained in the regiment were being threatened so forcefully that they tried not to show fear. At the same time, they took care to try to avoid doing anything that would lead to bloodshed. Fortunately for them, he wrote, "an old country quarrel" broke out among the men who were "most maddened by drink." Some of them were adherents of the Orangemen's movement; others were opponents of it. Members of the two groups momentarily turned their attention away from mutiny in order to fan the flames of long-drawn struggles in their native Scotland. In spite of this lull, Lusk felt that little significant progress had been made by early afternoon.

Stevens "called on the men for the last time to render obedience. Soberness and reflection had begun their work upon a few. These fell into their places, and were stationed around the camp as a guard over the others." This is the action with which Sickles was credited, though Lusk did not mention him in his first-hand account.

The lieutenant described himself as "quite exhausted" by the time "a body of cavalry and a line of infantry appeared, coming toward us." If McClellan's orders were followed, these regulars of the U.S. Army's famous 2nd Cavalry plus several companies of infantry were accompanied by a battery of field artillery.

As described for newspaper readers, the next act in the drama came quickly. Mutineers were scattered over a sparsely wooded hillside. One company of cavalry formed on top of the hill. Once they were in place, "the infantry marched past, and were drawn up on the side of the hill, the line extending to the base, and at an angle with the horsemen."

Stevens again called for all members of the 79th to fall into line; men facing loaded muskets and big guns "obeyed with reluctance." When the formation was complete, a detailed order was read to the mutineers:

> The General commanding has heard with the deepest pain of the acts of insubordination on the part of the Seventy-ninth regiment. Without attempting to enter into a discussion of the causes, it is sufficient to say that they are frivolous and groundless.
>
> These acts have thrown disgrace upon the regiment and the service, and taking place at this time, they give rise to the strongest suspicions of the most abject cowardice. The regiment has forced upon the Commanding General an issue which he is prepared to meet.
>
> The men are ordered to lay down their arms and return to duty. All those refusing to do so will be fired upon immediately. If they comply with the order, the ringleaders only will be punished.
>
> The colors of the regiment are taken from them, and will be returned only when their conduct in camp shall have proven that they understand the first duty of a soldier—obedience: and when, on the field of battle, they shall have proved their bravery. The names of the leaders in this revolt will be sent to the Governor of New York, to be placed in the archives of the State. A court-martial will be held forthwith. [McClellan, 99-100; RR, 2, doc. #184]

At Washington the colors (flag) of the 79th were taken from the regiment in a formal ceremony.

Leslie's Illustrated History of the Civil War

A private in one of the rear ranks yelled at the top of his voice in a distinct Scottish accent: "Let's keep the colors, boys!" Not a man responded to this challenge, so Porter requested Stevens to point out the leaders of the revolt. With a squad of men accompanying him, the colonel "went from company to company and designated the obnoxious members." The newspaper correspondent believed 40 or 50 men who were identified as leaders were placed under arrest; by this time, darkness had fallen, so he could not see all of the action. He did, however, hear Stevens order the regiment to "wheel by company into column and march to the [new] quarters in Virginia."

There was only an instant of delay. "Mutinous volunteers, evidently seeing that resistance was useless, reluctantly obeyed, and took up the line of march. The arrested leaders were taken to the guard house, while the remainder of the regiment was escorted by the cavalry and the battery." A line having been formed on the road at the base of the hill, "the regiment marched up Fourteenth street, with colors flying and band playing." A few men who were too drunk to march were left on the field to be picked up by a patrol. [*Philadelphia Press*, August 1861]

If a court-martial was held, the transcript of its actions was not preserved. Writing to his wife, Sherman said that 35 men were "placed in irons on board a man-of-war." He didn't say so in his letter, but these ringleaders of the biggest mutiny experienced by Federal forces up to that time were sent to the Dry Tortugas as prisoners. [Sherman, 212, 214]

Lusk described himself as "heartsick and much depressed." He said that most men of the regiment didn't have "the feelings of Americans," so he began "to repent bitterly" of having joined the Highlanders. He indicated personal eagerness for a battle that would give the regiment a chance to regain its colors that were stored in a hall at McClellan's headquarters. Yet the lieutenant also felt dread at the prospect of going into battle "now that our men are much demoralized." He fervently wished that it were possible for him to transfer into a Connecticut regiment. [Leech, 101, 110, 111]

In the capital, McClellan issued his General Order No. 4 as a precaution taken to prevent the spread of mutiny into other units. On August 16, "all passes, safe-conducts, and permits" given to enter or go beyond Federal lines on the Virginia side of the Potomac River were revoked. [McClellan, 100–101, here listed as Special Order No. 27]

One month after the mutiny was quelled by a show of force, the 79th New York went on reconnaissance near Lewinsville, Virginia. Importance of this village not far from Falls Church stemmed from the fact that five roads converged upon it. Capt. David Ireland, who was in field command that day, reported that his men came under "very severe" enemy cannonading during which three of them were wounded. He commended the conduct of officers and men as having been "cool and collected." Far from rebelling at any order, Ireland described them as having conducted themselves "more like veteran troops than volunteers." [Bailey, *Bloodiest*, 131; OR I, 5, 169–72, 175]

The successful foray of the 79th did not constitute a battle; it hardly merited classification as a skirmish. Yet fire of small arms and field artillery had been exchanged, and members of the regiment had earned the commendation of Ireland. With men believed to have incited the mutiny far away on the high seas or imprisoned on a desolate island, McClellan judged that the rest of the regiment needed encouragement. Hence he personally returned their prized colors to them. [CMH, 4, 181–82]

Reflecting upon the first major mutiny of the war and his handling of it, the commander of the Army of the Potomac was positive that he had done the right thing. The explosive and potentially lethal atmosphere that had prevailed on August 14 seemed to him to be due to "utter worthlessness of the officers." He was positive that from the beginning the 79th had "good material, but no officers."

[August 14, 1861, letter, McClellan to his wife; McClellan Papers, Library of Congress]

His optimism may have been a trifle greater than the complex situation warranted. A few days after having its colors restored, the 79th was again almost at the point of mutiny over pay. This time, prompt action by Gen. Benjamin F. Butler averted open mutiny (chapter 4). For the duration of the war, men in this regiment acquitted themselves with such bravery and honor that only about two hundred of them were left when hostilities ended. [OR III, 4, 56-57; D, 3, 1436]

8

Striking Back—Corps d'Afrique, December 9, 1863

"Tie 'em down. Right now."

Nodding obedience, members of the guard at Fort Jackson, Louisiana, gestured for two of their comrades to sprawl against a pair of old gun carriages. Once Harry Williams and Munroe Miller were in place about 5:30 P.M., their wrists were tightly tied to spokes of wheels.

At a gesture from Lt. Col. Augustus Benedict, guardsmen stepped aside. Looking as though he anticipated an interval of pleasure, the officer tested a mule whip by snapping it repeatedly in the air. Though complete with stock as well as lash, the whip was stiff from having hung in place for weeks without use. After three or four minutes, a nod of satisfaction indicated that it was judged it to have become sufficiently limber. Clearly a veteran user, Benedict made it give a snap almost as loud as a pistol shot before turning his attention to waiting culprits.

Muscles of their bare backs twitched during the warm-up, but neither of them moved. Both were musicians whose birth dates were not known. Williams looked as though he might be somewhere between 19 and 22; Miller was a few years older.

Benedict seemed initially to have planned to deliver alternate blows, but at the last minute he decided to take the offenders one at a time. By the time he stopped lashing Williams, who gritted his teeth and made no sound, Miller was writhing silently. As blow after blow fell upon him, the older musician sobbed before begging for mercy.

Col. Charles Drew, commandant of the fort, passed nearby during the punishment but averted his eyes and quickened his pace. So did three or four other officers whose business required them to go near the site. Five or six dozen soldiers, most of whom had been ordered into position by Benedict, watched with combined fear and rage. To them it seemed that Miller got a few extra lashes for having broken during his ordeal, but they were not sure. None of them could count past ten, and some knew no arithmetic at all.

When the two men were cut down, both dropped to the surface of the fort's parade and lay there briefly. Miller's sobs were no longer audible, but his chest continued to heave mightily. Williams briefly beat the stone surface with both fists, then suddenly rolled over and jumped to his feet. Without a word, a guard handed him his coat and shirt.

Benedict gave a bow to his assembled audience, almost as though he had been performing on stage. "That's all for today, soldiers," he called loudly. "Go to your quarters."

Though an estimated seven hundred Confederates had been based at Fort Jackson earlier, living quarters in the bastion were limited. Ex-slaves who formed two companies of the 4th Infantry, Corps d'Afrique, slept in tents just outside the walls. Security was supposed to be tight; any man quartered under canvas had to ask permission to enter the fort. When his tour of duty was over, a guard had to give him a nod before he could leave. None of the men quartered inside were supposed to leave except when going on an errand for an officer.

Organization of the Corps d'Afrique was launched in Louisiana in April, 1863, when the 1st Regiment of Engineers was organized at Camp Parapet. Twenty-five regiments of artillery, engineers, cavalry, and infantry came into existence very quickly; all were formed in Louisiana. Like the earliest South Carolina regiments made up of black recruits, the corps designation was dropped and regiments in it became labeled as U.S. Colored Troops.

Before the war ended, 138 regiments of black infantry had been established. The wide disparity between treatment of white officers and black privates of the 3rd Regiment, Corps d'Afrique, was presumably pervasive throughout Federal forces. [D, 3, 1718-40]

Benedict was sure he had seen both of the men he whipped slip out of Jackson after having told believable lies to sentries. He had been in command of the regiment less than 24 hours, transferring to it from Fort St. Philip across the Mississippi River. To him, it seemed right and proper to demonstrate immediately that he would tolerate no infraction of rules.

While at St. Philip he had made men stand stiffly at attention during the middle of a summer day while he slowly read the entire Articles of War to them. Striding toward his quarters after having replaced the whip he had taken from a rack, the lieutenant colonel decided he'd very soon schedule a reading of the Articles of War to the entire garrison of Jackson.

Enlisted men of the Corps d'Afrique, all of whom were black, were widely called "Buffalo Soldiers."

In October 1862, men of the 1st South Carolina Colored Regiment were attacked by bloodhounds.

That tentative plan was never implemented.

Almost exactly an hour after Benedict first gave a test snap with his whip, about two-thirds of those members of his command who were quartered inside Jackson burst out of their barracks. Most of them carried rifles, and one or two shots were fired before they emerged into the open parade ground.

By the time the entire body of belligerents surged across the parade a few words could be heard, intermingled with incoherent shouts. One officer clearly heard an unknown soldier yell "Kill him!" at the top of his voice. Another officer noticed that Williams seemed to be leading the pack. He was not positive, but he thought the musician screamed something about "getting Benedict."

Drew was in his office catching up with paper work when the riot began. He heard nothing, so looked up with surprise and a bit of annoyance when an aide burst into the room without knocking.

"You'd better come right now, sir," he was told. "Lots of the men are under arms! They're lookin' for trouble!"

The colonel started to reply, but said nothing. With the door open, he could hear occasional gunshots plus the muffled sounds of an angry crowd. Quickly taking off his side arm because sight of it could be inflammatory, he hurried to the parade. Benedict was there when the commotion started. Probably having heard his name shouted, he raced for his quarters on the parapet. Slamming the door shut and hastily bracing it, he made sure that his revolver was fully loaded. Then he reached for the handgun used by Maj. William Nye, with whom he bunked.

Outside, the commotion grew louder and gunshots became more frequent. To Benedict, it seemed for a moment that the surge of noise was headed toward the quarters of officers. He was positive that not a man in the command knew where he bunked, after having been there so short a time. That was small consolation to him. Unchecked, the mob of soldiers who had never been in battle could soon start looking for him, room by room.

Though that search may have been vaguely planned, it never took place. Drew pushed his way into the mob of screaming and cursing soldiers. Gesturing to emphasize the fact that he was unarmed, he managed to quiet two or three of them by warning that they faced severe punishment if they did not help him restore order. With the help of these men and three or four of his subordinates who rushed to the parade when they heard the commotion, he brought the mob of angry men under control in about an hour. A few shots were still fired into the air at intervals from outer fringes of the crowd, but men who were accosted one by one obediently put their weapons down.

No later than 8:00 P.M., order was restored. All of the rioters had relinquished their weapons and returned to their barracks. Though littered, the empty parade was now silent. Heaving a great sigh, Drew gestured for one of his captains to come to his side. He doubted that there would be another outbreak before morning, but knew that precautions were in order. At his direction, the captain hurried off to dispatch a telegram asking for help from armed vessels of the U.S. Navy.

At New Orleans, the commander of the Department of the Gulf immediately reported twice about the mutiny at Fort Jackson to Gen. Henry W. Halleck. Gen. Nathaniel P. Banks noted that Benedict's use of the whip had triggered the riot. Without military experience prior to the sectional conflict, he was widely known as "The Bobbin Boy of Massachusetts" because he went

Gen. Lorenzo Thomas headed the program aimed at recruitment and organization of black volunteers.
Photographic History of the Civil War

to work in a cotton mill at a very early age. He has been blamed for a number of Federal defeats, but his integrity was never questioned. [GB, 17–18]

Banks was not an ardent abolitionist, but he was a warm advocate of the use of black soldiers. In dealing with the incident at Fort Jackson, he took pains to stress that black soldiers were still useful and reliable and were urgently needed. Many regiments had been organized in his department, he reminded Washington, and he had taken keen personal interest in training them.

After tattoo was sounded early at Jackson, all insurgents went to their quarters. Their brief and potentially deadly disregard for discipline and for orders was believed by Banks to have stemmed in part from a visit made during the summer by Gen. Lorenzo Thomas. Thomas was head of the entire process designed to recruit ex-slaves and put them into uniform. While down river from New Orleans, he spoke at length to men at St. Philip. Some of them later transferred to Jackson, and undoubtedly remembered part of what he told them. Banks wanted officials in Washington to know:

> The negroes have been constantly assured, whether engaging in labor or enlisting as soldiers, that under no circumstances whatever were they to be subjected to the degrading punishment of flogging. This has always been made a condition by them, and

they have always received this assurance from officers of the Government. [OR I, 26, I, 456, 467]

Upon reporting to New Orleans by order of Drew, Benedict tendered his resignation but it was not accepted. Banks had already selected members of a military commission to look into the outbreak at the fort. It would be headed by Francis J. Herron. Elevated in rank early in 1863, at that time he became the youngest major general on either side. [OR I, 26, I, 459; GB, 229]

On the night of the outbreak, Banks had ordered two regiments of soldiers to go to the help of officers at Fort Jackson. Commodore Henry H. Bell of the West Gulf Blockading Squadron had responded to the urgent call for help by dispatching the USS *Kanawha* and *Arizona* down the river. According to Capt. J. B. Marchand, gunboats stopped at the quarantine station some distance up the river from the fort. There they received word that Drew did not want them to go beyond it. He was sure he could preserve order, he said, if neither gunboats nor troops came directly to the fort. [NOR I, 18, 714–16]

Gen. Francis J. Herron headed the military commission that investigated the mutiny in the Corps d'Afrique.
Harper's History of the Great Rebellion

Banks' report about findings of his commission went to Washington eight days after the mutiny. A lengthy transcript of its proceedings provided virtually all known details about events on the evening of December 9. He stressed that nothing in it served "to impair the confidence of the Government in the efficiency and reliability of black troops."

They revolted, in Banks' judgment, because men were subjected to punishment "contrary to the rules of war, and contrary to the orders constantly given in this department." Referring to what he now knew about Benedict prior to going to Fort Jackson, Banks labeled some punishments meted out there as "classed among the cruel and unusual punishments interdicted by the Constitution."

Drew was judged "derelict in reporting the conduct of some of his subordinate officers." In a lengthy dispatch of December 17, Banks devoted considerable space to an account of his personal efforts to recruit and train black troops. Yet he had no choice; he was required to treat "the affair at Fort Jackson as a case of mutiny against official authority."

Numerous officers were questioned by members of the commission, but no enlisted man was called before it. That meant, of course, that no soldier identified as a leader of the mutiny spoke to the commission in his own defense.

Drew believed that the issue of pay was simmering below the surface when the mutiny broke out. Black and white soldiers were rated at the same $13 per month at that time. This apparent equality was false, however, for whites in uniform got an extra $3 per month for clothing. The same amount was deducted from the pay of blacks, making their actual total pay $10 against $16 for whites. [OR I, 26, I, 461, 463]

According to the colonel, the mutiny was a spontaneous affair that was not planned in advance. He said he told mutineers that Benedict had done wrong, "but that was no excuse for their conduct." At one point during the melee, insurgents seemed to have thought guns of the fort might be turned on them. Drew took advantage of this false rumor by telling men that if they would go to their quarters he "would take no further steps at that time." [OR I, 26, I, 460-61]

Though he was reported as having been "mysteriously missing" during the mutiny, Maj. William E. Nye was questioned at length. He caught a brief glimpse of Benedict wielding a whip, but immediately closed a door and went back to his quarters. According to him, mutineers believed the lieutenant colonel had taken refuge on the army transport steamer *Suffolk*, which was lying near the fort at the time of the riot. He was under the impression that some blacks had tried to reach the vessel and was sure they would have killed Benedict if they had caught him. [OR I, 26, I, 464-65; NOR I, 20, 716]

Capt. James Miller estimated that half of the five hundred men in the regiment took part in the mutiny. A soldier known to him, Frank Williams, took two thrusts at him with a bayonet. Fortunately, both blows hit upon what he called his belt-plate, so he was not injured. According to him, Benedict often struck men under him and on the day of the mutiny whipped the two musicians severely with what appeared to him to be a rawhide lash.

Miller, like Benedict, was stationed at Fort St. Philip before being transferred to Jackson. At the installation on the east bank of the river he saw the lieutenant colonel mete out severe punishment. He "spread a man out on his back" before having stakes driven down to hold him in place. Once the offender could not move his arms or legs, molasses was spread over him to attract ants and flying insects. The fellow being punished lay there for a full day and part of the next. [OR I, 26, I, 466-68]

First Lt. George H. Kimball saw part of the whipping, but could shed no new light on what took place during the mutiny. With officers other than Benedict being called in descending order of rank, Sgt. George McFaul took the stand next. Unlike witnesses who turned their heads and hurried away when they happened upon the site of punishment on December 8, he stood and watched. Consequently he saw Benedict "strike Harry Williams from fifteen to twenty times with an army wagoner's whip or an artillery driver's whip."

During a period when both the lieutenant colonel and he were stationed at Baton Rouge in the summer, McFaul followed orders and staked out two men before smearing them with molasses. Having been officer of the guard at the time, he recalled hearing Benedict say that he didn't care if the men were kept in position on their backs until they died.

It was his impression that both were being punished for "stealing some corn to roast," but he was not positive that this was their offense. Though the matter did not come to light during hearings, Benedict is believed earlier to have slashed a man with his sword because of improper dress. [OR I, 26, I, 470-71; WWW, 49]

After having decided not to hear from any enlisted men, the commission established by Banks brought in Benedict and he was "duly sworn by the judge-advocate." His testimony was brief, and no questions were put to him concerning events of December 9 or earlier incidents in which he inflicted severe punishment. He denied that he was in his quarters during the entire riot, saying that men on the parade told him they wanted to be treated like soldiers. Alluding to Williams and Miller, he said he told insurgents that "Those boys were bad boys, and I treated them as such." According to him, rioters responded by pleading, "Don't shoot; don't shoot!" [OR I, 26, I, 473-74]

Throughout the hearing and in the report about it, the only label officers applied to black soldiers was "boys." Members of the body ruled that "the conduct of the men was more owing to an ignorance of their rights and the proper means of redress than to any preconcerted plan of revolt." [OR I, 26, I, 461, 462, 473, 475]

Despite this finding, a court-martial was convened at Fort Jackson on December 17. Its members sat for three days before delivering their verdicts, based in large part upon a transcript of hearings held by the Banks commission. As reproduced much later, the transcript runs to 15 pages of extremely fine print. [OR I, 26, I, 457-59, 460-74, 476]

Twelve black soldiers who were accused of having been leaders were charged with mutiny. Cpl. Henry Green plus Pvts. Jacob Kennedy, Volser Verritt, and James Hagan were found not guilty. Pvt. James H. Moore, charged only with insubordinate conduct, was found guilty and was sentenced "to hard labor for one month under guard."

Edward B. Smith, who like the two men who were whipped was a musician, was found guilty of mutiny and was ordered "to be imprisoned at hard labor for one year." Also convicted of having led the mutiny, Cpl. Lewis Cady was sentenced to two years. Pvt. Willis Curtis drew three years, Charles Taylor received a sentence of 10 years, and Julius Boudro was given 20 years at hard labor.

Williams, whose whipping was believed to have triggered the mutiny, had been seen urging his comrades into action. So had Pvt. Abraham Victoria, according to testimony by officers. Both men were found guilty and both were sentenced "to be shot to death with musketry at such time and place as the commanding general may direct." [OR I, 26, I, 476–79]

Benedict had been charged with "inflicting cruel and unusual punishment, to the prejudice of good order and military discipline." He entered a plea of "Not guilty," but members of the court ruled against him. As a result of this finding, he was sentenced "to be dismissed the service." [OR I, 26, I, 479]

Banks dissolved the court-martial and approved most sentences imposed by it. Finding evidence against Pvt. James H. Moore to be "conflicting and unsatisfactory," the man from Massachusetts ordered that he be released from confinement and returned to duty. He suspended execution of the sentences of Williams and Victoria "until further orders." Banks then directed that they be taken to Fort Jefferson, Florida, along with their comrades who had been sentenced to hard labor.

"In the case of Lieut. Col. August W. Benedict," ruled the man who was known as Bobbin Boy before donning a uniform, "the proceedings, findings, and sentence are confirmed. He ceases from this date to be an officer in the military service of the United States."

Viewed from the perspective of many decades, the gulf between the sentence meted out to Benedict whose brutality started the mutiny and the sentences of enlisted men who staged a violent protest appears to have been enormous. His only punishment consisted of having to take off his uniform and return to civilian life. Williams and Victoria probably were never executed but may have had their sentences informally and unofficially reduced to life at hard labor. If that is correct, mutineers spent two lifetimes plus 33 years and one month at hard labor as a result of having rebelled at what Banks himself regarded as "cruel and unusual punishment."

The revolt by men of the Corps d'Afrique gave Fort Jackson a unique place in annals of the war. It was the only installation in which there were two separate and unrelated mutinies. The first was staged by members of a Confederate garrison while under fire (chapter 5), and the second flared among Federal volunteers because they had seen and taken all the cruelty they could handle.

9

Three Disputed Weeks–20th New York, April 29, 1863

Camped near Falmouth, Virginia, U.S. Gen. Joseph Hooker consulted every attorney on his staff. He faced two thorny issues and did not wish to risk having his actions questioned by civilians. Though his plans were not yet firm, he had made up his mind to hit the Army of Northern Virginia very hard. It was possible that he could give "Granny" Lee and his secesh boys a blow hard enough to bring the war to a speedy end. Nothing must be left to chance.

Friction between army and navy commanders, always simmering, seemed about to boil over. Several disputes concerning jurisdiction had not been resolved. These centered in the lower Potomac and Patuxent Rivers plus inlets and mouths of rivers opening into Chesapeake Bay. At Hooker's request, Gen. Robert C. Schenck sent one of his commanders to Washington. Gen. Henry H. Lockwood was directed to see the secretary of war. The issue was too vital to be settled by one of his aides.

Hooker gave his personal attention to the second vexatious matter. The Army of the Potomac presently included 39 New York regiments whose members had volunteered for only two years of service. A few regiments held men who were obligated to fight for only nine months. Collectively, these units gave him 22,901 men. He absolutely had to have every short-term regiment for a few more weeks. His planned offensive wouldn't get off the ground if 20,000 or so men started back to the Empire State. On April 20, 1863, he drafted General Order No. 44 and larded it heavily with promises. Taking care that a copy of it went to Edwin M. Stanton, he directed that it be read "at the head of each company of the two years' and nine-months regiments serving in this army."

Six separate offers and stipulations were included in the order. (1) Re-enlistment of a company or regiment will guarantee retention of its officers plus a furlough. (2) If a regiment declines re-enlistment, it will be mustered out after turning in its arms and equipments. (3) When less than half of the men in a regiment re-enlist, the number of officers retained will be governed by General Order No. 86, of the War Department. (4) Part of the bounty offered for re-enlistment will be paid in connection with the first payment after returning from furlough. (5) In mixed regiments holding both two- and three-year men, the latter will be given special consideration about furloughs. (6) Three-year men in mixed regiments will be transferred to three-year regiments from the same state if two-year men do not re-enlist. [OR I, 40, 231, 233–34, 243; OR III, 3, 751]

Hooker's carefully prepared order covered all aspects of the situation except one. It failed to specify whether a regiment's service began when enlisted into state service or into federal service, always a few weeks later. Some New Yorkers who stood at attention while the detailed instructions were being read took it for granted that their service began when they signed up to become members of Empire State regiments.

One week after General Order No. 44 was circulated, the Army of the Potomac was poised to cross the Rappahannock River as the first move in a thrust designed to bring head-on collision with the Army of Northern Virginia. Officers at the head of a canvas pontoon train were directed to proceed slowly and conspicuously toward Port Conway. Hopefully, enough dust would be raised "to draw the enemy's force in that direction." Enlisted men were not to be informed of the reason for the movement. [OR I, 40, 234]

Officers of the cavalry corps were instructed to identify and remove "all men and animals not capable of performing long and rapid marches, day and night." President Lincoln was reminded that an immediate open thrust across the Rappahannock could involve great loss because water was very deep from spring rains. From Gen. George Stoneman, Hooker had just learned that even small streams were so swollen that without pontoons men and animals would have to swim across. Hence Lincoln was informed that his general planned to threaten a crossing at several points, so his men "could spring across the river when a suitable opportunity presents itself." [OR I, 40, 238, 245]

A confidential report from Dr. Jonathan Letterman, shared with the secretary of war, showed nearly one-tenth of the men in the First Corps to be sick because of "neglect of sanitary precautions and bad diet." In the Engineer Brigade, however, the percent of sick men was only a trifle more than half as high. [OR I, 40, 239–40]

Superintendents of military railroads in Virginia were told to use extraordinary precautions and accept no orders except from the general in command of a department if trains seemed in danger of being captured. Thaddeus Lowe and his Balloon Department were camped near Falmouth. On April 28 they were directed to get a balloon up after dark in order to spot the enemy's campfires. [OR I, 40, 245, 277]

At Winchester, a Rebel prisoner who had spent two days in irons broke and spilled everything he knew. He gave a detailed account of numerous forces, including estimates of their positions and the number of men in each. Gen. Robert H. Milroy was inclined to believe Andrew T. Leopold, he told Schenck, because things he divulged were "strongly corroborated by other

Gen. George Stoneman, who alerted other Federal commanders to the fact that Virginia rivers and streams were swollen from heavy rain

U.S. Army Military History Institute

circumstances and information." Near Warrenton Junction, Stoneman received what he considered to be valuable information from George W. Lake. A resident of Maine, he had managed to reach Stoneman's forces by way of Harrisonburg and New Market and had observed carefully as he traveled.

Hooker's response to Stoneman was almost disdainful in tone. He told his subordinate that "We have much more reliable information than [Lake] has furnished. We know the strength of the enemy in front, and he is looking for us to advance in this vicinity." Schenck was less confident that his commander. From Baltimore he confided to Gen. Henry W. Halleck than Hooker was "certainly mistaken" in some of his estimates of enemy strength. [OR I, 40, 252–55]

On April 26 officers and men of the XI and XII Corps were directed to be on the march at sunrise. Their movement was delayed, however, by a storm that Hooker labeled as severe. Telegraph wires were cut west of Piedmont, making it impossible to rapidly communicate in that area. Gen. Washington L. Elliott had been confident he would soon capture forces led by C.S. Gen. William E. Jones. He ruefully reported he was stopped by Lost River, which he found too

U.S. Gen. Daniel Butterfield, who notified Hooker that his balloonists had little to report

Buttre Engraving

C.S. Gen. William E. "Grumble" Jones and his men were protected by swollen Lost River.

Library of Congress

deep to cross without a bridge—and he didn't have the tools to build one. [OR I, 40, 256-61]

Men of the Second Corps were ordered to move toward Banks' Ford at sunrise on April 28. They were cautioned, however, not to attempt to lay bridges during the ensuing 36 hours. On the 29th, bridges must be "thrown across the instant the enemy may leave or be driven from the opposite side."

Simultaneously, commanders of three other corps were given instructions about crossing the Rappahannock. In every instance, Hooker wanted troops concealed "up to the moment the demonstration" began. Ambulances and wagon trains were to be parked behind a range of hills, so they would not be seen by the enemy. Gen. Henry W. Bentham was put in charge of laying two bridges at each crossing point. Hooker directed that they be ready for use before 3:30 A.M. on the 29th.

Wind was unfortunately high that day, making it impossible for Lowe and his men to make balloon ascents for observation purposes. Gen. Daniel Butterfield, who sent this unpleasant word to Hooker, seemed to be emotionally crushed by the weather, saying he'd feel "almost heartbroken if we were baffled again by a storm." At 5:00 P.M., rain was still coming down in sheets at Falmouth. Lowe managed to make several ascents that day, the 29th, but had little to

report "in consequence of the dense fog that envelops the earth."
[OR I, 40, 266-77]

In Washington, Stanton received a telegram from Gov. Andrew
G. Curtin of Pennsylvania. Expressing near desperation because a
section of the Baltimore and Ohio Railroad had been torn up by a
Rebel force, Curtin said he was "without arms, artillery, or ammunition." His message ended with a plea: "What can you do for us?"

The President took personal responsibility for responding to
the call for help from the vital Keystone State. From the War Department he sent a telegram to Harrisburg saying:

> I do not think the people of Pennsylvania should be uneasy
> about an invasion. Doubtless a small force is flourishing about
> in the northern part of Virginia on the "scewhorn" principle, on
> purpose to divert us in another quarter. I believe it is nothing
> more. We think we have adequate force close after them. [OR I,
> 40, 278-79]

Lincoln didn't know that mutiny had occurred in the Army of the
Potomac that morning. Had he been aware of it, he would have been
deeply concerned that it might spread quickly throughout the ranks
of fighting men in blue.

Camped close to the Rappahannock River, men of the 20th New
York had been talking and exchanging memoranda about their enlistment for at least a month. A petition drafted earlier was transmitted
to Col. Ernst von Vegesack soon after first light on April 29. A professional soldier who had fought in the Crimean War, he had been
put at the head of the regiment because he could communicate with
its members and was familiar with their thought processes. Known
in New York City as the United Turner Regiment, it was made up
entirely of Germans—some of whom spoke no English. Having
reached what they considered to be solid proof that they enlisted on
April 28, 1861, 201 men of the regiment indicated that they intended
immediately to go home.

Documentary evidence concerning their claim is somewhat contradictory. In some sources that are considered reliable, these men
are listed as having been organized on May 6, 1861, at New York City.
On July 10 of the first year of conflict, New York's Adjutant General J.
Meredith Read, Jr., notified his counterpart in Washington:

> It is proper to state that Companies A, B, C, D, and E of Colo-
> nel Weber's regiment (the Twentieth) are reported as mustered
> for three months, but I think that was an oversight, the muster-
> ing orders having been different. The rolls read "two years" in the
> caption and "three months" in Captain Smith's (Topographical
> Engineers) certificates.

Balloons took Thaddeus Lowe's "astronauts" up, but on some days they saw nothing of importance.

Three weeks later the secretary of war sent one of many calls for men to Gov. Edwin D. Morgan of New York. The President, said Cameron, wanted the chief executive of the Empire State to provide Companies A, B, C, D, and E of the 20th Regiment of New York Volunteers "for a service of two years." Cameron was careful to note that these companies had "heretofore been mustered into the service of the United States for three months only." [OR I, 122, 368]

Huddled together for warmth from the chilling rain, rebellious men of the 20th did not protest that there may have been irregularities concerning their term of service. They wanted it made clear that their enlistment had expired since the regiment had its official beginning on April 29—two years earlier to the day. Von Vegesack could not resolve the impasse between some of his men and their commanding general; his name first appeared in the table of organization, Army of the Potomac, on January 31, 1863. [OR I, 25, II, 25]

Had someone made careful plans, it would have been difficult to devise a more troublesome development for Hooker's forces. If word of discontent in the 20th should spread, it could very well become contagious. Each of New York's two-year regiments could be affected, as well as units from other states in which enlistment began very early.

According to clippings from German-language newspapers, most of which are undated and do not show the source from which they came, someone of higher rank than von Vegesack acted swiftly and decisively. On May 1, members of a hastily named court-martial held a brief session close to the Rappahannock River. It took them less than two hours to find all 201 protesting members of the 20th guilty of mutiny and to sentence them to become inmates of a military prison for the duration of the war. [Clipping files, USAMHI and National Archives]

Col. Ernst von Vegesack commanded the 20th New York.

No record of the court-martial is preserved in the OR. A single brief and easily misinterpreted memorandum appears in the May 31, 1863, table of organization of the Army of the Potomac. A footnote in type of microscopic size is attached to the makeup of the Third Brigade, Second Division, Sixth Army Corps. That terse memorandum makes no mention of mutiny or court-martial. It simply reports "The Twentieth and Thirty-third New York Regiments sent home for muster-out." In the case of the 20th, this reference perhaps applies to men who didn't mutiny. Their depleted ranks may account for the inept performance of the 20th New York in the Chancellorsville Campaign, during which it sustained 208 casualties. [OR I, 40, 581, 597, 609–10; Goolrick, 158; CV, 26, 161]

New York newspaper publishers Friedrich Kapp and Sigismund Kaufmann seem to have had a close if not an intimate relationship with Abraham Lincoln. Had he not been widely and enthusiastically supported by German-Americans in 1860, there is no certainty that he would have won the Republican nomination at Chicago. Having learned of the actions of Germans who refused to cross the Rappahannock, the influential publishers appealed directly to the man they helped to elect.

He soon discovered that the convicted culprits were prisoners at or near the Germantown, Maryland, headquarters of the Army of the Potomac. Some time in early August—approximately three months after men of the 20th were convicted of mutiny—Lincoln exercised executive clemency and ordered the release of all 201 men.

Had they adhered to Hooker's formula, men who rebelled at it would have remained in uniform an additional three weeks. That would have enabled them to take part in the humiliating Federal defeat at Chancellorsville. Actions of the President nullified the court-martial of sufficient German-Americans to fill two full companies. Chances are that Lincoln exercised his power without having been apprized of a legal ruling.

On April 24—five days before men of the 20th claimed that their enlistment came to an end—the solicitor general of the United States issued an opinion. It dealt directly with "Questions concerning the beginning of the terms of service of the New York two-year men."

The discharge dates of the numerous regiments in this category, said the solicitor general, should be two years from the date they were organized and mustered into state service. Had that formula been used, most or all of the mutineers would have gone home on April 23—nine days before they stacked their arms and said they'd obey no more orders.

10

False Allegations–2nd Maine, August 14, 1861

Abraham Lincoln's call for 75,000 volunteers needed for three months went out on Monday, April 16, 1861. Maj. Robert Anderson had surrendered Fort Sumter on the previous day. The effective strength of the U.S. Army was less than 15,000 men, so the huge pool of military manpower to be drawn largely from state militia represented an enormously large military force.

Eagerness to save the Union pervaded the entire North. Maine was far from the region directly affected by sectional strife, but patriotism ran high in the thinly populated state. At Portland, organization of a regiment of infantry proceeded rapidly. Mustered in for three months of service on April 28, the regiment was not ordered to Washington until June 1. Its men did not take part in the battle of Bull Run. Like numerous other bodies of volunteers, they were needed for defense of the capital. After remaining on duty there until August 1, without having experienced combat, they were sent home and were mustered out on August 5. [D, 3, 1219]

At Bangor, about one hundred miles north of Portland, recruitment for Federal service moved more slowly. Also responding to the call for three-month volunteers, the 2nd Maine left the state on May 14. Records indicate that at Willett's Point, New York, the regiment was mustered into U.S. service. Men who comprised it moved to Washington one day earlier than their comrades from Portland.

Upon reaching the capital, Maine's second body of men willing to fight for the Union was also assigned to help guard the city. Part of the time its members were stationed at a brand-new fortification, one of many that were hastily thrown up so that a threatened attack by secessionists could be stopped. Fort Corcoran was originally no

92

more than a set of earthworks. Men who moved into and around the spot held their heads high. The defensive work was named for Col. Michael Corcoran—the first Federal officer to be selected by lottery to serve as hostage for a captured Rebel seaman who was on trial for piracy.

Despite fears on the part of the President and some of his advisors, enemies made no visible move toward the capital. In the aftermath of the Federal debacle at Bull Run, Gen. P. G. T. Beauregard decided that his victorious troops were too worn out to pursue their enemies. New sets of rumors circulated throughout Washington and its environs every day, however. Men who were far from home soon found themselves becoming weary of sitting around and doing nothing except listening to gossip and taking part in drills and exercises.

Secession, which men from Maine and two dozen other states had come to quell, had broken out on the state level. Residents of Virginia who lived west of the Allegheny Mountains had taken steps to secede from the state. Though documentation is sparse, they were clearly encouraged to take this step by key national leaders. As early as August 8, Francis H. Pierpont of Wheeling was being addressed as governor of Virginia by military officials.

Even some men from faraway Maine probably knew that Richmond had been the capital of Virginia for many decades. They heard

Col. Michael Corcoran *(extreme left)* and officers at the fort named in his honor
U.S. Signal Corps

snatches of talk about the possible creation of a new state, but the matter would have been of little interest to them. [OR I, 5, 556]

Men who expected to go home very soon perked up their ears and listened when there was talk about a blockade, however. Lincoln had announced a blockade of ports located in seceded states, but at the moment did not have the power to enforce it. Rebels had reacted by establishing a blockade of the Potomac River that was quite effective for a time. Rations of men from Portland and Bangor may have been affected by a serious shortage of commodities that usually came to the capital by riverboats. August rains, notoriously heavy in 1861, had made some roads leading to the capital impassable.

Francis H. Pierpont led the movement to create West Virginia—and was sometimes addressed as governor of Virginia.

Lossing, *The Civil War in America*

Men from the Portland area had served three days past their enlistment period when they were released from Federal service on August 1. About eight hundred jubilant volunteers who made up this regiment were back in Maine on August 5, ready to resume their lives as civilians.

Word that their comrades had gone home stirred up a storm of indignation among men of the 2nd Maine. They had reached Washington at least two days ahead of the fellows from Portland; why on earth were they not headed north also?

Having little to do except sit around and grouse, the more men of the 2nd talked about the situation the madder they became. Clearly as a result of having made plans for several days and having fashioned a pact, many of them decided that if Uncle Sam wouldn't act, neither would they.

On August 14 the commander of the military Division of the Potomac, Gen. George B. McClellan, sent a report to Gen. Winfield Scott who was still in command of the U.S. Army. He told the aging hero of the Mexican War who had once been a candidate for the presidency:

> I am informed by Brigadier-General McDowell [now junior in rank] that 62 non-commissioned officers and privates of the Second Regiment of Maine Volunteers have formally and positively,

and in the presence of their regiment, refused to do any further duty whatever, falsely alleging that they are no longer in the service of the United States. I concur in the suggestion of General McDowell that this combined insubordination, if not open mutiny, should be immediately repressed; and I approve of his recommendation that the insubordinate soldiers should be immediately transferred in arrest and without arms to the Dry Tortugas, to perform such fatigue service as the commanding officer there may assign to them. [OR I, 5, 561]

Mutiny erupted simultaneously in the 79th New York. In the case of this regiment, cavalry, infantry, and an artillery battery were sent to their camp to subdue the insurgents (chapter 7). This show of force put an end to rebellion by eight hundred men in blue. Their punishment consisted of having the regimental colors taken from them briefly.

Dispatches concerning the two breaches of discipline on a single day were delivered by courier; unlike messages transmitted by telegraph, these have no time notations. Hence it is impossible to know which came to McClellan's attention first. In view of the way he handled their aftermath, it is likely that he was already angry about

Some mutineers in the ranks of the 79th New York are believed briefly to have occupied cells in the Washington Station House.

The Soldier in Our Civil War

mutiny among New Yorkers when he turned his attention to the 2nd Maine.

A McClellan biographer has characterized the major general's response to trouble in that regiment as "prompt and blunt." As he warned in his message to Scott, the punishment McClellan meted out this time was imprisonment at hard labor at an isolated fortress off the Florida Keys. He ordered 63 of the Maine volunteers to be taken there immediately. Writing to his wife about the matter, Gen. William T. Sherman said that 65 "were marched down to the Navy Yard and placed in irons on board a man-of-war." [Sears, 98; Howe, 215]

Gideon Welles, U.S. secretary of the navy, was kept informed about the shipment of mutineers.

U.S. Army Military History Institute

Regardless of whether McClellan or Sherman was correct in the exact number of mutineers subjected to harsh punishment, not all of them were on their way to prison immediately. On August 26, Cmdr. Maxwell Woodhull of the U.S. Navy sent a dispatch to Gideon Welles, secretary of the navy. Upon reaching Hampton Roads the previous day he had received orders to transport to the Dry Tortugas as many mutinous soldiers as the USS *Connecticut* could handle. After consultation with a military leader, Woodhull decided that 50 mutineers constituted "a number quite as great as I have the means properly to guard and keep in subjection." At the end of his message he noted that he was not even provided with "a sufficient quantity of irons" and could not obtain them. [NOR I, 27, 361]

The log of the warship temporarily serving as a supply vessel has been preserved. It covers the period August 23, 1861, to October 5, 1865, but yields no clue concerning mutineers taken aboard at Newport News. Since it was operating off Key West in November, prisoners were presumably delivered to the Dry Tortugas before then. Their ultimate fate—and that of the 13 or 15 whom the *Connecticut* could not transport, is unknown. [NOR I, 27, 684–85]

Men of the 2nd Maine refused to obey orders because they had seen their comrades go home and were convinced that terms of enlistment of the two regiments were identical. McClellan, who probably had no documentary evidence on which to base his verdict, considered their claims to be "false allegations."

Strangely, Dyer's record adds to the confusion instead of clearing it up. According to his findings, men of the 2nd were "mustered into U.S. service for two and three years May 28, 1861." Two aspects of that notation are puzzling.

President Abraham Lincoln was on record as having promised Congress that if given the men and money he needed, the conflict would be "a short, and a decisive one." He incorporated this idea into his July 4 message to the special session of Congress. That being the view of the Federal commander in chief of military and naval forces, there seemed to be no need for two- or three-year terms of enlistment. [CW, 4, 431]

A notation made in New York that some men of the 2nd signed up for two years and others for three is equally difficult to understand. At this stage in the conflict, all of the men who made up a regiment almost invariably signed up for the same length of service. [D, 3, 1219]

No wonder the fellows from Bangor were puzzled, if they were aware of either of these two matters. They mutinied because they vowed that they owed Uncle Sam three months of service, no less and no more. Is it possible that some recruitment officer at Willett's Point plied all of them with whisky and then got their shaky signatures upon two sets of documents?

Perhaps. It is possible, but not provable, that "false allegations" quite different from those of which men of the 2nd Maine were accused originated with a zealous Federal official. Long before Bull Run, he may have guessed that Lincoln was wrong; men would be needed for much longer than three months. That being the case, someone—somewhere—may have tampered with the muster record of mutineers from Bangor. Severely punished mutineers from the North Star State must undoubtedly have cursed the day they offered to give the Union three months of military service.

11

"Galveston Pox"—A Two-Year Epidemic

A dispatch to superiors in Houston from C.S. Col. X. B. Debray, who in command at Galveston, said that on August 10, 1863, the 3rd Texas "yesterday refused to drill and to obey the orders of their officers, evincing tumultuous and riotous evidences of insubordination." This report came to him from Maj. J. H. Kampmann, their commanding officer.

Debray, who was an acting brigadier, was drilling his own regiment at the time he learned of the trouble. He considered it to be "all-important to crush this movement in the most summary manner." Hence he ordered his men to their quarters to procure ammunition, directing them to rendezvous on Broadway.

Simultaneously, he dispatched a light battery led by Capt. O. G. Jones to the same spot. As an extra precaution he told Col. H. M.

The powerful USS *Westfield* was blown up when Rebels seized the harbor.
Official Records (Naval)

Elmore to "get his three companies under arms" and follow him to the trouble spot. He reached the court-house square, which was used as a parade ground, just as the parade of the 3rd was ending. Debray moved forward, with cavalry exhibiting loaded carbines at both flanks of the column of mutineers. His artillery parked in front of them, where gunners unlimbered and loaded their pieces with canister.

So fortified, Debray "advanced to the front of the regiment, and addressed a few words to these misguided men." He stressed that military discipline must be observed, regardless of what it might cost in lives to make it respected. Then the acting brigadier ordered: "Stack . . . arms!"

Mutineers moved slowly, but obeyed. He then directed them away from the area where their muskets were stacked, marched them to their quarters and posted a guard around the premises. Men were quiet and orderly during the night and drilled without arms for two hours the next morning. Unable positively to discover the cause of the mutiny, he ordered a board of inquiry to make a thorough investigation and try to identify the ringleaders. He wrote:

> The movement was general, with the exception of one company (Company C), but I am convinced was brought about, as is always the case, by a few men having influence upon the mass, and there are doubtless many who already regret the part they have taken. I am informed that this is not the first time this regiment has behaved in this way when they wished to gain a point, and that on each previous occasion or occasions it has ended by a compromise between the officers and men, a course, which, of course, I would never consent to adopt. [OR I, 41, 242-43]

The following day he was less optimistic. After mentioning actions of the 3rd and the fact that its men had been disarmed, he said that "Cook's regiment refused to leave the batteries which they now hold." He ruefully noted that he had only 150 men of Elmore's regiment with whom to launch an attack. Guns of men in the 3rd had been deposited in the armory, but Debray had no force to guard the weapons. "The sappers and miners, I am just informed, refused to work," he added, noting that they claimed that their pay was six months in arrears.

After less than a day, he had discovered the "alleged cause" of the misconduct—"the want of bread, the corn-meal now issued to the men being old and weevil-eaten." He acknowledged that no flour was on hand and that the meal was "of inferior and detestable quality." Still, he was sure food did not trigger the mutiny. Debray attributed it to three factors: "seeds of discontent sown by bad citizens," plus speeches by men seeking political offices and "the talk of paroled prisoners from Vicksburg" whom he characterized as being "very demoralized and dissatisfied."

Gen. P. N. Luckett, who was in personal command of the brigade that included the 3rd, fortunately arrived late on the afternoon
of their mutiny. He immediately promised good rations, and because
the weather was unbearably hot suspended drill for a few days. Debray
characterized his own position as difficult, since he could depend
only upon his regiment of about three hundred men. Matters were
complicated by the fact that these men were "obnoxious to the balance of the garrison." [OR I, 41, 243]

A dispatch filed by Lt. Col. E. F. Gray, who headed the 3rd in
Luckett's absence, may not have made any impression upon Debray.
Writing a full week before the mutiny, Gray complained that "good
and wholesome flour are in depot at Columbus and Harrisburg." Yet
rations of his men consisted of beef, molasses, and cornmeal. He
described the cornmeal as being "sour, dirty, weevil-eaten, and filled
with ants and worms." Though he did not say so, he made the chief
item in the diet of his men sound as though they were prisoners of
war instead of members of a garrison. [OR I, 41, 241]

By August 12, Debray had decided that "the cause of the mutinous feeling among the men" was bad food. This matter he believed
to have been "seized upon by a few designing men, who are using it
in order to suit their own bad purposes." Unless the movement was
checked he feared an "open and general revolt."

For some time he had been doing his best to get better flour
and meal, he said, but had failed. These commodities that reached
the Galveston garrison, he said, were "very bad and utterly unfit to
be issued; the flour is sour, and the meal sour and absolutely filled
with weevils and worms."

Instead of subsiding, general discontent had spread into Cook's
regiment; men of the battery led by Jones also seemed to be "inclined to sympathize with the malcontents." As far as Debray could
tell, all cavalry regiments were loyal to their officers and their colors.
Since Luckett was now on hand, he wrote, it would be "out of his
province" to dispatch an additional report about the mutiny. [OR I,
41, 244]

Luckett's account, filed the following day, said that word of the
mutiny reached him by telegraph. He immediately took a train to
Galveston, where consultation with officers revealed that "great discontent and dissatisfaction pervaded almost the entire garrison."
Men of the 3rd had refused to drill, and their movement had been
joined by members of a company of artillery plus one company of
infantry at Fort Magruder and another at Fort Bankhead.

Most officers told Luckett they saw no signs of genuinely "disloyal sentiments amongst the men." Hence he directed Debray to
have their arms restored to them. He attributed the mutiny to bad

food plus excessive drilling in unbearably hot weather. Gen. W. R. Scurry had reached the city, he noted, and ended by saying that at the moment he saw "no cause of alarm." That meant he judged the mutiny to have been quelled by means of a strong show of strength that did not involve firing upon malcontents. [OR I, 41, 245–46]

Gen. John Bankhead Magruder, commander of the District of Texas, New Mexico, and Arizona, was astonished and outraged at what had taken place. His General Order No. 139, issued on August 24, said he felt deep mortification at having learned of mutinous and insubordinate conduct at Galveston. Most of the men involved had fought under him the previous January. He said he could hardly believe that soldiers "who shed so bright a halo of glory around our holy cause" could so quickly become "unmindful of their high obligations."

Magruder scolded mutineers for having taken things into their own hands instead of communicating with him. Noting that he'd never yield to force, he revealed that without knowing of dissatisfaction among his regiments he had been planning to try to trade with cotton. He hoped to exchange it for "the full ration of coffee for all the troops on this side of the Mississippi, and to improve the ration in other respects."

He commended conduct of men in the units that helped to suppress the mutiny and asked all members of the garrison to be "willing not only to shed their blood in the service of their country, but to endure every hardship and discomfort without a murmur." Commanding officers of regiments, battalions, and separate companies were directed to read the entire order to their men. Newspapers were, however, forbidden to publish it. [OR I, 41, 246–48]

C.S. Gen. John Bankhead Magruder was mocked behind his back as "Prince John" because of his arrogant ways.
Century War Book

A few months earlier, Magruder and his men had been feted throughout the Confederacy. A squadron of U.S. naval vessels led by Cmdr. William B. Renshaw had captured the vital port in October, 1862. Federal forces held the city for less than three months, however. In November, Magruder—whose arrogant ways led some subordinates to mock him as "Prince John"—began planning a joint land/sea attack.

Very early on January 1, 1863, the Rebel assault got under way. Most of the Federal troops on shore were captured, along with the USS *Westfield* and *Harriet Lane*. The latter vessel, a converted revenue cutter, was named for bachelor President James Buchanan's niece who was his Washington hostess. As a result of the coup led by Magruder, he received the Thanks of the C.S. Congress and Rebels held the major port until after Appomattox. "Prince John" was indignant that "gallant men who so nobly supported him on the 1st of January" should have "exhibited a spirit of insubordination" from what he termed petty motives. [OR I, 21, 147-51, 200-227, 614-15, 837; OR I, 41, 246; NOR I, 24, 242]

One month after the outbreak led in the city by the 3rd Texas, trouble erupted at Camp Kelsoe Springs in Colorado County. Lt. Col. John C. Robertson of Terrill's Texas Cavalry received orders from Magruder to take his riders to Galveston. He informed his 340 men that they were to move immediately—without their horses. Hearing grumbling in the ranks, he assured cavalrymen that this was a temporary measure, only. They would be in Galveston temporarily in order to help repel an expected invasion, he explained.

When Robertson finished talking, Capt. C. G. Murray of Co. F asked to say a few words to him. For one, he growled, he was not willing to part with his horse—and he'd promised his men they'd never be dismounted. Murray said he'd been fooled earlier, and never regained his animal. While he was gesturing excitedly as he argued with his commander, Murray was constantly interrupted by cheers from the troops.

It was apparent to Robertson that "fermentation" had proceeded so rapidly he couldn't stop it without use of arms—and he hardly knew what men he could trust with them. Hence he dismissed the parade and hoped for the best. Though boisterous for a time, the troops soon appeared to have become quiet.

On the morning of September 12, Robertson was astonished to see that many horses were saddled and that their riders were preparing to leave. He called them into formation and addressed them again, apparently quieting them by a promise to call for volunteers to go with him to Galveston.

"My object in this was to gain time, and in moving our camp to once more get control of the men by proper influences," he said in his detailed report. Believing that his ruse had succeeded, he returned to his quarters—where he soon got word that Murray and about one hundred men had ridden out of camp. "I hastened up the line; found it was true," he wrote. "I was powerless without arms, and at that time did not suppose I could get men to use them if I had them."

Two hours later he learned that Murray and some of his followers had taken clothing, baggage and saddles of men in other troops who had already gone to Galveston. He then listed the mutineers:

The troops under Captain Murray left in a body and consisted of his own company, 25 men; of Captain James E. Gray's company, 4 men; of Captain Israel Spikes' company, 30 men; of Captain William C. Hurley's company, 30 men; and Lieutenant J. G. Chancellor, who was in command of them. [OR I, 41, 238-39]

According to Robertson, Chancellor "did very much in fermenting and inciting the troops to insubordination by false representations and putting in circulation false reports." Robertson was confident that many of the mutineers "who were led away in the excitement" would soon see the error of their ways and return. There is no record that even one of them did so, however. [OR I, 41, 239]

About the time of the August mutiny, Adj. and Insp. Gen. J. Y. Dashiell made public a serious problem he faced. Some conscription officers had found that in order to get the men they needed, they had to "guard the avenues of departure with a military force until the enrollment was completed."

News of this matter came to the attention of a newspaper correspondent who hoped soon to dispatch word that Federal forces had attempted an invasion and had been repelled. To readers of the *Charleston Mercury*, he confided that the spirit in the West was far different from that in the East. Texans, he said, seemed to have become infected with a spirit of rebellion and mutiny, which he termed "the Galveston pox."

Postwar Confederate analysts attributed the outbreak of mutiny to belief on the part of troops that Gen. E. Kirby Smith was about to order them to surrender. Resorting to use of a nautical metaphor, men who left their camps openly in daylight instead of deserting during the night, were described as acting:

not with a disaffected spirit in mutiny against their superior officers; but it was as in the case of the wrecked vessel slowly sinking; when the captain's power of control had ceased by common consent, the manning of the boat any longer was seen to be hopeless, and the personal safety of each man on board was the common concern, to be secured if practicable each in his own way. [CMH, 15, 139; OR I, 41, 170]

At the time "the Galveston pox" was coined, cavalrymen who were ordered to Galveston had not yet rebelled and ridden off in a body. If the spirit of mutiny really was contagious among Texas forces, the epidemic lasted two full years. In May, 1865, there was a third mutiny at Galveston that Magruder termed "serious." Though

Rebels who had seized Galveston from Union forces mutinied when they believed the port was about to surrender.

Harper's Weekly

it may have been quelled at the time of his May 12 dispatch in which he mentioned it, he anticipated "a recurrence" that would lead to the fall of the city. [OR I, 48, 1300]

A fresh outbreak of rebellion against military authorities by Rebel soldiers was not the only problem Magruder faced. An otherwise unidentified officer whom he termed "General Walker" must have been commandant of a body of Texas state forces. In a dispute with C.S. Gen. Hamilton P. Bee, brother of slain Gen. Bernard Bee, Walker refused to yield command. This occurred despite specific orders from departmental headquarters.

Magruder did not go into detail about this dispute. He went on record, however, as hoping that the third Galveston mutiny would "prevent another mutiny and save Houston." To him, it seemed "a burning injustice" that mutiny deprived him of cavalry he desperately needed "under these trying circumstances." [OR I, 48, 1309]

Despite Magruder's fears, troops that remained obedient to their officers held out to the bitter end. Galveston was not surrendered until June 2, 1865, when Smith turned the city over to U.S. naval forces. The Texas port holds the dubious distinction of being the only city in the South or the North that was central to three separate mutinies in a period of only two years. [NOR I, 19, 440-54; NOR I, 22, 214]

12

Insubordinate Officers–6th Missouri Cavalry, October 22, 1863

At Cape Girardeau, Missouri, Col. J. B. Rogers first learned of serious trouble on October 22, 1863. Maj. Samuel Montgomery, who commanded the 6th Missouri Cavalry, sent him a terse message that morning at 9:00 A.M. According to it, troops at Bloomfield were "in open mutiny, headed by officers."

A battery commanded by Lt. V. B. S. Reber was planted in front of Montgomery's headquarters. He had been placed under arrest by some of his subordinates. A guard had been stationed to watch over the telegraph instruments and their operator. Capt. William H. Crockett was giving orders to mutineers, but Reber appeared to be the chief instigator of it. The brief message of the major ended by a notation that he, "of course, refused to recognize their arrest." [OR I, 32, 709]

Lt. Herman J. Huiskamp got off a much longer report to Rogers nearly twelve hours later. He said Crockett woke him up at 7:00, telling him that Reber wished to see him at headquarters in an hour. When he reached Reber's office he noticed that the battery horses had been harnessed. Crockett, Capt. John H. Paynter, Lt. E. J. Burross, and Lt. Luther D. Potter had arrived ahead of him. Among them, only Crockett was unarmed.

Huiskamp was asked to take a seat, after which Reber read him a lengthy statement that other officers present had already signed. According to it, they regarded Montgomery to be a traitor who should be arrested at once. The lieutenant was so stunned that none of the charges against the major registered mentally with him. Requested to add his name to the document signed by five of his comrades, Huiskamp flatly refused. He said he didn't believe the charges and considered actions already taken to be "hasty and wrong."

106

Crockett walked a short distance with the lieutenant when he left Reber's office and confided that he had counseled against action the previous night. Having been overruled, he believed "it was too late to back out now." As they walked and talked, a battery was planted in front of their headquarters and dismounted cavalrymen prepared to service it. Montgomery appeared and Huiskamp told him what had happened.

Paynter having seen the major and the lieutenant, four men from each company formed a special detail to arrest their commander. They moved slowly and seemed to Huiskamp to be acting reluctantly, apparently being far from eager to act against Montgomery—who was characterized as being old. Potter called upon the major to surrender, saying that Crockett was taking command of the post.

"The major," continued Huiskamp, "refused to recognize the arrest, as coming from an inferior officer." He turned, however, and walked toward headquarters "closely followed by a guard of 16 men." Upon reaching his destination three of the guards went inside to prevent the telegraph operator from sending dispatches. Crockett soon sent members of the guard to their quarters and released the telegraph operator.

"The main instigator, Lieutenant Reber, has been drunk ever since the occurrence," Huiskamp reported. "The men were not aware, as a general thing, what they were ordered out for and a great many deserted the ranks upon finding out. The whole thing has thus far resulted in a grand fizzle." [OR I, 32, 710-11]

Fizzle or not, Rogers considered the matter to be of utmost gravity. He immediately dispatched Lt. Col. Hiram M. Hiller to take command at Bloomfield with orders "to arrest the leaders of the revolt." Notifying Gen. Clinton B. Fisk of his actions, he wondered whether it would be better to leave the mutinous officers at their post or to have them brought to Cape Girardeau. Fisk offered no guidance on this matter. [OR I, 32, 709]

When the written complaint that had been signed by five officers reached Rogers, he found it to be tediously long. According to it, a majority of commissioned men at Bloomfield held a conference on the evening of October 21 and reached four conclusions. First, they considered it doubtful that the post could be held against Rebels with Montgomery in command. Second, they considered him to have entered into an alliance with leading traitors of the region. Third, they decided that it would be necessary to render Montgomery harmless "until this fearful and disgracing condition of things can be reported to the proper authorities." Fourth and last, they signified their resolve to arrest Montgomery the following morning and hold him until their action could be reported and orders could be received. To facilitate this goal, they sent their message and a lengthy set of complaints to Cape Girardeau by courier. [OR I, 32, 708]

With the mutiny having been nipped in the bud as a result of Rogers' actions, nothing else about it appeared in the OR until December 21. That day paragraph X of the War Department's Special Order No. 564, ordered that 2nd Lt. V. B. S. Reber be dishonorably discharged "with loss of all pay and allowances." This step was taken as punishment for his "mutiny, disobedience of orders, neglect of duty, and desertion while under arrest." Though taken in the name of the President, it is unlikely that Lincoln's aides referred so trivial a matter to him for his personal verdict. No mention of it appears in his *Collected Works.* [OR I, 32, 718]

Summary treatment of Reber may have stemmed from the fact that he commanded the artillery that drew up before the headquarters of the 6th Cavalry, then occupied by Montgomery. Four of the lieutenant's fellow mutineers were given the benefit of a court-martial that was held at St. Louis during January. Each member of the quartet faced six separate charges, to which detailed specifications were attached. Though language varied slightly in some instances, the charges and specifications were for practical purposes identical in each case.

The first charge against Paynter, Crockett, Burross and Potter was mutiny. In the case of an enlisted man, conviction could bring a sentence of death; officers did not fall under the same code. Each member of the quartet of men holding commissions was charged with having been "a chief actor and a leader" in the "unlawful, unwarrantable, and wanton arrest and forcible dispossession from command and authority" of Montgomery.

The second charge accused these officers of having been present at a mutiny and not having used "utmost endeavors" to suppress it. Their failure to act was considered to have caused Montgomery to be arrested and deposed.

Charge #3 centered in alleged "knowledge of an intended mutiny" and failure immediately to notify the commanding officer about it.

Charge #4 intimated that the four officers on trial had individually offered violence against their superior officer—that is, Montgomery.

Charge #5, conviction on which would have resulted in punishment far less drastic than that associated with mutiny, was simply "conduct to the prejudice of good order and military discipline." The sixth and final charge against officers already branded as mutineers was mere "disobedience of orders."

Paynter and Crockett were convicted on all six counts; their fellow mutineers were found not guilty of disobedience of orders

Gen. John M. Schofield, who confirmed sentences that had been given to mutineers

Harper's History of the Great Rebellion

but were convicted of the five earlier charges. With individual names and ranks stipulated, each member of the quartet from the "Sixth Regiment Missouri Cavalry Volunteers" received an identical sentence—dismissal from the service of the United States. [OR I, 32, 711-18]

Gen. John M. Schofield, an 1853 graduate of West Point who was serving as commander of the Department of Missouri, solemnly confirmed each sentence. To him, to Rogers, and to members of the court-martial, it appeared that the case was closed. They soon found that they were very, very wrong. Missouri Congressman S. H. Boyd circulated documents to other lawmakers and found 35 members of the state legislature who joined him in "praying the restoration of these officers to their former rank and command in the Sixth Missouri Cavalry."

All lawmakers who signed the petition expressed "disbelief that they [the four convicted officers] were guilty of willful mutiny, or could possibly be, as they are true patriots, who have from the outbreak of the rebellion devoted themselves to the cause of their country. "They were praised for having demonstrated their patriotism and valor" during Missouri and Arkansas battles at Lebanon, Wilson's Creek, Sugar Creek, Pea Ridge, and Prairie Grove.

The lawmakers' petition was summarized by Democratic Kentucky attorney Joseph Holt, who had become judge advocate general of the United States. His detailed findings that were prepared for the President listed five factors that to Holt seemed to palliate—that is, make less serious—"the very grave offense of which these officers were found guilty."

Following the usual pattern of legal documents, the summary by the judge advocate general listed five separate sets of actions by Montgomery, here greatly condensed, that seemed pertinent to the cases. First, the colonel at the head of the 6th Missouri Cavalry had permitted numerous Rebel deserters to come back home "without requiring them to take any oath or give any bond for their future loyalty."

Pea Ridge, fought in March, 1862, had put the 6th Missouri Cavalry to an arduous test.

The Soldier in Our Civil War

Second: While at Bloomfield, the major constantly associated with "the most dangerous and notorious rebels." Third: He habitually cursed and abused high military and civil officers, including Abraham Lincoln and Gov. Hamilton R. Gamble.

Fourth: When supervising the sale of contraband goods "he favored a notorious secessionist" who wore an emblem on his hat that signified his views. Fifth. Major Montgomery "married one of the two most notorious rebel women in the country [around and about Bloomfield]." [OR I, 32, 719-20]

Holt would not have devoted time and attention to the case of the mutinous officers without a directive from the President. His summary was ready for the attention of attorney Lincoln on April 15. Despite being constantly bombarded by military matters of the gravest national importance, the chief executive studied the Holt paper carefully. As a result, on May 17 Thomas M. Vincent, assistant adjutant general, sent a brief memorandum to the governor of Missouri. In it he said:

> by direction of the President of the United States the disability resting upon J. H. Paynter, E. J. Burross, Luther D. Potter and William H. Crockett . . . by reason their dismissal from service under sentence of general court-martial, is hereby removed, and they may be recommissioned if Your Excellency so desires." [OR I, 32, 721]

Since not one of the four mutineers is again mentioned anywhere in the OR, men who compiled it late in the 19th century noted that "It does not appear that any of these officers re-entered the service."

To 20th-century civilians without legal or military training, the outcome of this mutiny by commissioned officers probably seems somewhat bizarre. One man was summarily dismissed without the benefit of a hearing; four of his comrades were booted out of U.S. service and presumably had no desire to return to it.

Maj. Samuel Montgomery, against whom the Union's judge advocate general leveled five sets of accusations that mirrored those of officers who rebelled, remained in command of the 6th Missouri Cavalry. There is no record that he received even a verbal slap on the wrist for having conducted himself in such fashion that subordinates felt duty-bound to arrest him.

13

Summary Executions–Galvanized Yanks, December 15, 1864

About 260 prisoners, foreigners, at Florence [S.C.] have volunteered for our service. In consultation with General Beauregard I recommend and ask that Maj. Henry Bryan, assistant adjutant-general, and Capt. J. H. Brooks, of Nelson's battalion, Hagood's brigade, be ordered to Florence without delay to organize them into a battalion. Many others may be obtained. I will await your instructions before taking any other steps in matter. [OR I, 129, 694]

That dispatch went to James A. Seddon, C.S. secretary of war, on September 30, 1864. Sent from Charleston by Gen. Samuel Jones, the brief report indicates how desperate Rebel leaders had become. Seddon had earlier approved the idea of enlisting "Irish and other foreign prisoners." His only stipulation concerning implementation of the plan was that Brooks' superior officer should get an explanation of why he was needed for special service. [OR I, 129, 694]

Union leaders still had an abundant pool of manpower, which was constantly boosted by thousands of immigrants arriving every month. Gen. U. S. Grant, whose forces included a great many of them, was using large numbers of ex-slaves as well. Despite the heavy losses brought about by his determined push to bring the Confederacy to its knees, there had been no significant decrease in the number of men fighting in blue uniforms.

That was not the case in the South, however. Governors of most seceded states were jealously guarding what little manpower they still had—men past 45 plus underage boys and severely handicapped veterans. Prisoner exchange having been halted by Grant, no conventional system could possibly augment the constantly shrinking size of Rebel forces.

Irish-born C.S. Gen. Patrick Ronayne Cleburne believed he had at least a partial solution for the dilemma. While encamped at Dalton, Georgia, during the winter of 1863–64 he drafted a lengthy paper. In it, he urged that during more than two years of struggle, Rebels had gained "nothing but long lists of dead and mangled." Leaders initially hoped quickly to enlarge the geographical size of the C.S. Instead of that being done, Cleburne insisted that "we are hemmed in to-day into less than two-thirds of it, and still the enemy menacingly confronts us at every point with superior forces." [JSHS, 31, 215, 219]

Gen. Ulysses S. Grant, who often took his wife and son into the field with him, used tens of thousands of immigrant soldiers.

Library of Congress

Slavery, said the Irishman, was a chief source of strength for the South at the beginning of the war, but had become "one of our chief sources of weakness." As a result of these considerations, he suggested that no men in gray should be released until war's end and:

> we immediately commence training a large reserve of the most courageous of our slaves; and further, that we guarantee freedom within a reasonable time to every slave in the South who shall remain true to the Confederacy in this war. [JSHS, 31, 222]

In Cleburne's judgment, the only way to get enough men into Confederate forces was by "making the negro share the dangers and hardships of the war." Soon he became a virtual soapbox orator, crying in writing:

> For many years—ever since the agitation of the subject of slavery commenced—the negro has been dreaming of freedom, and his vivid imagination has surrounded that condition with so many gratifications that it has become the paradise of his hopes. To attain it he will tempt dangers and difficulties not exceeded by the bravest in the field. The hope of freedom is, perhaps, the only moral incentive that can be applied to him in his present condition. . . . The slaves are dangerous now, but armed, trained, and collected in an army they would be a thousandfold more dangerous [to the enemy]. [JSHS, 31, 225]

Having framed a plan that he believed would "save our country," the Irish Confederate submitted it to his officers for their consideration—with his signature attached. Soon it was endorsed by Gens. D. C. Govan, M. P. Lowry, and J. H. Kelly. Four colonels, two lieutenant colonels, three majors and Capt. J. H. Collett of the 7th Texas affixed their own signatures to the lengthy document. [JSHS, 31, 227–28]

W. H. T. Walker, a major general, denounced the Cleburne proposal as dangerous to the point of being incendiary. He was so enraged that he requested permission to send a copy to Jefferson Davis, whose written notation concerning it was brief. "While recognizing the patriotic motives of its distinguished author," noted the President of the C.S., "I deem it inexpedient, at this time, to give publicity to this paper, and request that it be suppressed." [JSHS, 29, 173; 31, 217]

All copies were believed to have been destroyed. Years later, however, a single copy surfaced and was sent to the Confederate Record Office of the U.S. War Department. Irving A. Black, who was assistant adjutant general on Cleburne's staff, soon attested to its authenticity. According to him, Gen. Joseph E. Johnston refused to forward it to Richmond on the grounds that it "was more political than military" in character. Subsequently, former Confederate Gens. William J. Hardee and John B. Gordon lauded the suppressed proposal. [JSHS, 18, 265; 29, 173; 31, 157]

After having refused to make Cleburne's proposal public, new reverses on battlefields caused Davis to re-think it and to act upon it. On November 7, 1864, he proposed to the C.S. Congress that radical changes should be made at once. Carefully selected slaves should immediately begin to get military training, he suggested. Satisfactory battlefield performance of such men should put them into a program of gradual emancipation, with compensation to owners. Opposition to the Davis proposal was quick and violent.

Though it had no immediate chance of passage, it did not die. As the ranks of his Army of the Potomac grew thinner and thinner, Robert E. Lee lent his enormous influence to the concept of recruiting black Confederate-fighting men. On March 13, 1865, desperate Rebel lawmakers enacted enabling legislation by which to implement the idea. Two days later, Richmond newspapers carried notices that slaves were now eligible to become soldiers. A few black units seem to have been recruited and organized; their training had just started when Lee surrendered at Appomattox, so none of them went into combat.

No public hue and cry resulted from a related but different idea. An unidentified leader adopted Cleburne's position that something radical must be done in order to increase Confederate manpower. This led to a proposal that Union soldiers of foreign birth who were languishing in stockades and prisons would probably welcome an opportunity to fight in exchange for their freedom. [OR I, 129, 694]

Rebel lawmakers found the idea attractive, but were cautious. In order to implement it, a man with impeccable credentials who was willing to lead former Federal soldiers must be found. Clearly, it would add greatly to public support of the novel experiment if the man chosen to implement it was widely known and respected.

A brief search turned up an experienced soldier who met all the criteria for leadership of "galvanized Yanks." This term stemmed from then-novel galvanization processes by which a thin layer of rust-resistant zinc was placed over cast-iron and steel surfaces.

John H. Brooks of Edgefield, South Carolina had won region-wide reflected glory as a result of 1856 actions by his brother. During debate in the U.S. Congress over the Kansas-Nebraska Bill, Sen. Charles Sumner of Massachusetts delivered on May 20 an impassioned speech that became famous as "The Crime Against Kansas." In the course of his oration, he made disparaging remarks about Sen. Andrew Pickens Butler of South Carolina. After adjournment of the lawmaking body, Rep. Preston S. Brooks stalked into the Senate chamber seething at what had been said about his uncle. Using a gutta-percha cane as a weapon, Brooks beat Sumner into insensibility.

On June 2, a movement to expel Brooks from the House of Representatives fell short of the required two-thirds vote required for passage. Despite this factor, Brooks resigned in a huff. He then went into a civil court and pled guilty of assault and paid a fine of $300. After making speeches to his constituents about the affair, he was presented with a gold-headed cane and re-elected to the House of Representatives. Because Brooks was lauded throughout the South, his brother was widely known and admired. [WWW, 76]

Capt. John H. Brooks helped to recruit and then led a body of South Carolina soldiers to Virginia. At Drewry's Bluff he fought in May, 1862, with such distinction that he was cited for gallantry. Though wounded three times, he refused to leave the field until he was ordered to the rear by Gen. Johnson Hagood. [CMH, 6, 322; CV, 23, 459; JSHS, 12, 231]

While recuperating in his native state, he recruited enough men to form a company of partisan rangers. When commanders of such units were ordered to send rolls to Gen. Samuel Cooper in Richmond, he was one of only two in South Carolina who complied promptly and efficiently. During the October, 1862, battle of Old Pocotaligo he and his rangers fought bravely and well. [OR I, 14, 649; CMH, 6, 104]

Sen. Charles Sumner, as satirized in
Vanity Fair magazine

Congressman Preston S. Brooks was hailed as a hero in the South after
having beaten Sen. Charles Sumner with a cane.

University of South Carolina

Brooks had all of the qualifications to lead galvanized Yanks—provided that he was willing to do so. When approached about taking such a command, he readily acceded. At the immense prison camp in Florence, South Carolina, inmates were notified that those of foreign birth who were willing to fight in gray would be set free.

Men of Irish extraction were preferred, but there were not enough of them to form a fighting force. In addition to Irishmen, numerous Germans, at least one Italian, and several natives of the U.S. North who posed as Englishmen were accepted for service under Brooks. As a result, nearly three hundred former prisoners of war formed in October, 1864, what some Rebels called Brooks' Foreign Battalion. Men who made up the six companies of the battalion were experienced soldiers, so needed little training. [Brooks, 95-138]

Mustered into Confederate service in mid November, the foreign battalion was immediately sent to Summerville, South Carolina. One company having been left at that base, the remainder of Brooks' men marched toward Savannah, Georgia, early in December. With the city menaced by Federal forces under Sherman, Confederates believed that a holding action could prevent the capture of the port whose prewar cotton exchange was second in size only to that of London, England. On December 18, Jefferson Davis notified Robert E. Lee that Sherman's demand for the surrender of Savannah had been refused. [OR I, 44, 940, 966]

Moving closer to Savannah through marshes and woods, numerous members of the Brooks-led unit tried to desert in order to return to Federal lines. Many of them were quickly caught, however, and were told they'd be shot if they made another attempt to escape. Desperate, an undisclosed number of galvanized Yanks mutinied in the absence of their commander. While they were battling with some of their officers, Brooks rode up at the head of a company of infantry. With rebellion having been quickly quelled, officers of the battalion held a drum-head court-martial.

All of the mutineers received the same sentence—death—which came to them immediately after the unofficial conference of officers ended. Bodies of galvanized Yanks who had tried to break Confederate military control were presumably dumped into a swamp. [Brooks, 135-64]

Lt. Col. John G. Pressley was under the impression that some officers of the foreign battalion lost their commissions as a result of the mutiny. If so, records concerning them were destroyed or lost. On December 18, Hardee dispatched a directive to Gen. Samuel Jones: "Send back to Florence all that part of Brooks' Foreign Battalion now at Somerville, under guard, and turn them over to the officers commanding Federal prisoners, to be confined as prisoners of war." [JSHS, 14, 38; OR I, 44, 966; Brooks, 170-74]

Their surviving comrades who had marched deep into Georgia but had not taken part in battle soon rejoined them in prison. On the day before Christmas, Hardee disclosed his decision that the field use of the Brooks' Battalion had constituted "a fair test" of galvanized Yanks. His terse recommendation concerning such troops insisted that "all authority to organize similar commands be revoked." The great Confederate experiment in use of foreign-born Union soldiers had ended with summary execution of mutineers. [OR II, 7, 1268; Denney, 326; WWW, 76]

By now notable in his own right as well as still lauded for being the brother of Preston, John H. Brooks became an ardent supporter of veterans' movements in postwar years. As commander of the Abner Perrin Camp at Edgefield Court House, the former captain's name appeared regularly in the *Confederate Veteran* magazine. [CV, 1, 359; 2, 24, 55, 88, 134; 9, 270; 10, 244; 17, 34]

Gen. William J. Hardee announced a premature verdict according to which "galvanized Yankees" made good Rebels.

Hall Engraving

14
Passwords and Grips–The Peace Society, January 5, 1864

At Gonzales, Alabama, one out of five Rebels in a detachment mutinied on January 5, 1864, informing their captain that "they would do no service." He responded promptly and decisively by placing 60 men who had been on picket duty near Pensacola under arrest and sending them to Pollard, headquarters of Gen. James H. Clanton.

Clanton seems earlier to have realized that his brigade included numerous men who held membership in the state's Peace Society. With men stationed at Pollard plus mutineers drawn up at attention, he made an impassioned speech on January 7. At his urging, about one hundred men who were not under arrest confessed to membership in the society. Saying that they were deceived into joining it, they asked their commander's pardon and apparently got it.

At least to his own satisfaction, Pollard identified and ironed "those who were ringleaders in the contemplated rebellion." Without going into details, he described the mutineers and their friends as having been "badly whipped." That evening he sent three "peace men" to Mobile in irons and said 70 more would follow on the next day. In his judgment, virtually all of the culprits deserved to be shot. Private Tulman, member of a regiment not based at Pollard, was believed to be another ringleader. Hence Clanton requested Col. George G. Garner, chief of staff to Gen. Dabney H. Maury, to have this man arrested also. [OR I, 42, 552-53]

Alabama, home of the Peace Society, included large numbers of citizens who opposed secession. Believed by Confederates to have been organized at Cumberland Gap by the enemy, the society had links with at least three other bodies. Like Freemasonry, all of these groups operated in secret. In North Carolina they called themselves

119

Heroes of America. This body, plus the Peace Society, was extremely strong in eastern Tennessee. Arkansas residents who were ardently opposed to the war formed their own Constitutional Society, but some of them also belonged to the Peace Society. [OR I, 42, 552; EC, 3, 1183]

Clanton's quick suppression of mutiny may have been due to vigilance that followed a raid by U.S. Col. Abel D. Streight of the 19th Indiana. Eight months earlier Streight and a band of men mounted on mules had raced toward Rome, Georgia, site of a foundry and served by a major railroad. During their move through northern Alabama, strength of the blue-clad force was considerably augmented by anti-secessionist civilians who joined their ranks. [CV, 35, 452–54]

Every state in the Confederacy included individuals—some of whom were very prominent— plus groups who opposed secession. Even Charleston, where the war started, was no exception to this rule. In the port city, Judge James L. Petigru never ceased to criticize the movement that was led by his native state.

Col. Abel D. Streight led his Federal force across northern Alabama on mules.

In Alabama, Winston County tried to secede from the state as a gesture of protest against secession. One of the state's congressmen, Williamson R. W. Cobb, resigned his seat on January 30, 1861. Elected to the Confederate Congress, he was expelled by unanimous vote after having refused to take his seat in the body.

Reporting to the secretary of war in Richmond, Maury brushed the Pensacola affair aside as being unimportant in itself. He noted however:

> it will be greatly magnified by rumor; will increase the anxiety of our own people, already too despondent, and will encourage the enemy. The fact is established that an organized opposition to the war exists in our midst; that a secret association has been formed in the army, and with many members in the country, seeking peace on any terms. . . .
>
> . . . many of them have bound themselves to each other by solemn oaths never to fight against the enemy; to desert the service of the Confederacy; to encourage and protect deserters, and

to do all other things in their power to end the war and break down the Government and the "so-called Southern Confederacy." [OR I, 42, 551-52]

Except for soldiers in blue plus warships that were blockading Southern ports, the C.S. faced no greater threat than that exposed by Clanton's mutineers who belonged to a subversive society with adherents in at least three states. Since it was wholly secret, few persons loyal to Richmond knew anything about it except that it existed.

Clanton triumphantly reported having "bursted the institution." Without revealing what techniques he used to break the wills of mutineers, he said he "secured the names, oaths, pass-words, and grips [secret handshakes] of the concern." With this knowledge in hand, he wanted a regiment not present at Pollard to be sent back "that I may give them the grip and pass-word [to identify Peace Society members] and purge it of all impurities."

According to the brigadier, Peace Society members "refused a fair fight which I tendered them yesterday with their guns loaded." He was eager to have all regiments that might include such men to be put under his command. When that was done, he assured Maury through Garner, "I will do the Confederacy signal service, and in the spring wipe out their disgrace with blood upon the battlefield." [OR I, 42, 552-53]

Maury informed Richmond that he was not surprised that the mutiny had developed among Clanton's men "when we consider the elements of which it is made up and the manner in which they were brought into service." According to him, about a year earlier Clanton received authority "to raise a legion" whose members would be recruited from among men exempt from military service.

When the big unit was formed, its members enlisted for six months of service within their state; subsequently, they "agreed to serve for the war and to go anywhere." Having been promised by Richmond that he'd be made a brigadier upon enlisting 40 companies, Clanton worked very hard and succeeded in forming "a large brigade of men who have entered the army very reluctantly."

According to Maury, the body included some conscripts as well as some substitutes. He charged that "unusual inducements and influences" were used by Clanton. Men under his command, he said, had been kept near their homes, "have received many indulgences, and have never been in real field service." [OR I, 41, 551-52]

Born in Hungary, U.S. Gen. Alexander S. Asboth considered the break in ranks of the enemy to be significant. From Barrancas, Florida, he reported it to Gen. Charles P. Stone. According to him 75 Rebel soldiers laid down their arms at the 15-mile station on the Pensacola railroad "and refused further service." [OR I, 65, 453-54]

C.S. Gen. Joseph E. Johnston's knowledge of the trouble in Alabama was probably limited to what he learned from Maury. From Dalton, Georgia, he sent a January 15 memo to Richmond recommending that "Clanton's troops should be dispersed and sent as far from home as practicable." According to him, their commander's incompetency had been demonstrated by the conduct of men under his command. [OR I, 42, 553]

Word of Johnston's proposal and of Maury's stinging report must have reached Clanton before the end of the month. From Meridian, Mississippi, he addressed to Gen. Leonidas Polk a request for a brief interview at any time the lieutenant general might designate. If Polk did not have prior knowledge that the man from Alabama had earlier clashed with Gen. Braxton Bragg, he learned of this matter from a letter sent to him by Gov. T. H. Watts of Alabama. A former attorney general in the Davis cabinet, the chief executive of the state said that Clanton led the 1st Alabama Cavalry at Shiloh with gallantry. His disagreement with Bragg was on such a level of intensity that he resigned his commission and returned to civilian life for a time. Later he recruited the brigade in which the mutiny occurred. [OR I, 42, 554; WWW, 696]

Among all Confederate commanders, few were more intimately acquainted with Bragg-related problems than was Polk. As a corps commander in the Army of Tennessee, along with Gens. James Longstreet, William J. Hardee and others he had become embroiled in a bitter dispute with Bragg more than a year prior to the Alabama mutiny.

Part of the discontent among Bragg's subordinates stemmed from his failure to follow up after the great Confederate victory at Chickamauga. In addition, he appeared to be indifferent to the needs and wants of his officers and men. Col. James Chestnut, military secretary of Jefferson Davis, was sent in September, 1864, to assess the situation in Alabama. From that vantage point he surveyed relatively nearby forces and became so alarmed that on October 5 he sent Jefferson Davis a telegram. His presence with the Army of Tennessee was urgently needed, Chestnut informed the President. [Davis, 518]

Though Chestnut didn't know it when he called for Davis to come, Polk and 11 more of Bragg's generals had signed a petition calling for his removal from command. Davis took his time in going to Tennessee, so did not reach Atlanta until October 8. By then the long-simmering animosity between Polk and Bragg had erupted into a public quarrel. Furious at being relieved by a commander who charged that he had been disobedient at Perryville, Polk had demanded a court-martial. The trial was never held because the President countermanded Bragg in this matter. [Davis, 517-19]

Rebels scored a great victory at Chickamauga, but Gen. Braxton Bragg did not follow it up.

Bragg and Davis had long enjoyed an extremely cordial and a very close relationship. When the President left Richmond, he took with him the Pennsylvania native who was despised throughout the South for having surrendered Vicksburg. News that the chief executive was headed toward Chattanooga with Gen. John C. Pemberton in tow traveled faster than they did. This led many of Bragg's subordinates to conclude that their commander had agreed to let Davis replace Polk with Pemberton.

Already widely rebellious against Bragg and sullen at having to serve under him, the Army of Tennessee now began seething with discontent. Gen. James H. Longstreet, who would soon be charged by his commander

Gen. Braxton Bragg enjoyed a long and close friendship with the Confederate President.

with disobedience, described the mood of officers and men as being "disaffected." Later analysts considered that to be one of the gross understatements of the war. According to this view, the Army of Tennessee was closer to mass mutiny than any large fighting force had been since soldiers of the Pennsylvania Line mutinied against Gen. Arthur St. Clair during the American Revolution. Their action had led to St. Clair's court-martial; it appeared that Davis might be thinking of promoting Bragg instead of censuring him. [Longstreet, 466; McHenry, 365; Eaton, 187]

Before fierce infighting among top Confederate officers ended, Polk was transferred, Longstreet offered his resignation, and numerous regiments were shifted from one command to another. These moves by Bragg were taken in an attempt to reduce the influence of Longstreet, Gen. John C. Breckinridge, and other officers who wanted a new commander.

Gen. Simon B. Buckner, who had been at the head of the Department of Tennessee, was largely stripped of power by being assigned to head a division of the army. Gen. Daniel H. Hill was relieved of his command of a corps and Bragg persuaded the President not to submit his name for promotion to the rank of lieutenant general. [Longstreet, 469; WWW, 68, 86, 309-10]

The struggle that was literally tearing the Army of Tennessee apart ended only when Bragg asked to be relieved of his command in order to become an advisor to Davis with an office in Richmond. By that time, Polk was far away—serving as commander of the Department of Mississippi and East Louisiana. [Davis, 528; WWW, 512]

No officer in gray knew better than Polk that Bragg was volatile, temperamental, arbitrary, stubborn, and vindictive. Yet in his new role, no longer under Bragg's command, Polk seems to have had little patience with the Alabama officer who earlier quit the army because of Bragg. Probably influenced by views of Maury, he concurred in the view that the best way to handle Clanton was to take him out of his native state and "distribute his regiments among other troops." [OR I, 42, 552-53]

In his lengthy request for an interview with Polk, the man under fire because a mutiny had occurred in his ranks referred to what he termed his "persecution by General Bragg." At the same time, he ventured to say that Polk knew Bragg better "than any [other] general of our army." Citing a few of his own many accomplishments, Clanton noted that he raised and for 10 months commanded Alabama's first regiment of cavalry. His new battalion had fought at Chickamauga, where he said its colors "were pierced by eighty-two balls."

In addition to the cavalry regiment and the infantry battalion, the Alabaman said he organized two batteries of artillery. Altogether, he said, he had "raised about 5,000 men during this war under the greatest difficulties." He estimated that of this number at least two thousand—in whom the Tuscaloosa Cadets were numbered—were not subject to conscription. In Mississippi against his wishes, he had been deprived of most of his men and said he had only a few hundred left. Clanton did not mention he had discovered "the pass-words and grips" of the Peace Society, thereby making it easy to detect its members. [OR I, 42, 552, 555–56]

Along with his lengthy set of arguments in his own defense, the officer who was now far from home sent Polk a detailed statement from four judges of Maury's military court. Claiming to have heard many cases involving mutiny, the quartet said that no blame whatever rested upon Clanton's shoulders. They had found evidence that the Peace Society did not originate in his command. What's more, they commended him for his display of "commendable zeal and efficiency in having guilty parties properly prosecuted." He had rendered additional valuable service, in the opinion of Judges Thomas J. Judge, Samuel J. Douglas, Andrew Herron, and E. J. Fitzpatrick. Some officers in his brigade had been profiting from "illegal substitute transactions." These men, said the Mobile justices, had been ferreted out, prosecuted, and punished by Clanton. If Polk granted the requested interview, records concerning it were lost. Soon, though, he brought the Alabama leader to his headquarters staff as an aide. [OR I, 42, 557; E, 565; *The Atlanta Century*, January 10, 1864]

Clanton was in the limelight only briefly after having broken a major mutiny and discovered the secret signs used by members of the Peace Society. Once in Mississippi, he dropped out of sight and nothing else from him or about him entered the OR. [E, 565; *The Atlanta Century*, January 10, 1864]

15

Switched Allegiance—Texas Partisans, 1863-64

At the camp of the 33rd Texas Cavalry on the San Fernando River all was routine during the morning of October 28, 1863. That afternoon, Col. James Duff designated two privates to serve as messengers. Following his orders, Litteral and Dashiel of Co. A set out for Boca Del Rio. They took a written directive addressed to Capt. A. J. Vidal.

Vidal led a company of partisan rangers who had volunteered for six months of service to the Confederacy. He and his men had been on picket duty. Now Duff wanted them to move to nearby Fort Brown and report to its commander.

Five or six hours after Duff's messengers left headquarters, one of them returned. Gesturing because he had been shot through both jaws and could not speak, Litteral managed to convey dreadful news. His comrade, Dashiell, had been killed by some of Vidal's men; he signaled that he was lucky to be alive. Possibly but not positively resorting to writing words and phrases in lieu of relying upon gestures, the soldier informed his commander that Vidal and some or all of his men had mutinied.

Duff jumped to the conclusion that the renegade officer "was acting in concert with the hundreds of renegades and deserters harbored on the other side of the Rio Grande River." If that was the case, the fort—which normally had only a small garrison—was a likely target.

Lt. J. R. Vinton was ordered to take 10 men of Co. A and locate the mutineers. He was told not to engage them under any circumstances. His job was to find them and then fall back and report. He didn't get back to headquarters until 10:00 P.M., at which time he said an unidentified party of at least 70 men had chased him and his men "to within half a mile of the post."

Duff had only about 30 men upon whom he was sure he could rely. Expecting the renegades to advance very soon, he formed a defense with troopers he could trust and simultaneously sent word to Brownsville that he needed help. An estimated one hundred civilians, most or all of whom had been accustomed to use of firearms since boyhood, responded to his call. Pickets were soon thrown around the town in a move designed to make it difficult for a small band of men to conduct a successful raid there. [OR I, 26, I, 439-40]

When within about a mile of Brownsville, some of Vidal's men discovered that pickets were in place. As a result they moved some distance away. On the following morning they crossed the river into Mexico at a point about nine miles from Brownsville. That meant they were seeking refuge in the Tamaulipas district. Clearly, they found it, for when a party of soldiers under Capt. Richard Taylor approached the riverbank, they spotted "a large body of cavalry" made up of renegades and deserters from nearby Texas counties. Not until later did Duff learn that during the hours when he could not follow their movements, Vidal and his followers had "committed several atrocious murders on unoffending citizens and soldiers." [OR I, 41, 440, 450]

From Fort Brown, Acting Asst. Adj. Gen. E. R. Tarver sent word to Ringgold Barracks that Vidal and about 60 of his men had shown themselves to be "base traitors." They had "rebelled against the military and civil authorities," his dispatch said. After having murdered an unknown number of persons, perhaps as many as half a dozen, they had moved up the river. While en route to it they had impressed a number of rancheros into their ranks. All signs suggested that they were moving to join the Mexican leader Cortinas, who had been branded as a traitor by Confederate authorities. [OR I, 41, 447]

Gen. H. P. Bee immediately sent a detailed account to headquarters of the District of Texas. Most or all of Vidal's men were Mexican citizens, he wrote. Once

Gen. H. P. Bee discovered and reported that most of Vidal's men were Mexicans.

Texas State Archives

he succeeded in getting two heavy guns into position, he felt that he could defend Brownsville against any number of assailants. By noon on the following day he was sure that he faced no force except Vidal and his company plus a few rancheros.

He reported that the identified murdered were Pvt. D. H. Dashiell, a well-known Captain King who had lived at Galveston for many years, "Mr. Barthelow, former sheriff of Cameron County," and a Mr. Cruz who was identified only as having been "a trustworthy friend of his country, much esteemed." Two days later, Mexican Gov. Manuel Ruiz told him that "the victims numbered at least 10."

To the surprise of Confederates who considered Cortinas a traitor, he and his men had made prisoners of 22 renegades who followed Vidal's leadership. Ruiz had promised full cooperation as well. He dispatched two units of his cavalry to reconnoiter the left bank of the river on the day after the mutiny. This development probably surprised mutineers, believed by Bee to have planned to attack and plunder Brownsville.

It was a logical target, he wrote, because its warehouses were "filled with valuable supplies for the army." According to him, "millions of property, invaluable to the soldiers of our army, and the plunder of the city, was the stake for which Vidal played." [OR I, 26, I, 448–50]

Taylor believed on October 31 that "the danger of the effects of this outbreak" had passed, thanks to Ruiz and his troopers. Still he offered for the capture of Vidal a reward that he considered to be large. He personally led a body of soldiers to hunt the outlaws. They spent one night on a ranch belonging to Fermie Gonzales, who was believed to be a supporter of the renegade captain. On the following day they encamped about noon at Palmito Ranch—destined in 1865 to be the focus of the last battle of the Civil War.

Most of the excitement created by the mutiny and its aftermath had subsided by November 8, when Bee brought Duff's regiment

Brownsville, Texas, at the time Vidal and his men were believed preparing to seize it and plunder

Leslie's Illustrated History of the Civil War

into headquarters. These men and their horses needed a few days of rest, he pointed out. Men of Cos. A, B, D, and F had worked long and hard—and not a single desertion had occurred in their ranks. It was possible to relieve them because at Houston Gen. John Bankhead Magruder had ordered two companies of cavalry and a battery of artillery to Bee's Santa Gertrudas headquarters. [OR I, 26, I, 403-4, 435, 444, 450-51; OR I, 26, II, 408; OR I, 53, 111, 910]

In order to encourage friends and keep enemies quiet, Bee proposed on November 12 to "march in three days for Rio Grande City with all the available force" he could muster. This demonstration was considered by him to be essential—partly in order to safeguard large shipments of cotton then en route for Laredo. He knew he would be taking a risk by this action, for Yankee forces were in the region and he did not know their precise location. U.S. Gen. Nathaniel P. Banks was reported by a Mexican informant to have been at Brownsville recently. Said to have paid a formal visit to Cortinas, where Vidal and other traitors were now being sheltered, the Federal force was rumored to be headed for Corpus Christi. [OR I, 26, II, 408; OR I, 34, II, 890-91]

With December just around the corner, Russell reported that only two regiments of Federals went to Corpus Christi. They were believed to have left behind at Brownsville "about 3,000 or 3,500" soldiers of occupation, some of whom were Negro troops. Confederate dispatches no longer devoted space to mutineer Vidal and his followers; for all practical purposes, they seemed to have vanished. [OR I, 34, II, 890-91; OR I, 53, 917]

The renegades must have decided that their best policy was to lie low for a period, then try to play an ace. Apparently they succeeded in doing so, for on December 2 Vidal's name cropped up once more—this time in a dispatch by U.S. Gen. N. J. T. Dana. Reporting to Gen. Charles P. Stone in New Orleans, he said simply:

> Vidal's command has been mustered in, armed, and equipped to the number of 89 men, for one year. One of them was killed yesterday in a brawl, and I propose to make an example of the murderer. By the day before Christmas, Vidal and his men—now termed scouts and protected by large Federal forces—had returned to Brownsville from a foray into the interior of Texas. [OR I, 26, I, 830-31, 876]

On January 31, Vidal surfaced again in records of the Department of the Gulf, U.S. Gen. Nathaniel P. Banks, commander. At that time the Confederate mutineer headed one company of Texas Partisans in the brigade led by Col. Edmund J. Davis.

Once he changed sides, the mutineer's activities were seldom mentioned in military records that were preserved. His former comrades were unable completely to forget him, however. A May 25 notation made at Ringgold Barracks by C.S. Col. John S. Ford for Gen. J. E. Slaughter at Houston said:

> A party of Vidal's men crossed to the Mexican side the other day near Reynosa, attacked a train of cotton carts, but were repulsed by the Mexican soldiery. A lieutenant of Vidal's was wounded in the face. [OR I, 34, II, 195; OR I, 53, supp., 994]

Nearly a month later, the renegade and his force were still on the prowl. Ford ruefully reported that Vidal had once more crossed the Rio Grande "with some 60 men, armed, mounted and equipped." Had it not been for the rise in the river brought about by heavy spring rains, the Confederate officer was positive that "400 others would have gone with him, carrying with them ten wagons and teams." [OR I, 34, IV, 685]

Nothing in existing records indicates whether Vidal planned in advance to change uniforms when he led the largest mutiny among Texas cavalry. Since a considerable time elapsed before he began to wear blue, it is possible that he was recruited by Banks during the period the Federal commander was in and out of Brownsville. Whatever the case, members of no other large band on either side successfully switched their allegiance, found protection, and continued to plunder for months after having staged a landmark mutiny.

Like most partisans, Vidal's men did not wear uniforms and they preyed on civilians without mercy.

16

Eight Thousand Watched–The XVIII Corps at Cold Harbor, June 3, 1864

"As Petersburg is now uncovered you will take your movable column, prepared for that purpose, and cross the river by the pontoon bridge and attack Petersburg." Directed to U.S. Gen. William F. Smith, Gen. Benjamin F. Butler's terse order marked the end of days of preparation. Petersburg, next to Richmond in importance in Virginia, seemed likely to fall to the Army of the James.

Before the Union XVIII Corps got under way, Smith received a second directive. He was now told to turn his back upon the Virginia city and head for tiny White House landing on the Pamunkey River, a prewar home of Mrs. Robert E. Lee. This sudden and dramatic change in plans, said Butler, came about as a result of "imperative orders from General Grant." With 16,000 men having been given another assignment, Petersburg would have to wait.

Smith's response to Butler was curt and to the point: "I have the honor to request that the orders for the movement of to-morrow, for my command, may be furnished to me to-night in writing." [OR I, 36, III, 286]

Had it not been for his eagerness to reduce Petersburg, Butler would have been glad to get Smith out of his army. A native of Vermont and a high-ranking 1845 graduate of West Point, the officer widely known as "Baldy" was famous—or notorious—for saying what he thought. He did precisely that after the frontal assault upon Rebel lines at Fredericksburg collapsed in December, 1862. With Gen. William B. Franklin as co-signer, a lengthy letter was posted.

Ignoring the long-established chain of command, the proposal went directly to President Abraham Lincoln rather than to Gen. Ambrose E. Burnside. It said their commander's plan of campaign

131

for the immediate future "cannot possibly be successful." Franklin and Smith then presented a detail set of proposals for movements of the Army of the Potomac. [OR I, 21, 868–70]

Three days before Christmas the chief executive whose military orders typically identified him as commander in chief of the U.S. Army and Navy responded. His brief letter, almost curt in tone, dismissed their proposal as riddled with old difficulties. Lincoln closed by saying he remembered clearly that when he was at Harrison's Landing the previous July, Franklin had espoused a quite different set of operations. Franklin tartly responded four days later by saying that circumstances were quite different after nearly six months. [CW, VI, 15–16]

Gen. William B. Franklin signed a letter of protest that went to the President.

Nicolay and Hay, *Lincoln*

Unlike his comrade, Smith did not challenge Lincoln's appraisal of their plan. As a corps commander who had spent years in uniform, he had been notified in July that he had been nominated for the rank of major general. He was furious when he learned that the U.S. Senate had failed to confirm the nomination. As a result, he did not move up in rank—and in March was reduced to the command of a division in the Department of the Susquehanna. [WWW, 608–9]

During a later period of service in Mississippi, he had a violent disagreement with Gen. William S. Rosecrans. Yet his skill as an engineer was unquestionably great. As a result, he won praise from Gens. William T. Sherman, George H. Thomas, and U. S. Grant. Their influence probably led to a second appointment as major general. This time, it was confirmed, and he took command of the XVIII Corps. Very late in the war a bitter argument with Gen. Winfield S. Hancock led to his removal from command. [GB, 463; WWW, 608–9]

Five days after being told to take his force to White House, he refused to obey an order from Gen. George G. Meade—a matter about which he wrote boldly many years later. Had this been made public at the time, he would have been subject to court-martial on a charge of mutiny. His disobedience of an order was apparently unknown at

Gen. Winfield S. Hancock *(right of tree)* caused William F. Smith to lose his command.

U.S. Signal Corps

the time except to an aide or two. Hence he was one of the highest-ranking officers who engaged in mutinous conduct without receiving severe punishment.

Debarking at the Pamunkey River site began on the morning of May 30, 1864. It proceeded slowly, however, because wharf facilities were severely limited. Large Rebel forces were known to be near. Hence the landing of troops was guarded by Lt. Cmdr. Charles Babcock of the U.S. Navy and vessels of the North Atlantic Blockading Squadron. From Grant by way of Gen. Henry W. Halleck, Smith received orders to rebuild the railroad bridge at White House.

During the morning he was ordered to New Castle, on the south side of the river. Leaving Gen. Adelbert Ames and 2,500 men to guard White House, he set out for the new destination about 3:30 P.M. with 10,000 men and 16 guns but without adequate wagons to carry ammunition and supplies. [NOR I, 10, 102-3; OR I, 36, I, 998-99; Smith, 222]

A six-hour march during blistering heat caused some of his men to straggle, but most of them were within three miles of important

New Castle ferry when they halted for the day. Sending word to Grant of his position, he waited for fresh orders and received them the following morning. He and his men were told to proceed to New Castle, and a tone of urgency pervaded Grant's dispatch. As a result, officers and men of the XVIII Corps marched without having breakfast.

Upon arrival at his new destination, the man who had entered the Engineers upon graduation from West Point in 1845 surveyed the surrounding countryside as best he could. He didn't like the looks of the place, since it was surrounded by hills within artillery range. If occupied by Confederates, he was sure that the hills could be carried only by assault.

Greatly perturbed, Smith sent Capt. Francis U. Farquhar of the Engineers to Grant's headquarters with an oral message. "There must have been a mistake in orders," he was instructed to say as a prelude to a request for a correction. Long before he returned, Lt. Col. Orville E. Babcock of Grant's staff rode up with word that there really had been a mistake in orders. Smith and his force were supposed to be at Cold Harbor, about 15 miles from Richmond by road but only half that far away as the crow flies. [OR I, 36, 999]

Men of the XVIII Corps, few of whom were accustomed to long marches, returned to the vicinity of the ferry. After a brief rest they headed to Cold Harbor on a day that Smith later described as having been "intensely hot, the dust stifling, and the progress slow, as the head of the column was behind the [wagon] trains of the VI Corps." Numerous members of his command fell out from exhaustion, reducing his ranks to no more than 9,500 men—possibly less. While on the march he received a new order—the first sent to him by Gen. George G. Meade. Under its terms, the XVIII was instructed to cover the approximately three miles between Bethesda Church and Cold Harbor—and be ready to join in an attack. Though he was the commander of the Army of the Potomac, the Gettysburg victor was subordinate to Grant. [Smith, 223]

Many officers and men in gray were taken by surprise at Grant's move to interpose his forces between them and the Rebel capital. Sgt. Maj. George C. Eggleston of a Virginia battery wrote for thousands of his comrades when he expressed both surprise and disappointment. After the long and brutal contest in The Wilderness, Rebels had expected men in blue to retire for a period. Instead, here they were—apparently headed toward Spotsylvania.

That showed Grant had no intention of retreating. Furthermore, the usual pattern of actions in Washington had not been followed. That meant failure or defeat would not remove the new Federal lieutenant general from command. He could be expected to continue his war of attrition, regardless of losses sustained by his own forces. [Eggleston, 230]

Only an occasional cabin was found in the three-mile front between Bethesda Church and Cold Harbor.

The Soldier in Our Civil War

Smith's reasoning may have been along a similar line, but he failed then or later to reveal what he was thinking as he headed toward Cold Harbor. Upon arrival there, he saw that the Federal position was as bad if not worse than it would have been at New Castle. Correctly believing the enemy to be established in a dense wood, he noted that it could be reached only by crossing an open field whose width was about three hundred yards at one point but was estimated at 1,200 yards elsewhere. He was positive that if Rebels launched a massive assault, he didn't have enough men to "fill the space" between the two points at which he was directed to anchor them. Men of at least one of his regiments were armed only with heavy and unreliable Austrian-made weapons. To make matters worse, soldiers had no ammunition except that in their cartridge boxes. [OR I, 36, I, 1001; Smith, 223]

An adequate supply of ammunition eventually reached the XVIII from Gen. Horatio G. Wright of the VI Corps. Yet about noon on June 2, Smith saw that much of their front consisted of only one line of battle. As a result, he sent a terse dispatch to Gen. Andrew A. Humphreys, Meade's chief of staff. He had no idea how long he could hold his position if vigorously attacked, so said he had to leave this matter to the commanding general. Soon afterward the commander of the XVIII Corps acted much as he had at least twice before. As he remembered it, he told Meade that the planned afternoon attack "would be simply preposterous." [Smith, 224]

Despite his views, the general advance ordered by Meade and Grant began about 4:30 P.M. on June 2. Officers and men commanded by Gen. Thomas C. Devins formed the front line of the Federal assault. Smith castigated the movement as providing conclusive proof of the "entire absence of any military plan" among Federal forces. Despite "a murderous fire," men in blue managed to reach the edge of the woods, where the second line caught up with them. They overcame some Confederate rifle pits and took an estimated 250 prisoners. Resuming their advance, they burst into a second clearing. Here the enemy fire was so heavy that they fell back. According to U.S. Gen. Gilman Marston, any additional attempt to have advanced would have brought about "useless slaughter." [OR I, 36, I, 1006; Smith, 223]

The Vermont native, whose initial assessment of the field of potential battle had proved to be correct, was alert to the danger that roads on his right might be taken by Rebels. When units were detailed to guard them, the extended front of the XVIII meant that "only one thin line of battle" was opposed to barely visible but extremely stout enemy works. The outcome of the afternoon struggle was predictable; some Federal units managed to hold positions they had gained, but they and their comrades suffered numerous casualties. [OR I, 36, I, 1000]

Meade's brusque orders had made it clear that he placed great importance upon dislodging and if possible routing the enemy before entrenchments could be dug. Smith's request for ammunition brought a response that was typical of the man widely known as Old Snapping Turtle. "Why the hell didn't he wait for his supplies to come up before coming here?" Meade demanded of his own subordinates. Despite his obvious anger, he made arrangements for a substantial quantity of ammunition to go to the XVIII. [OR I, 36, I, 1001-2]

Smith reasoned, perhaps correctly, that Meade was chafing at having to take a subordinate role after his monumental victory in Pennsylvania. His treatment of a newspaper correspondent had so angered all members of this body that they entered into an unwritten conspiracy. Meade's name was never mentioned in connection with a victory, but was always made prominent in reports of defeat or failure. Years later, Smith was still convinced that Meade's battle orders at Cold Harbor resulted partly from the fact that "the papers were full of the doings of *Grant's* army, and he was tired of it, and was determined to let General Grant plan his own battles." [Smith, 228]

Whether the decision was made by Grant or by Meade, orders soon came for a full frontal assault at 4:30 on the following morning. Smith saw the Rebel position as being more than merely formidable, saying:

After the fall of Vicksburg, Gen. Ulysses S. Grant was depicted as vanquishing all foes.

Harper's Weekly

In front of the center was a line of Confederate earth-works like a curtain [which had been dug overnight], with a flanking arrangement at either end—that on the right being somewhat exposed to the fire of the artillery of my right division, that on the left opposed to the left of the Eighteenth and right of the Sixth Corps. Near the center was a small stream with marshy sides running toward the enemy's lines. On its right was a bluff a few feet in height affording to the troops moving down the stream partial shelter from a cross-fire on the right. [Smith, 225]

Generations later, Jeffrey D. Wert characterized the Rebel works at Cold Harbor in two words: "nearly impregnable." Other late 20th-century analysts generally agree that this may have been the strongest defensive position occupied by Confederates during 1861–65. [E, 150]

Impregnable or not, orders were to take the Confederate works. Diaries and letters reveal that on the night before the scheduled grand assault, large numbers of men in blue wrote their names and addresses on slips of paper and pinned them to their shirts. This information would be essential if bodies of the slain were to be shipped home to their relatives.

Precisely at 4:30 A.M. on June 3, Martindale's forces "moved down the stream, out of the woods, and against the earth-works." Repulsed by a combination of frontal and cross fire, they fell back to the edge of the woods. This left them within easy musket range of the enemy's line. Dozens of other Federal units had experienced comparable setbacks. Gen. George J. Stannard's brigade made three separate assaults in a matter of a few minutes; each was repulsed with heavy losses.

Soon afterward it became generally known that the Federal move at Cold Harbor, whose width is variously estimated at having been from one-half mile to six miles, lasted less than 10 minutes. During that time, men in blue became casualties at the rate of about 16 per second. Pickett's Charge at Gettysburg is far better known and may have involved more casualties. Yet no other Civil War action approached Cold Harbor in its June 3 per-minute casualty rate of approximately one thousand men.

Smith dashed off a dispatch to Meade in which he reported the triple repulse of one body of Federals. His own forces were "very much cut up," he said and added that there was no hope that they could carry the works in front of them without relief from galling Rebel fire. In reply, he received orders to move forward "without reference" to adjoining bodies of troops. Later in the day a courier delivered an oral command that he lead another assault. "That order I refused to obey," Smith later confessed.

Because the leader of the XVIII flatly disobeyed his commander, some eight thousand men in blue—more or less—watched as their comrades were once more mowed down. There is no reason to believe that the outcome of the move against Robert E. Lee's forces would have been affected had trouble-making Smith done as he was told to do.

In the melee of battle, it is unlikely that anyone except a handful of loyal aides knew that he had defied Meade. If his action had been known at headquarters and regulations had been followed, his disobedience would have led to a charge of mutiny.

As it was, a clearly mutinous act by a top-rank officer went unpunished and probably unknown at the time. That it saved hundreds or even thousands of lives was beside the point; he had knowingly engaged in disobedience. Smith never wavered in his conviction that the order for a parallel advance at Cold Harbor was "murderous." In his opinion, "complete ignorance or culpable neglect" marked "the logistics that brought the Army of the Potomac to the battlefield of Cold Harbor." [Smith, 229]

That scathing denunciation of Meade—and of Grant by implication—may or may not have been accurate. Regardless, disobedience at Cold Harbor by Maj. Gen. William Farrar Smith has no precise parallel among actions of hundreds of Union and Confederate general officers.

Part III
Quick Fuzes

17

Reorganization—William H. C. Whiting, October 24, 1861

General Order No. 15 came from Richmond on October 22, 1861. Under its terms the new Department of Northern Virginia was established to include the Valley, Potomac and Aquia Districts. Commanders were directed to brigade troops in the Potomac District and form them into divisions. This action stemmed chiefly from the desire of President Jefferson Davis to brigade all Mississippi troops together.

According to the directive from the office of the adjutant and inspector general, the second brigade of the first division was to be led by Brig. Gen. W. H. C. Whiting. Whiting's command was to consist of "five Mississippi regiments." The same structure, spelled out in slightly great detail, was repeated three weeks later in General Order No. 18. [OR I, 5, 913, 960]

Whiting, a Mississippi native who graduated first in the West Point class of 1845, hit the ceiling. He probably knew that in May then-Col. Thomas J. Jackson had refused to obey a War Department

No gunner ever said "Stonewall" Jackson had a slow fuze; as a colonel, his anger flared at Gen. Joseph E. Johnston.

Leslie's Illustrated History of the Civil War

order transmitted through Gen. Joseph E. Johnston. Regardless of
whether or not he was influenced by Jackson's example, two days
after being directed to head the newly formed division, he wrote to
Gen. Gustavus Smith. Raging, he said:

> I had heard that attempts were on foot to organize the regiments
> into brigades by States—a policy as suicidal as foolish. For my
> own part, I shall protest to the bitter end against any of my regi-
> ments being taken from me; they are used to me and I to them,
> and accustomed to act together. . . .
>
> If they persist in Richmond in their purpose to reorganize
> the brigades, they will be guilty of inconceivable folly. For one, I
> am not disposed to submit for one moment to any system which
> is devised solely for the advancement of log-rolling, humbugging
> politicians—and I will not do it. [OR I, 2, 872; WWW, 711; GG, 334;
> Lee's, 1, 119; JSHS, 26, 150-51]

On December 19 he addressed a dispatch to Jefferson Davis. Though
it was lost, the President's response indicates that it was much like
the one received and saved by Gustavus Smith. [OR I, 5, 893]

Whiting had good reason to doubt that he would be severely
punished for his refusal to obey an order from his commander in
chief. As the son of an officer of the U.S. Army, he had enjoyed high
professional prestige from the day he was assigned to the Engineers.
Two months prior to the reorganization, he had been almost as ad-
mired and feted as Gen. P. G. T. Beauregard. [Lee's, 119]

At Harpers Ferry, Virginia (now West Virginia), Gen. Joseph E.
Johnston had put him in charge of getting Rebel troops to Manassas
Junction. Major Whiting pored over maps for hours before deciding
that it would be impossible to rapidly cover the distance on foot.
Hence he came up with an idea that had never before been tried—
use of commandeered railroad cars for transportation of troops.

Thanks to Whiting's ingenuity and engineering skill, Johnston's
men began arriving at the Bull Run battlefield during the early afternoon of July 21. Their presence was widely credited with having led
to the Confederate victory that put a pall over Washington and sent
residents of Richmond into the streets to dance and celebrate.

C.S. President Jefferson Davis was a former U.S. secretary of
war who would have preferred to command armies rather than deal
with lawmakers. He was so deeply concerned about events a short
distance west of the new Rebel capital that he went to Bull Run to
see some of the action in person.

Keenly aware of the crucial role played by Johnston's men who
arrived thanks to Whiting, the chief executive took an extraordinary
step. He conferred one of his rare battlefield promotions that day, jump-
ing Whiting three grades and making him a brigadier. The President's

Transportation of soldiers by rail was a major factor leading to Confederate victory at Bull Run.

action, soon confirmed by Confederate Senators, was taken as a gesture of gratitude for Whiting's role in transporting Johnston's men to the scene of the action. [WWW, 711; GG, 334; EC, 3, 1711–12; JSHS, 26, 139]

Had Whiting been quizzed barely two months later, he probably would have confessed that he was sure Davis had not forgotten how the tide was turned at Bull Run. He probably felt wholly secure in voicing his refusal to obey an order that originated with the chief executive. Probably he did not know that some gunners had begun to call the President "Quick Fuze" because of his hair-trigger temper. Other events suggest that the brand-new brigadier was as rash as he was self-assured.

He was at Dumfries, Virginia, the day General Order No. 18 began to circulate. In a brief dispatch to Gen. Samuel Cooper he addressed a different matter and stormed in writing that unarmed regiments being sent to him would only get in his way. "Please to put these new regiments somewhere else," he demanded. "They can do no good here, and will only seriously embarrass all operations." [OR I, 5, 961]

Older and far less volatile, Johnston had not protested nearly a month earlier when subjected to the same arbitrary treatment. C.S. Secretary of War Judah P. Benjamin notified him on October 23 that he was sending him immediately "1,000 unarmed men." There is no record that Johnston voiced an objection or a complaint—though he may have shared Whiting's views.

The fledgling general officer must have realized that action designated as mutiny in military regulations would not go unpunished. Five days after he wrote the lost letter of December 19, the secretary of war sent a dispatch of considerable length to Johnston, commander of the Department of Northern Virginia. It was sent at the request of Davis and said:

> The President has read with grave displeasure the very insubordinate letter of General Whiting, in which he indulges in presumptuous censure of the orders of his commander-in-chief, and tenders unasked advice to his superiors in command.

Davis, continued Benjamin, had no desire to force Whiting to command a brigade "which it was supposed he would feel honored in accepting." Because he took offense, Benjamin told Johnston:

> ... you are requested to issue an order relieving Brigadier-General Whiting of the command of a brigade of five Mississippi regiments as assigned to him by General Orders, Nos. 15 and 18.
>
> As there is no other brigade in the [Confederate] Army of the Potomac not already provided with a commander under the general orders of the Department, the services of Brigadier-General Whiting will no longer be needed for the command of troops. The President therefore further requests that Maj. W. H. C. Whiting, of the engineer Corps of the Confederate States, be directed by your order to report for duty as engineer to Major-General [Thomas J.] Jackson, of the [Shenandoah] Valley District, where the services of this able engineer will be very useful to the Army.

Benjamin closed by scolding Johnston for having forwarded a letter from a subordinate "having so obvious a tendency to excite a mutinous and disorganizing spirit in the Army."

Davis could not strip Whiting of his stars. Yet removing him from command and sending to the Engineers as a major meant a drop as rapid as his earlier rise. [OR I, 5, 1011–12; Lee's, 1, 120]

Shortage of experienced general officers was so great that Whiting was back at the head of a division by the time of Second Bull Run. He was away from his command immediately after the battle, so missed a power struggle within ranks headed in his absence by Gen. John B. Hood.

Gen. Nathan G. ("Shanks") Evans, in command of a new brigade of South Carolinians, managed to get it assigned to Whiting's division on September 1, 1862. His commission was conferred on October 21, 1861, but Hood did not become entitled to wear stars until

March 3, 1862. Evans therefore took command of the division. He quickly demanded that ambulances captured by Hood's men must be turned over to the quartermaster of his South Carolina troops. Hood refused to obey, so Evans relieved him of command and put him under arrest. [CV, 6, 275]

If Whiting thought he would have no more trouble over rank, he found himself mistaken. Sent to fever-ravaged Wilmington that fall, he superintended the construction of Fort Fisher. Back in Virginia and accused of being drunk at Walthall Junction, he requested to be relieved so he could go back to North Carolina. [CV, 6, 208; EC, 4, 1711–12]

Under his leadership, Wilmington became one of the most strongly fortified of Confederate positions. Yet Davis—who seldom forgot a grievance—sent his close friend Gen. Braxton Bragg to take command at the port city. Years later, Gustavus Smith branded the President's action as having been "a sad mistake." [JSHS, 26, 154]

Though Whiting was now a major general, he ended his military career as a subordinate to Bragg. Other officers had up-and-down careers. Few of them, however, matched the frequency and speed of Whiting's changes that were initiated by his commander in chief who was as fast as a quick fuze.

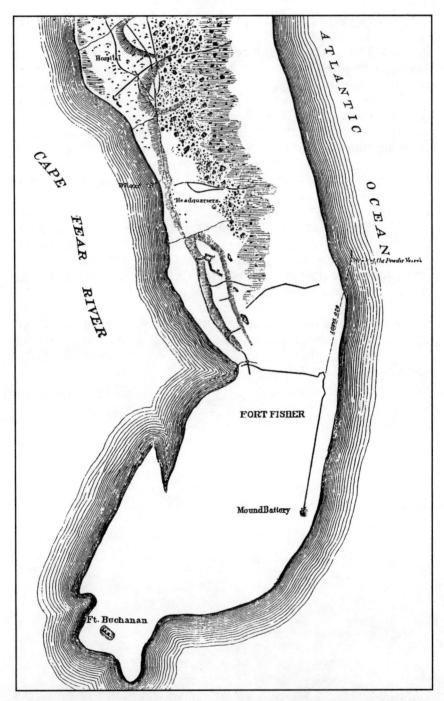

Built on Cape Fear near Wilmington, Fort Fisher was the last big Confederate
port to remain open.

Harper's History of the Great Rebellion

18

Obey, or Die!–Army of the Potomac, June 30, 1863

Officers and men who made up the Federal Army of the Potomac knew that they had a three-fold mission. They were expected to defend Washington regardless of any other actions that might be under way. At the same time, their offensive goals were to take Richmond and master Rebel forces, of which the Army of Northern Virginia was the most prominent.

Upon the outbreak of war, many career military officers in blue hoped that someone from their ranks might be chosen to head Federal operations. They were badly disappointed, Abraham Lincoln assumed his constitutional role as commander in chief and devoted the majority of his time to it for month after month. Gen. Irvin McDowell's defeat at Bull Run led to the elevation of Gen. George B. McClellan, who took command of forces around Washington. Later field commander of Federal forces, he headed the Army of the Potomac for only 15 months before being removed by Lincoln.

His successor, Gen. Ambrose E. Burnside, lasted just 90 days and was replaced in January, 1863. Almost from the start of his tenure, Gen. Joseph Hooker questioned decisions reached by Gen. Henry W. Halleck, who had become commander in chief in July, 1862. By June, 1863, there were many signs that suggested Robert E. Lee was planning or had begun covert moves designed to foster his second invasion of Union territory. [CW, 6, 78-79; 249, 281-82]

Halleck notified Hooker on June 5 that Lee was likely to move with light supplies, so Federal forces should be prepared to do the same. Lincoln personally discouraged Hooker's suggestion that he push south of the Rappahannock River in order to pounce upon Richmond. "I would not take any risk of being entangled upon the river,

Gen. Ambrose E. Burnside commanded the Army of the Potomac for less than 90 days.

like an ox jumped half over a fence and liable to be torn by dogs front and rear," the chief executive advised. [OR I, 27, I, 31]

Five days later Hooker reverted to his plan to take the Rebel capital, saying that it was defended by only 1,500 men. Lincoln practically snorted a response to this notion, stressing that Lee's forces rather than the capital should be the objective of the Army of the Potomac. Though it was not necessary for him to do so, Halleck endorsed the views of the President. [OR I, 27, I, 35]

A few days later, Hooker complained that a telegram from Washington seemed to indicate that Confederates were mounting an invasion. If so, he said it was not in his power to prevent it. Earlier, the chief executive had sounded out Gen. John F. Reynolds concerning his willingness to replace Hooker. When Reynolds found that final decisions would be made in Washington rather than by him, he turned down the opportunity to command. Probably but not positively at this point, Lincoln began considering the elevation of Gen. George G. Meade. He did not, however, take action.

On June 15 Hooker conceded that invasion seemed to be the "settled purpose" of Robert E. Lee. Almost simultaneously, he complained to the President about Halleck's lack of confidence in him. Lincoln's 10:00 P.M. response to mention of this source of friction was terse and to the point. He said:

> To remove all misunderstanding, I now place you in the strict military relation to General Halleck of a commander of one of the armies to the general-in-chief of all the armies. I have not intended differently, but as it seems to be differently understood, I shall direct him to give you orders and you to obey them. [OR I, 27, I, 43, 45-47]

Lincoln may have hoped to receive Hooker's request to be relieved; if so, he was disappointed. The commander of the Army of the Potomac continued to label news from Pennsylvania as "too confused and contradictory to be relied on." He quarreled with Halleck over newspaper coverage of his campaign, then reverted to his idea of striking "in the direction of Richmond." [OR I, 27, I, 50-55]

New orders from Halleck directed him to protect the capital plus Harpers Ferry and simultaneously to strike at Lee's forces. Hooker protested that he was unable to comply with this order and requested to be relieved at once. The general in chief replied that this was a matter that could be handled only by the President, but very early on the morning of July 28 Meade was awakened by a courier. The message delivered that morning was from Lincoln, who put Meade in command of the Army of the Potomac. Both men knew that a major battle was in the immediate offing, but neither of them knew where it would take place.

Harpers Ferry, Virginia (now West Virginia) was considered vital to the safety of Washington.

Popular History of the Civil War

Meade immediately headed toward Pennsylvania and soon established headquarters at Taneytown, Maryland. He had been there for some hours before he got word that a major conflict was shaping up in the village of Gettysburg, Pennsylvania—roughly a dozen miles north of Taneytown. [OR I, 27, I, 61-71]

Highly skilled at keeping his ear to the ground, Lincoln must have known that Meade's quick and violent temper had led many of his men to call him "Old Snapping Turtle." His selection of Hooker's replacement was made hastily and under great stress. In elevating Meade, he was aware that this general seldom wavered and never tolerated anything approaching insubordination. [CW, 6, 347, 356, 400, 414-15, 441-43, 459-61, 478, 481-82, 491-92, 506, 515-16, 561]

Meade's General Order No. 67, of June 28, was probably not yet on file in Washington. He informed his officers and through them his men that the President's elevation of him was "totally unexpected and unsolicited." Now it was his duty and that of the Army of the Potomac to relieve the Union "from the devastation and disgrace of a hostile invasion," he said. [OR I, 27, III, 374]

Some time on the following day Meade prepared for his entire force a document that was labeled as a "circular." In it he ordered all commanders to address their troops, explaining to them "the immense issues involved in the struggle." After a brief exhortation, he added a single sentence of warning to all of his enlisted men: "Corps and other commanders are authorized to order the instant death of any soldier who fails in his duty at this hour." [OR I, 27, III, 415]

Officers who had served under Meade for 60 days or more were not surprised by the blunt directive. Early in May, a disturbance took place among men of the 8th Ohio. Learning of it, Meade demanded that Gen. John Gibbon immediately send him an account of the affair in which he understood that "certain men declined to do duty." Gibbon replied that the rebellion had been quashed and that "12 of the ring-leaders were placed in irons."

Meade quickly issued General Order No. 23, in which he labeled conduct such as that among men of the Ohio regiment as open mutiny. In the future, he said, it would be "punished with death without trial" unless protesters "promptly returned to duty."

As though he feared he had not made himself clear, he added:

> . . . hereafter, any soldier who refuses to do duty on a plea [such as that his term of enlistment has expired] will instantly be shot without any form of trial whatever. [OR I, 36, II, 331]

Only an expert in military regulations and legal interpretations of them could have said whether or not Meade acted properly. He used slightly different language but conveyed the same warning on June 29. His actions in May and on the eve of Gettysburg were not unique. Other commanders had threatened to have rebellious soldiers shot on the spot. [OR I, 12, III, 577; OR I, 14, 669, 883; OR I, 27, III, 790; OR I, 34, II, 175; OR I, 34, III, 376; OR I, 35, III, 66; OR I, 36, III, 229; OR I, 41, III, 406; OR I, 47, III, 37; OR II, 4, 235-36; OR II, 8, 386]

Meade was in command of the Army of the Potomac barely two days before it went into the biggest battle ever fought on the North American continent. All of his troops marched into Pennsylvania, subject to his terse order concerning instant death without

Gen. John Gibbon put a dozen men in irons when they refused to do duty.
U.S. Army Military History Institute

trial as punishment for any action that could be construed as mutiny. Since an estimated 90,000 men were covered by the directive, it is likely that some of them ignored it.

Whether or not some men in blue were summarily executed as mutineers is a matter of conjecture. There are no records concerning such actions, but any commander who had a man shot for disobedience would have liked to keep the matter quiet. Significantly, references to Federal stragglers who abounded on many a battlefield are conspicuously lacking from accounts of the Gettysburg Campaign.

Did Meade's inflexible attitude toward mutiny contribute to Federal victory in and around the little town at which the Confederacy reached its high tide? No one knows, but the possibility that it did is an intriguing question concerning the great battle won by a commander who had been in the saddle barely long enough to get it warm.

19

Companies B & K–4th Connecticut, September 8, 1861

Early recruitment and organization of Connecticut volunteers centered in Hartford and New Haven. The state's first infantry regiment left Hartford one week after Lincoln's April 15 call for 75,000 90-day men. Organized at New Haven, the 2nd and 3rd Connecticut went to Washington on May 7 and May 14. Regiments 1, 2, and 3 saw the elephant at Bull Run and were mustered out on July 31, August 7, and 12.

Though it was organized at Hartford on May 21, the 4th Connecticut did not leave the state until June 10. Men of the regiment were on duty at Chambersburg, Pennsylvania, and Hagerstown, Maryland, until July 4. August was spent marching from one small post in Maryland to another and early September found them briefly at Darnestown. By that time, many members of the regiment were openly disgruntled. Basing their calculations upon movements of other units from their state, they fumed that they should have gone home no later than August 19.

On Sunday, September 8, some men let it be known that they wanted to sleep late the next day. They said they had been shifted from one place to another so many times they were still tired from marching. Lt. Col. James White snorted that he didn't intend to put up with laziness, so ordered the bugle to sound at the usual time. While eating their breakfast, men of Co. K swapped complaints with one another. Some of them grumbled that their Connecticut State Militia uniforms were too ragged to wear after returning home. One big fellow said he'd split his trousers and hadn't been able to get another pair.

From Samuel Colt's factory, Hartford looked larger than it was.
The Way It Was in the U.S.A.

Someone whose name did not get into the record stood up and shouted at the top of his voice: "I wanta go to Hartford! Our time is up, boys!"

Two or three dozen of his comrades lifted themselves to their full height and began screaming. Since their words were not coordinated, the result was not a chant but a melee of nearly meaningless noise. Only one word could be heard clearly at intervals: "Home!"

Capt. Sam Lepprell ran to his men and ordered them to move into the company street for the usual two hours of morning drill. With their muskets in their hands, they formed a ragged formation. "Shoulder . . . arms!" Lepprell ordered.

Not a man in the company lifted his weapon. Most stood stiffly silent, but a few mumbled curses under their breath. Lepprell tried three or four other orders, but was sullenly disobeyed.

Racing to White's quarters, the captain arrived with barely enough breath to spit out just one word: "Mutiny!"

A later inquiry revealed that the mass insubordination was spawned by certainty that the regiment was just like its three predecessors. Men were dead sure that they, too, had been mustered into Federal service for 90 days and that their term had expired some time ago.

Officers of the regiment never were able fully to clear up the question of how long the 3rd was supposed to serve. Clerks in the War Department found confusing and contradictory records, so were of no help about the term question. On the day of the mutiny, no man or officer had any documentation with which to try to quell the outbreak of sullen disobedience.

Yet White, whose fuse may have been even shorter than that of high-level leaders like George G. Meade and Jefferson Davis, was said to have hesitated less than a second after Lepprell reached him. Knowing Co. B to be in its street close by, he dashed over and signaled for the drill in progress to halt.

"Men of B," said their commander, "you are about to be put to the test. We do not face Rebels, but rebellion has broken out here. You will soon have a chance to show the stuff you're made of. Any man not ready and willing to obey orders can step two paces forward."

No member of Co. B accepted that offer.

White immediately marched the entire company to the street of Co. K. There he halted his command precisely in front of the mutineers and only five or six paces from them. About the time the formation was completed, it dawned upon him that the Sharps rifles carried by men of Co. B were not loaded.

To men of Co. K, who were armed with muskets, White snapped: "Shoulder arms!"

No member of the company obeyed, so he turned to Co. B and ordered: "Load for action!"

Men who had drilled for most of the time they were out of Connecticut opened their cartridge boxes and went through the prescribed set of precise movements involved in preparing their pieces for action. Chambers of rifles were closed and hammers were thrown back to half-cock in a matter of seconds.

"Company B, ready!" White ordered. With quick movements, according to a detailed account of the action-filled morning, "Every hammer went up to full-cock."

"Aim!" White directed.

Obedience to that order left each soldier in Co. B looking down his rifle barrel at a member of Co. K, a few feet away from him.

White gave mutineers another chance by repeating his order to shoulder arms. Again, they remained motionless.

Their commander pulled a watch from his pocket, and flipped open the lid of the time piece.

"I gave an order to Company K," he said. "That order must be obeyed before the second hand moves full circle. If it is not, there will no longer be a Company K in the 4th Connecticut."

Waiting soldiers estimated that about thirty seconds passed without any sign of movement among men of Co. K. Then scattered members of the unit began lifting their muskets. They were followed by a rush of comrades, so that every man stood at "shoulder arms" before the sixty seconds had passed.

To Co. B, White ordered: "Recover arms."

Turning back to Co. K he directed, "Order arms." This time, he was promptly and properly obeyed by every man, so he snapped, "Stack arms."

With muskets properly stacked, he commanded members of the mutinous unit: "Two paces to the rear; march!"

When this simple maneuver had been executed, men of Co. B were filed between rebellious comrades and their weapons. Mutineers were then marched to headquarters as prisoners. Each man's hands were tied with rope, after which the entire company was sent to the provost marshal. Gen. Nathaniel Banks, who then commanded a division in the Military District of the Potomac, kept men of the rebellious company in confinement for a time.

There is no record that about 80 men who had briefly defied orders were tried by a court-martial. Banks seems to have considered their imprisonment to have been adequate punishment, so upon their promises of future obedience he released them.

Soon the 4th Connecticut was ordered to Washington to help defend the capital. There, many of its members responded to an invitation to form a new unit, Connecticut's first regiment of heavy artillery. Probably because of this unusual development, nothing about the 4th Connecticut found its way into the OR. The story of a full-fledged mutiny that was instantly quelled by a commander who made lightning-fast decisions appears in some editions of *The Popular History of the Civil War*, which was issued under at least three different titles.

Dyer's exhaustive research yielded no clear evidence about the term of service for which men of the 4th Connecticut enlisted.

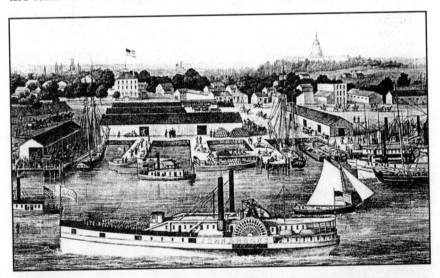

Washington bustled with military activity by the time the 4th Connecticut came to help defend it.

Mutineers vowed that they had not received any pay, uniforms, weapons, or accouterments from Federal sources at the time of the outbreak.

Veterans of the infantry unit who formed the regiment of heavy artillery remained in uniform until September 25, 1865. Two officers and 49 enlisted men were killed in battle or received mortal wounds. Four officers and 172 enlisted men succumbed to disease.

Some of the many battles and campaigns in which former mutineers fought were: siege of Yorktown, Hanover Court House, The Seven Days, Gaines' Mill, Malvern Hill, Fredericksburg, Chancellorsville, Gettysburg, Brandy Station, Mine Run, Dutch Gap, Petersburg, and Fort Fisher. [D, 3, 1006-7]

Numerous other groups of soldiers in the South as well as in the North mutinied during disputes about terms of enlistment. Much evidence suggests that Union and Confederate authorities sometimes tampered with records, making it impossible to authenticate some data. In other instances, military commanders simply ignored the terms upon which men had been recruited and enlisted, forcing them to fight after their enlistments expired. On both sides, fierce determination to keep on fighting and hoping for final victory led to flagrant disregard of the rights of thousands of fighting men.

After conducting a successful siege, men in blue put these new defenses around Yorktown, Virginia.

20
The C.S. Conscription Act–27th Virginia, May 15, 1862

Cadets at the Virginia Military Institute snickered about Prof. Thomas J. Jackson behind his back. Some of them wavered between calling "Old Blue Light" eccentric or regarding him as looney. All of them were keenly aware that it was not healthy to cross him. Jackson wanted things done his way and precisely on his schedule. Turning his back on the classroom in order to fight for Virginia, his inflexibility plus his ferocious temper led to more than one notable quarrel with a subordinate.

Strangely, however, during his weeks as a relatively lowly colonel of Virginia Volunteers he didn't hesitate to defy orders from a Confederate brigadier. Following Virginia's secession, he was briefly in command at Harpers Ferry, Virginia (now West Virginia). C.S. Gen. Joseph E. Johnston reached the post late in May to take command and send a memo to Colonel Jackson. In it he asked the former V.M.I. faculty member to put C.S. Maj. E. E. McLean in charge of the quartermaster's department. At the same time, he wanted Maj. W. H. C. Whiting (later a major general) to oversee work of the Engineer Corps.

Jackson replied to Johnston immediately, saying that he was responsible to Gov. John Letcher and Gen. Robert E. Lee. Not yet a Confederate officer, he tartly informed the new commander that he would not transfer his command or publish the Johnston order.

A general officer of the brand-new Confederacy who was less mature than Johnston would have set out to take the hide off a brash colonel of state forces. He apparently ignored behavior that in later months Gen. "Stonewall" Jackson would not have tolerated from a subordinate for an instant. To the strange military genius who typically refused to tell his officers and men where they were going or

160

why, any breach of discipline was a cause for a volcanic eruption. [OR I, 2, 871-72]

According to Maj. Robert L. Dabney, the Virginian who was figuratively speaking a walking Vesuvius, spewed with rage less than a year after he defied Johnston. Lt. Col. Andrew Jackson Grigsby led Jackson's 27th Virginia, one of the regiments in the famous Stonewall Brigade. Size of the 27th varied from a low of 150 men to a peak of more than four hundred. On or about May 15, 1862, men of the unit marched from McDowell, Virginia, to Mount Solon. Much of the journey was made in pelting rain that was cold enough to make many men miserable. At some point on the march Grigsby was faced with open rebellion. [OR I, 12, I, 753-54; OR I, 12, III, 879; WWW, 270]

A number of his men, constituting most or all members of several companies, had for some days been complaining that their time was up. They had volunteered for twelve months, they insisted, and a full year had passed.

Grigsby did his best to calm them by offering an explanation. Members of the C.S. Congress, he told them, had passed very important legislation almost exactly one month earlier. It did not become law until it was fiercely debated at length. Later entitled the Conscription Act, it was the first measure ever enacted that was designed to force Americans to fight instead of being asked to volunteer. Under terms of the legislation, Grigsby informed his men, their enlistment papers no longer meant anything. Like it or not, they were in uniform for the duration. [OR I, 10, II, 444, 480; OR I, 13, 944; OR I, 15, 919; DxD, 200]

This news sent some of the men of the affected companies into a fit of rage. As a gesture of defiance, one man after another threw his musket to the ground. Their action dramatized the fact that Congress or no Congress, these fellows didn't intend to serve another day.

Probably throwing up his hands to signify helplessness, their leader referred the matter to Jackson. According to Dabney, the general's face became as hard as flint while he listened. Then he spoke firmly and to the point.

"Why," he stormed, "does Colonel Grigsby refer to me to learn how to deal with mutineers? He should shoot them where they stand."

Jackson presumably took matters into his own hands. Mutineers were made to parade before other companies of their regiment whose members held loaded muskets. Charges and penalties were read and recalcitrants were offered two choices: instant submission, or instant death. All of them immediately wilted and Dabney wrote that there was no other "attempt at organized disobedience in the [Shenandoah] Valley army." [Dabney, 354]

Numerous biographers have used the brief account of the mutiny, making it well known despite the fact that it is not mentioned in the OR. In at least one account, the number of rebellious soldiers drops from "several companies" to 17 Irishmen. [REL, 1, 362; Farwell, 269; Henderson, 231; Bowers, 197]

Though an earlier action was not officially termed mutiny, Jackson had dealt in March with men who didn't want to fight. By that time it was public knowledge that conscription was being debated in Richmond and that legislation of some sort would come soon. Members of an anti-war religious body in Rockingham County tried to evade conscription by seeking to find Indians who would serve as their substitutes.

In the same county, some members of the Virginia militia took to the heavily wooded mountains in order to avoid being forced into Confederate service. According to Douglas Southall Freeman, "Jackson did not hesitate for an hour." At his direction, four companies of infantry and some cavalry surrounded hiding places of men trying to avoid conscription. Then two guns that had been sent along by Jackson went into action.

These pieces went to work shelling the woods in which draft resisters were hiding. One of them was killed, 24 hurried out to surrender, and their leader was captured while on the way toward Federal lines. This "insurrection" was put down 60 days before the May mutiny in the 27th Virginia. Having already shown that he didn't mind spilling blood in order to gain obedience, Jackson put a very quick end to trouble in his brigade. [Lee's, 1, 323]

The Conscription Act of April 14, 1862, was signed by Davis on April 16. Under its terms the President was given extraordinary powers, since he was specifically authorized to:

> call out and place in the military service of the Confederate States for three years all white men, who were residents of the Confederate States, between the ages of eighteen and thirty-five years at the time the call or calls may be made who are not legally exempted from military service. [OR IV, 3, 848]

Wording of the act was carefully framed to include men already in uniform whose terms had expired or would expire in the future. The measure was vigorously debated at great length before being enacted. [JSHS, 45, 26-33, 203-11, 213-16, 250-54, 263-65; 46, 32-36, 49-54, 68-72, 74-79, 108-11, 148-56]

Rebel soldiers were already confused and angry over the long list of exemptions that had been issued earlier. There were so many of these that it was all but inevitable that the phrase "rich man's war, poor man's fight" should be coined and gain currency. A common

Jefferson Davis *(center)* had the support of most of his cabinet members concerning the Conscription Act.

Harper's History of the Great Rebellion

complaint by older civilians stressed that young men were being called from the fields, when the government didn't have weapons for them. [OR I, 10, II, 480]

The Confederate conscription law was modified twice before being rescinded in March, 1865. During one period it extended even into the Chickasaw Nation, whose leaders had made an alliance with Richmond. The statute was so complex that it included more than 30 sections. Dates of muster, bounties, election of officers, service of 90-day men and 12-month men were among the multitude of matters with which it dealt. [OR I, 24, III, 1055; OR I, 52, II, 319, 406; OR IV, 1, 1103, 1150; OR IV, 2, 1056]

In addition to confusion and chaos created by complex statutes plus changes in them, civil and military leaders were authorized to suspend enforcement under some circumstances. These factors often contributed to or created nightmares for regimental commanders. [OR I, 28, II, 483; OR I, 53, supp., 985, 1026; OR IV, 2, 107]

In one instance, all men who re-enlisted for 30 days upon expiration of their terms were furloughed and went home. More than one hundred who initially refused to re-enlist were persuaded to change their minds later—under duress of the Conscription Act. Inevitably, men who thought they were fighting as volunteers and were forced into lengthy service were sullen and prone to mutiny. [OR I, 10, II, 444]

Though thousands of men in gray were illiterate or semi-literate, most regiments included at least a few well-educated men. These kept abreast of widespread objection to conscription among civilians, some of whom tried armed resistance to it. Inevitably, news about reaction to laws that directly affected them was shared with men who couldn't read or write. Inadequate food and clothing, unbearably long marches, and the risk of death in combat added fuel to fires of discontent over the various Conscription Acts. [OR I, 33, 403, 604]

Many civil officials disliked what members of the C.S. Congress did to secure soldiers and some of them branded all of the Conscription Acts as unconstitutional. Others feared that residents of states governed in part from Richmond would become "utterly powerless to protect their own families even against their own slaves." Extreme proponents of states' rights such as Gov. Zebulon Vance of North Carolina screamed to high heaven. [OR IV, 1, 1082, 1129; OR IV, 2, 129]

One of the longest official protestations addressed to Jefferson Davis came from Georgia Gov. Joseph E. Brown, who was in Atlanta on June 21, 1862. In an earlier exchange, Davis had sent his attorney general's response to Brown's questions concerning constitutionality of the act. Far from being satisfied, the state executive raised new questions and revived old ones. He quoted at length from James Madison, John C. Calhoun and the famous Virginia resolutions of 1798. Much of his tediously long argument was directed against Richmond's plan to use the Conscription Act to force members of state militia into Confederate service.

Brown probably realized that he was tilting against windmills, so brought his letter of more than eight thousand words to a close by challenging the President's handling of questions and complaints. He was surprised, he said, to find that Davis had released part of their unfinished private correspondence "upon a grave constitutional question" to newspapers.

John C. Calhoun of South Carolina was quoted when the Conscription Act was defended.
Harper's History of the Great Rebellion

He probably knew he was wasting ink by requesting in conclusion "that as an act of justice all newspapers which have published part of the correspondence [should be told to] insert this reply." [OR IV, 1, 1156-69]

Barely a year after leaders in Richmond resorted to use of force in an attempt to fill the ranks of its military forces, Washington followed suit. Exemptions, commutation clauses, and provisions for substitutes contributed to anger that erupted in draft riots, the most notable of which took place in New York City in July, 1863. Numerous analysts consider conscription to have been among the most notable failures of the Lincoln administration. According to Patricia Faust, only about six percent of men in Union states whose names were drawn in draft lotteries actually became soldiers. [OR I, 15, 503; OR I, 27, II, 932; OR III, 3, 241; DxD, 384-85; E, 160-61]

Jackson was not alone in being challenged by rebellious men. Dozens of commanders in gray and in blue had to deal with conscription-linked mass disobedience and defiance that was widely termed mutiny. Relatively few of them quashed rebellion in the ranks the instant it surfaced, however. The quick and violent "knee-jerk response" of the commander of the Stonewall Brigade was characteristic of the enigmatic man whom Robert E. Lee called his "right arm."

New York City erupted in riots when conscription went into effect in the Union.

Harper's Weekly

21

No Consolidation!–2nd Rhode Island Cavalry, August 30, 1863

U.S. Gen. Nathaniel P. Banks, commander of the Department of the Gulf, was requested by Washington to explain his decision to consolidate the 2nd Rhode Island Cavalry with another regiment. Writing on October 16, 1863, he admitting that he had no authority to take this action "except such as the necessity of the situation" gave him.

Most enlisted men of the unit were New Yorkers, he explained. Their officers were, however, Rhode Islanders. By late 1862 the tiny state was having difficulty meeting its draft quota. As a result, a substantial bounty was offered and this led drifters and vagrants from New York to become members of the outfit that was organized at Providence. [OR I, 26, I, 272; D, 3, 1627]

Ordered to New Orleans immediately, the 2nd Cavalry saw duty at Baton Rouge and Port Hudson before being frequently moved to rural spots such as Algiers, Franklin, Opelousas, Simsport, Monett's Plantation and Bayou Sara. Banks described the regiment as being "composed mostly of men entirely beyond control." Their frequent marches to spots distant from New Orleans probably made it possible for them to ignore prevailing Federal standards of conduct. Banks said that "Their depredations and robberies were frightful," but were brought to a halt when the unit returned to a camp near Port Hudson in May, 1863. During the lengthy siege of the river city, wrote Banks, his force was "continually in a disturbed and disordered condition" as a result of actions by members of the Rhode Island regiment.

Officers acknowledged their inability to control their men, so offered their resignations. Their impending departure from the

New Orleans, where men of the 2nd Cavalry reported on being sent to the
South

At Baton Rouge, cavalrymen from the North were awed by the size of river steamers.

William Waud in *The Soldier in Our Civil War*

regiment promised to leave it with "only 100 or 200 men." Hence Banks took an extraordinary step. Fully aware that state loyalty and state pride were inextricably linked with organization of regiments, he issued Special Order No. 209. Under its terms, the 2nd Rhode Island Cavalry was ordered into the ranks of the 1st Louisiana Cavalry. [OR I, 26, I, 262, 272]

Lt. Col. Harai Robinson of the Louisiana unit was given the responsibility of implementing the directive from Banks. According to testimony he gave during proceedings of a military commission, officers of the Rhode Island body "had full control of their men up to August 29." They then notified Robinson that all inventory records and muster rolls were ready for his use.

At 4:00 P.M. that day, the 1st Louisiana Cavalry assembled for dress-parade. Officers of the 2nd Rhode Island Cavalry formed their line in front of the Louisiana unit, facing it and about 40 yards away from it. With men of the 1st Louisiana at "order arms," their adjutant read the Banks' order to them. At Robinson's direction, he then turned and read the same directive to men who made up the remnant of the 2nd Rhode Island.

During the joint army/navy siege of Port Hudson, members of the 2nd Rhode Island Cavalry kept Federal camps in an uproar.

F. B. Schell in *The Soldier in Our Civil War*

"Instantaneously, and as if by accord," Robinson testified, "a tumultuous and general 'No, No' was uttered from one end of the line to the other." He responded by taking personal command and ordering that they present sabers. They hesitated and wavered but finally obeyed. He then ordered sabers to be carried and returned. As soon as these actions were completed he directed men of the Rhode Island unit to dismount "and form ranks as preparatory to fighting on foot." Men of the Louisiana regiment then "relieved horse-holders" by taking all of the animals to another spot. [OR I, 26, I, 263, 267]

Five non-commissioned officers obeyed directions to station themselves "at intervals of 10 paces from each other, on a line at right angles with right company guides." First sergeants then called the roll and men took their places in five squads that soon "formed on the left of the different companies of the First Louisiana Cavalry." Once the parade was dismissed, Robinson told his officers to take care that men from the now-dissolved Rhode Island body must not leave the camps of the companies to which they had been assigned. [OR, 26, I, 262–63]

Quiet reigned during the night. On the morning of August 30, however, Acting Reg. Q.M. Lt. Thomas Maher started to receive the property that had been assigned to the Rhode Island body. He was surprised and angry to find that as fast as he received horses, animals were "cast loose from the picket rope by the enlisted men of the late Second Rhode Island Cavalry, who were also carrying off other public property."

When this state of affairs was reported, Robinson went to the camp that had been occupied by men of the Rhode Island body. He found them assembled there, rather than remaining with the companies of the 1st Louisiana Cavalry as ordered. He rode up to them and directed them to "take up their packs and join their respective [new] companies."

Not a man responded to the command of their new lieutenant colonel. Two of them, he later testified, got on their feet and stormed that they had enlisted in the Second Rhode Island Cavalry and, by God, would serve in no other regiment. Their comrades who were seated on the ground gave a loud murmur of approval and none of them obeyed Robinson's directive. His detailed account of the incident said:

> I immediately ordered out the First Louisiana Cavalry, one company mounted, three on foot. The mounted company was ordered to encircle the camp, and the three on foot to form a line facing the mutineers. I then rode up to the mutineers, taking with me a German interpreter, who, after I had addressed them myself

in English, Spanish, and French, and ordering them to join the companies to which they had been assigned, communicated the same order to them in German. Not a man of the mutineers stirred. I then told them emphatically that if they did not rise up and form line, I should order them to be fired on. They then arose, and I picked out the two ringleaders, one of whom had used mutinous and seditious language the evening previous at the consolidation. Some decisive action was necessary.

Some members of the body had deserted earlier that morning. Most of the men in three companies of the 1st Louisiana were raw recruits "who had not been a month in camp" and hence were judged to be incapable of giving satisfactory service as guards. Robinson had reason to believe that the mutineers would have welcomed confinement in a body. Hence it was his reasoned opinion that "nothing but fear could prevent them for turning into a band of marauders." [OR I, 26, I, 263]

In this dilemma, Robinson decided to take "severe and instantaneous measures." He had the dismounted men of two companies of the 1st Louisiana "to form line on the wings and at right angles with the line of mutineers." He then dashed off a penciled order in the saddle, by which Adj. Edward B. Hall was named provost marshal and given command of the third company. His hastily framed directive read:

> First Lieutenant Hall, adjutant of the First Louisiana Cavalry, is hereby appointed provost marshal of the day, and is charged as such with the execution of Private Richard Murphy, Boston *alias* Richard Smith, and of private Frederick Freeman, *alias* William Davis, mutineers—a military necessity.

Men who were to be executed were placed 10 paces in front of the center of the two platoons charged with carrying out Robinson's orders. They were blindfolded, after which the adjutant took down their real and their assumed names plus their final requests. He gave them time to pray, after which he gave a signal and members of the two platoons that made up Co. F fired successively. [OR I, 26, I, 263–64, 267–68]

Hall was questioned a few days later during the brief hearing held by the military commission. All five of its members were from the Empire State, serving in the 159th, 91st, and 131st New York. A member of the commission was informed in a two-word sentence that Robinson gave his orders in "a cool, soldierly manner." Hall was then asked two more brief questions: "How long a time elapsed from the commencement of the mutiny on the 30th until it was quelled?" and "What quelled it?"

The lieutenant who had served as provost marshal for a day responded: "From what I saw of it, I should say [the mutiny lasted] not over half an hour." He then said that it was quelled by "Shooting two of the ringleaders on the spot." [OR I, 26, I, 266]

Officers who made up the hastily formed body of inquiry returned three brief verdicts. They said that the mutiny in the 2nd Rhode Island Cavalry was caused by the reading of the order of consolidation on August 29. The course of the uprising, they ruled, was from the time of that reading until the executions on the following morning. Finally, they commended Robinson for the "prompt and efficient manner" in which he suppressed the mutiny. [OR I, 26, I, 268]

Nothing in the published record indicated that it was in any way unusual for a mere lieutenant colonel to order the execution of two men within half an hour of their public show of disobedience. If a member of the court considered it a violation of regulations to have a pair of soldiers shot without so much as a perfunctory drumhead court-martial, he said nothing for the record that was published as Special Order No. 266, Headquarters Department of the Gulf, October 24, 1863. [OR I, 26, I, 269]

Gov. James Y. Smith of Rhode Island, who did not then know that two men had gone before firing squads, was furious at the idea of consolidating the regiment from his state with the 1st Louisiana Cavalry. In a letter of protest to Edwin M. Stanton, U.S. secretary of war, he urgently requested revocation of the consolidation order. Even the officers who had surrendered their commissions stood to lose if they should re-enter Federal service, he pointed out. They "would lose rank by date of commission," while all men remaining in their regiment would "lose all their identity with their native State" upon being "cooly thrust into a new organization." [OR I, 26, I, 270]

Replying through one of his aides, Stanton sent Smith a copy of a letter from Banks. A month later, Smith stormed to Stanton that "this is a matter, sir which cannot be lightly dropped and thought no more of." Possibly not yet being aware of the executions, the governor branded the consolidation of regiments as "an outrage to Rhode Island."

This time, the chief executive of the tiny state received a one-sentence reply from General in Chief Henry W. Halleck. Smith was told that a copy of the Banks' report of November 15 "shows the necessity of his order." The importance attached to the entire set of events by Banks is indicated by the fact that by November he was under the impression that the 2nd New Jersey was "consolidated with a New York regiment" and had forgotten the role of the 1st Louisiana Cavalry. [OR I, 26, I, 271–72]

Consolidation of regiments was a desperate expedient used only when a unit had dropped far below regulation strength due to deaths, desertions, or both. Even when two units from the same state were involved, members of one or both were likely to voice violent objections to the change. In numerous instances that commanders did not treat as mutiny, resistance to consolidation was at least as great as in the case with which Robinson dealt so swiftly and harshly.

Part IV
Trouble from Start to Finish

22

1861–Nine Months of Defiance of Authority

April—7th New York

Gustavus Vasa Fox, who planned the unsuccessful attempt to resupply Fort Sumter in April, 1861, was amply rewarded for his work. Abraham Lincoln had a new post created for him and saw to it that he became assistant secretary of the U.S. Navy Department. Even before assuming that position, his intimate relationship with the President gave Fox access to information that today would be termed "classified."

Writing to his wife in early May, 1861, he became almost ecstatic in his praise of Massachusetts Volunteers, saying:

Gustavus V. Fox, assistant secretary of the navy, didn't want rebellious conduct of soldiers to be known.
Nicolay & Hay, *Lincoln*

The communication [between Washington and the North] is open thanks to the Masstts troops. The famous N.Y. 7th declined a duty because an overwhelming force were *said to be in advance,* declined the order in writing. So the Masstts troops took the rejected duty FOLLOWED by the 7th. Don't say anything about this because there must be no quarrels now. [Fox, 42]

This "almost adored" body of 985 men who made up the 7th New York "left for Washington amidst the greatest enthusiasm" on April 19. Six days later, the regiment reached the capital and "marched up Pennsylvania avenue to the President's house." On April 27 officers and men "took the oath to support the Constitution" and immediately went into action trying to restore severed communications between the capital and the North. Five employees of the Washington Navy Yard were arrested for having filled shells with sand and sawdust. [D, 3, 1408; RR, 1, d34, d45, doc 81–82, doc 148–54]

Written refusal of the 7th to obey orders followed almost immediately. Even a few months later this would have resulted in severe penalties. At the time, public notice of the mutiny might have led to quarrels between leaders of loyal states, so it went unpunished.

May—Ohio Volunteer Militia

According to Gen. Joshua H. Bates, defiance of orders by very early volunteers from the Buckeye State also went unpunished because he quelled it very quickly. Members of regiments at Camp Harrison near Cincinnati were issued brown-barreled muskets that had been altered from flint to percussion locks. Men of one company flatly refused to accept the "Brown Bess," saying they wanted rifles but would rather have clubs than the old-fashioned weapons. Bates ordered the company to be disbanded and sent its members from camp as mutineers whom he termed "unworthy to be soldiers." According to Bates, his prompt and decisive action caused them quickly to change their minds and return in order to "take very kindly to Brown Bess." [MOLLUS, vol. 1, Ohio, 132]

June—39th New York (Garibaldi Guard)

This regiment was organized at New York City under the leadership of Col. Frederick G. d'Utassy, who called himself a count. Almost all of its 830 officers and men were natives of European nations. They formed one company each from France, Italy, Switzerland, and Spain, plus three companies each from Hungary and Germany. [RR, 1, doc 210]

Soon after reaching Washington in early June, nearly one hundred men mutinied when they were issued arms that they considered worthless. A number of U.S. Army companies formed in front of the mutineers, whose resistance soon wilted. Their colonel quickly quarreled with Capts. Francis Takatas and Louis Tassillier, resulting in news coverage in both the capital and New York City. Enlisted men whose defiance melted under the rifles of regulars seem to have escaped punishment.

The St. Louis riot was witnessed by civilian Ulysses S. Grant.

Leslie's Illustrated Weekly

Their colonel was not so fortunate; along with a number of other officers he was placed under arrest and according to the *New York Herald* did not rejoin his command until early April. Somewhat chastened, the colonel, his former mutineers, and their comrades fought at Bull Run. [ACW, 5/95, 56; OR I, 2, 427]

June—21st Illinois

Though it was minor and local, the mutiny of men who made up this regiment was one of the epochal events of the war. Illinois had been asked to provide only six regiments in the aftermath of Lincoln's call for 75,000 volunteers. One company was raised at Galena, and leather store clerk Sam Grant was offered its command, which he refused. This company eventually became part of the 11th Illinois. When the legislature authorized Gov. Richard Yates to accept 10 additional regiments for state service, it was Grant who mustered in these troops.

Soon after having been a witness to the St. Louis riot, from Galena the former U.S. Army officer offered his services to Col. Lorenzo Thomas at Washington, who was then serving as adjutant general. Thomas never replied to the overture, so Sam went to Cincinnati in order to see Gen. George B. McClellan. He later confessed to "some hesitancy" about seeking the rank of colonel—but knew himself to be much better qualified than many Illinois and Indiana commanders of regiments. After two futile days spent in trying without success to see McClellan, he returned to Springfield.

While Grant was away from the state capital, Lincoln called for three hundred thousand more men. As a result, all regiments then in the service of the state were put into Union forces. Without exception, Illinois units had elected all of their own officers "from the highest to the lowest." Most enlisted men were satisfied with these choices, but members of the 21st Illinois—earlier called the Seventh District Regiment—were different. Soon after donning uniforms its members found that they didn't like Simon Goode, whom they had selected as their colonel.

Goode had issued bread that they considered to be inferior, so they mutinied and refused to eat it. When he announced that the offenders would be punished, they and their comrades burned the guardhouse to the ground. Men who had volunteered for 30 days were now being asked to sign up for three years. Almost to a man, members of the regiment sullenly refused to take this step.

Grant had mustered the unit into service at Mattoon, so was familiar with many of its members. Probably through the influence of Congressman Elihu B. Washburne, on June 15 Yates offered Grant the command of the mutinous regiment and he took over on the following day. Soon he and six hundred sullen men were camped "on the fair grounds near Springfield."

A member of the regiment later wrote that though their new colonel took over very quietly, "He reduced matters in camp to perfect order" in only a few days. He did it by telling his men that their infractions of rules might have brought a fine and a short term of imprisonment in a time of peace. Stressing that they were now members of a fighting force that would soon go to war, he warned that new acts of mutiny could be punished by death. On June 28th he swore them in as three-year men.

Once in uniform again, Grant quickly demonstrated unusual ability and was promoted rapidly—eventually becoming the first U.S. lieutenant general since George Washington. Had men of the 21st been willing to go to war under their first colonel, the story of events during 1861-65 might have been quite different. [Grant, 231-43; WWW, 261; Nevin, 45; Perrett, 128-32]

July 11—44th Virginia, C.S.

Henry M. Price, who was there, watched a dramatic struggle at Beverly, Virginia (now West Virginia). According to his account, C.S. Gen. Richard B. Garnett sent three hundred "college boys" to hold a mountain top. There they were attacked by a Federal force of about five thousand. Members of the 44th Virginia could see the site of the struggle, and knew that it was hopeless for Rebels. Garnett, who could have ordered them into action, demanded that they be "idle witnesses." In this emotion-charged situation, wrote Price, "stern men" wept in agony at their inaction and reached the point of mutiny before the surviving "college boys" scattered into surrounding woods. [JSHS, 27, 38-39]

July 17, 1861—Stonewall Brigade

D. B. Conrad was on hand at Bolivar Heights when the Virginia Brigade was formed in May, 1861. The new unit was made up of five Virginia regiments—the 2nd, 4th, 21st, 27th, and 33rd. Their commander, widely known for his eccentricity, seemed never to sleep and walked about with no companion. After a skirmish near Martinsburg, the brigade that later took the nickname of its colonel as its own fell back upon Winchester.

About 3:00 P.M. on July 17, the long roll was beaten and men under Col. Thomas J. Jackson were directed to form a hollow square in order to surround a number of tents. Soon it was evident that the brigade enclosed a body of troops as well as the tents; these were soon identified as a battalion of mutineers.

Following Jackson's orders, a subordinate read a statement he had prepared. After expressing surprise and regret that officers and men had refused to obey orders, he warned that they must give "instant obedience." Facing five regiments of men who looked as though they knew how to use their weapons and were ready to do so upon order, the mutineers wilted. There is no record that they were punished for having defied commands of their own colonel. [Conrad, 83-86]

July 19—Erie Regiment

Stationed near Pittsburgh, members of the Erie were reported in the press as displaying "a rather ugly, mutinous spirit." Discontent stemmed from the fact that $17.23 due to each of its members from the state had not been received. Colonel McLane addressed his men, saying that he had spent $1,000 without receiving one cent in return. "There is one thing I want you to understand," he stormed, "and that is, that *I intend to command this regiment.*" His quick and decisive action apparently brought an end to talk of mutiny. [RR, 2, 92]

July 21, 1861—12th New York

According to the *New York Times* the 12th regiment made up of men from the state left New York City on Sunday, April 21. As they marched along Broadway they received "cheers from ten thousand voices welling in prolonged chorus." Men of the 90-day unit saw no action until their term of enlistment was about to expire.

On July 18 they were involved in heavy but relatively unknown action at Blackburn's Ford, near Bull Run. Under fire the green troops fell back "out of the woods in disorder." According to Col. Israel B. Richardson of the 2nd Michigan, only about 60 of the New Yorkers remained in line—and they were retreating when seen. Action of men who made up the regiment was regarded by Richardson as so important that he reported about it to Gen. Daniel Tyler. Despite its retreat, the unit sustained 34 casualties—the largest number of any Federal body engaged that day.

Three days later, Col. Louis Blenker of the 8th New York received a peremptory order that was not explained to him. Following instructions, he sent two companies of the 8th New York to disarm members of one company of the 12th. This action was presumably taken because enlistment of the 12th had expired and though it was on the battlefield, some of its members had refused to fight. No punitive action was taken against these mutineers, who returned to New York and were mustered out on August 5. [OR I, 2, 313-14, 427; D, 3, 1409-10]

July 24—13th New York

With enlistments of numerous regiments having expired or about to expire, Gen. John A. Dix became desperate. From Ft. McHenry he visited a number of camps and succeeded in persuading members of the 26th Pennsylvania to remain in uniform one week longer. Gen. Nathaniel P. Banks had a similar response from the 6th Massachusetts, whose men promised to stay where they were until August 2.

At the camp of the 13th New York, Dix found that men had already adopted a resolution to go home the following day. He used every argument he could devise "and by the most urgent remonstrances and by strong appeals induced them to stay another week." This rebellious body of men reluctantly kept their pledge to Dix, but were mustered out on August 6. [OR I, 2, 759-60; D, 3, 1410]

Men of the 6th New York, stationed at Annapolis and Manassas Junction, were not due to be released until August 19. Dix found them just short of mutiny, describing them as being "dissatisfied and demoralized." In an urgent appeal to Washington he listed other regiments whose time had expired or was about to expire: 18th Pennsylvania, 19th Pennsylvania, 22nd Pennsylvania, 13th New York Militia, 20th New York Militia, 6th Massachusetts, 8th Massachusetts, a Massachusetts battery of light artillery, and the 3rd Battalion of Massachusetts Rifles. In near frenzy, Dix demanded fresh troops because he knew that if those listed were not released some or all were likely to mutiny. [OR I, 2, 760]

August 22—Gen. John Pope

Discontent at a dangerously high level was not limited to enlisted men. Writing to V. B. Horton, Gen. John Pope penned a thinly veiled threat of a general mutiny. Simultaneously defending his men and blasting the administration, he wrote:

They [fighting men] find themselves neglected, abandoned, and humiliated by the President they have themselves put into the White House, and they have resolved to endure it no longer. . . . They warn [Lincoln] that neither Banks nor Hunter will be suffered to take command of Illinois troops, and that if it is attempted the whole of the Illinois force will march back into the State and have no more to do with war.

We are certainly cursed with the rulers in this country and especially at such a time.... By neglect, corruption, and outrage, the States of the West will be driven to group together and act without reference to the authority of the Central Government. [Quoted, Nevins, I, 321-22]

U.S. Gen. John Pope put into writing a hint that he was ready to lead a general mutiny.

Battles & Leaders

October—Fort Sumter's Garrison

According to a report that circulated among Northern newspapers, Pvt. James Cahel of the Fort Sumter garrison let it be known that he planned to spike guns if a Union fleet should appear. News of his idea reached Capt. A. B. Rhett, who took summary disciplinary action. He had Cahel tied to a gun in order to receive "one hundred and twenty-five lashes, well laid on."

Other members of the garrison mutinied in reaction to the harsh punishment, and Rhett was forced to call for help from Fort Moultrie in order to restore order and discipline. [*Milwaukee, Wisconsin*, October 30]

August—Pennsylvania Volunteers

Immediately after Bull Run, 90-day men began returning to the Keystone State. Numerous regiments whose men were waiting to be discharged camped near Harrisburg. No provision had been made for their housing, their food, or their pay. As a result, members of several regiments became mutinous.

They prowled about the capital in search of shelter and rations, then began to talk openly of breaking into business establishments. Gov. Andrew Curtin knew he faced a crisis, so called a regiment of three-year men to the capital to protect it. Mutinous units were dispersed throughout the state, and at their new places of encampment were eventually paid. [Nevins, 1, 232]

Mid October—9th New York

Col. Rush C. Hawkins of the 9th New York Zouaves found his hands very full as soon as he took command of Fort Clark at Hatteras Inlet, North Carolina. On September 7 he notified Gen. John E. Wool at Fort Monroe that some officers and men of the 20th New York had acted as vandals. Immediately upon reaching North Carolina, men of the regiment had begun "breaking open private houses and stores." With his own eyes, Hawkins saw some of them come into the fort loaded down with the results of their plundering" despite his stern orders forbidding such practices. [OR II, 2, 61-62]

By early October, the 20th Indiana was a major source of vexation to Hawkins. This regiment arrived without roll-books and officers admitted they didn't know the names of their men. Because he had complained earlier without effect, Hawkins now railed out against Washington officials he considered guilty of "criminal neglect" in failing to respond to him. "I feel that I have an ungrateful and unappreciating Government at my back," he told Wool. [OR I, 4, 622-23]

Matters became much worse when a new commanding officer arrived. He reached Hatteras Inlet on October 13 and quickly launched a fresh and extremely tough schedule of daily activities. Within a week, Hawkins requested a transfer from "this infernal place" but did not get it.

A relationship already simmering came to a boil when Williams assigned a newly arrived captain to the 9th New York. When Hawkins refused to accept him, Williams arrested the colonel and sent him to Fort Monroe to await a court-martial.

In the absence of Hawkins, his men defied regulations by burning their new captain in effigy. Their mutiny was so violent that the newcomer resigned and gave up his appointment. Members of the Zouave regiment might have been severely punished for their actions had their colonel failed to see Abraham Lincoln. He voiced so eloquent a plea for his men and for the continued defense of Hatteras that the President reportedly had him address his cabinet. Probably at Lincoln's insistence, Hawkins was restored to command of his once-mutinous regiment on December 22.

Bustling Fort Monroe, where a rebellious colonel was sent to wait for a court-martial

J. H. Schell in *The Soldier in Our Civil War*

Men whose violent insubordination had forced the resignation of a captain were not punished. Williams, who soon left Hatteras, stirred up a commotion in Louisiana during August, 1862. There he had five of his officers arrested, charging them with having "excited a mutiny" among troops at Baton Rouge. Other officers drew up a set of 31 specifications according to which Williams was guilty of official misconduct.

Nothing came of either set of allegations, since the man who had stirred up mutiny among Zouaves was killed before courts of inquiry could be established. Rumor had it that the stern disciplinarian had his head blown off when his own men held him in front of a cannon. If Hawkins and his mutineers learned of this story, they must have beamed with joy that "the bastard got what he deserved." [CW, 5, 59, 305; CWT, 7/75, 5–9; WWW, 719]

October 21—71st Pennsylvania (Baker's California Regiment)

Col. Edward D. Baker, whose military experience was limited, rode toward a Confederate camp at Leesburg, Virginia, with a commission in his pocket. The document named him as a major general, but he had neither accepted nor declined that rank. To accept would mean giving up his seat in the U.S. Senate, and he was reluctant to yield it. Strong ties with Abraham Lincoln accounted for his commission; while in Springfield, the Illinois attorney had named his second son Edward as a tribute to Baker.

Once war became a certainty, Baker declined the offer of a commission as brigadier but on June 22 took command of a regiment. Raised in Philadelphia and New York, the 71st Pennsylvania became known as the California Regiment because its commander had been a leading figure in that state before going to Oregon. Not a man in the regiment was a native of California and it is doubtful whether any officer or soldier other than Baker had even been in the far West. [D, 3, 1597; WWW, 27; GB, 16]

Col. Edward D. Baker, some of whose men mutinied under fire at Ball's Bluff

Nicolay & Hay, *Lincoln*

On October 21 Baker led his men toward Leesburg as commander of the 3rd Brigade in the division of the Army of the Potomac that was led by Charles P. Stone. Under orders to make a demonstration, he took his brigade across the Potomac River and placed them on top of Ball's Bluff. At this exposed point, they were ideal targets for Rebel marksmen hidden in adjacent woods. Shots from men they couldn't see began felling men in blue and chaos soon reigned among them.

According to eyewitness accounts, two companies of the 71st Pennsylvania dropped their weapons, fell to the ground, and hugged it in a futile effort to get out of the line of fire. In the heat of battle, Baker could do nothing about the mutiny that took place under his personal leadership while he was trying to rally his men.

Earlier, malcontents in the regiment were judged to have been at the point of mutiny while in camp. Hence on August 20 Gen. Andrew Porter had been authorized by Gen. George B. McClellan to use force if necessary in order to quell the mutiny. It did not erupt when expected, but on the field of battle members of the regiment ignored orders from their commander. This chain of events confirmed views held earlier by Gov. Andrew Curtin. He had hesitated to accept the motley regiment for service as a Pennsylvania unit, and did so only under pressure from the President. [OR I, 5, 574–75; CWT, 5/89, 19]

During a September 28 affair at Munson's Hill, Baker had commended his officers and men for "high personal bravery." Since he took four Rebel balls simultaneously, all of which were considered to have been fatal, he may never have known how badly some members of the California Regiment behaved at Ball's Bluff. Despite mutiny under fire, the regiment's loss of 281 men was topped only by that of the 15th Massachusetts. [OR I, 5, 217, 308, 328]

McClellan was furious at the unexpected disaster, not having authorized the crossing of the river. In a report to the secretary of war he emphasized that he had ordered no more than "a slight demonstration." Judah P. Benjamin, C.S. secretary of war, reported 155 Rebel casualties against 2,110 among men in blue.

Baker, intimate friend of the President, had fallen on the field during the Federal debacle in the first significant clash after Bull Run. Probably because of the known intimacy between Baker and Lincoln, blame for the fiasco fell upon Charles P. Stone. Arrested without charges, he was held incommunicado for about six months. His request for a court of inquiry was ignored, so his career was ruined without having been charged with an offense. There is no record that any punishment was given to men from Pennsylvania and New York who fought as Californians and who mutinied while battle was raging. [OR I, 5, 290; OR IV, 1, 796; WWW, 27–28, 626; E, 34; GB, 16, 480–81]

Early Autumn—11th Tennessee, C.S.

A mutiny so small that it is not recorded in the OR took place at Blair's Creek near Cumberland Gap, Tennessee. Lt. Alexander H.

Vaughn of Co. H, 11th Tennessee, had been sent to Tazewell to restore order to the village. As provost marshal of the town, he demanded obedience from unruly members of his own regiment. At a
spot about five miles from the village, mutineers killed him when he
tried to arrest them.

Three leaders of the mutiny were captured and taken to
Cumberland Gap in irons. When Rebels under Col. James E. Rains
withdrew from that spot, they took along the three mutineers "se-
curely chained to a wagon and under a strong guard."

One of them subsequently died from an unspecified illness and
another made his escape to Federal lines. According to Tazewell resident B. F. Schultz, the third mutineer was jailed at Knoxville before
being tried by court-martial at Bean's Station. Found guilty and condemned to die, "The stern and horrible decree of the court was executed by the comrades of the slain officer." [CV, 8, 518]

November 21—Justice of the Peace William H. Suydam

John A. Kennedy, superintendent of police in New York City,
was the first person to notify the U.S. Department of State that a
civilian official was under arrest. Officers of the 1st U.S. Lancers, a
regiment then encamped in Kings County, had alerted Kennedy to
what was taking place there.

According to soldiers, Justice of the Peace William H. Suydam
had worked actively "to disorganize the command" and had succeeded in inducing large numbers of men to desert. Two of the Lancers signed affidavits according to which Suydam "had counseled the
men of said regiment to mutiny."

A November 21 telegram from William H. Seward ordered that
the man advising mutiny should be arrested and committed to Fort
Lafayette. On December 16, a State Department telegram directed
the release of Suydam but gave no explanation for this action.

Federal officials soon had good reason to fear that Seward or
his aides had made a dreadful mistake. While residing at the Howard
House in East New York in early February, 1862, the justice of the
peace tried to act as a negotiator. Seeking the release of notorious
Rebel leader Richard H. Thomas, aka Zarvona, he suggested that he
be exchanged for one of his friends.

Though documentary evidence is lacking, the friend of whom
he wrote is believed to have been Irish-born Col. Michael Corcoran,
later made a general. Corcoran was the first man selected by lottery to serve as hostage for a captured Rebel privateersman. When
most other hostages in this group were released months later,
Corcoran languished in prison because he refused to sign a parole.

Had the civilian who was arrested for trying to persuade Lancers to mutiny succeeded in his role as negotiator, he would have

been hailed in both the South and the North. Zarvona was a popular hero among Rebels and Corcoran was held in such esteem by Federal forces that a Washington fortification was named for him. [OR II, 2, 321, 389; B, 176; WWW, 143-44]

November 25—11th Indiana

Stationed at Paducah, Kentucky, a group of Hoosiers under the command of Gen. Lew Wallace ignored the state's announced neutrality and forcibly raised the Stars and Stripes over "the house of a resident" of the city. Gen. Charles F. Smith, who knew that a Rebel flag had been flying, had ordered that no attention be given to it. Hence he sent an aide to Wallace with orders to have the Federal emblem removed. Smith's commission had been issued on August 31, but Wallace did not receive his parchment until September 3.

Col. Michael Corcoran, proposed for an exchange by an official who tried to incite mutiny.

Though outranked, Wallace indicated that he had no intention of obeying Smith's directive. As a result one of Smith's staff members got into a fist fight with a Wallace aide and was knocked down. Smith then issued General Order No. 36, in which he warned Hoosiers that they had subjected themselves to prosecution under the Articles of War. This was "the first proceeding of a mutinous character that ever happened with troops under his immediate command" during his 37-year military career, Smith wrote.

His thunder on paper may have given him a bit of satisfaction, but when he issued it he knew he could not force Wallace to obey. Neither the general who later wrote the famous novel *Ben Hur* nor members of his own Indiana regiment received punishment for the act of overt mutiny in a neutral state. [OR I, 4, 287; RR, 3, d89, doc 190; WWW, 601, 687]

December 4—New Orleans Tigers

Organized at New Orleans by Chatham Roberdeau Wheat who became their major, five companies formed a battalion that became famous as the Tigers. Wheat's Battalion may have been the most polyglot of all Confederate units. No member of the body used English as his primary language, and eight or ten nationalities were represented in its ranks.

During the first week of December, two members of the Tigers paid with their lives for insubordination. At Shepherd's Hill, Virginia (near Centreville) these unidentified Rebels "were shot for mutinous conduct and an assault upon the officer of the day." [*The Richmond Examiner*, December 9, 1861; CV, 19, 426-27]

Early December—4th Louisiana, C.S.

When Henry Watkins Allen donned the uniform of a Confederate private he had no idea that he would later become Louisiana's last wartime governor. Soon elected lieutenant colonel of the 4th Louisiana, he and his green troops were sent to Ship Island. There he quelled a mutiny about which little is known, but his handling of the matter may have led to his elevation in rank. As colonel of the regiment, the future state executive joined P. G. T. Beauregard in Tennessee in time to fight with distinction at Shiloh. [E, 7; WWW, 7; CMH, 1, 723-24; 13, 292-94]

Late December—53rd New York (D'Epineuil's Zouaves)

Under great pressure to meet increasingly heavy demands for men, officials of New York expressed concern that organization of the state's 53rd regiment of infantry proceeded unusually slowly. Though formation of the unit was launched at New York City on August 27, the regiment was not organized until November 15. Among Rebel units, its closest counterpart was Wheat's Tigers. Men of about a dozen nations signed up for service in the 53rd, often under financial pressure or some other form of duress.

It was probably the only regiment of the war that included an entire company of Tuscarora Indians who were recruited in extreme western sections of the state. Lionel J. D'Epineuil was elected colonel of the unit despite the fact that its ranks included Vigneur De Monteil. A veteran of European wars and 10 years older than D'Epineuil, De Monteil was chosen as lieutenant colonel.

Three days after its organization was completed, the body widely known as D'Epineuil's Zouaves left for Washington. The regiment stayed there only a few days before being moved to Annapolis and placed under the command of Gen. Ambrose B. Burnside. By that time, the unit was plagued with serious problems that included desertion plus a high level of friction between its two top-rank officers.

When De Monteil was accused of having neglected his duties, he angrily demanded a court of inquiry and got the promise of it. His name was eventually cleared, but while he was waiting for a hearing the regiment got completely out of hand. Late in December, a band of privates seized several of their officers and put them in irons during the last mutiny of the year.

Members of the 11th Connecticut came to the rescue of captured officers and brought the uprising to an end. Though the reputation of the 53rd had been permanently blackened, Burnside reluctantly consented to permit it to take part in his North Carolina expedition. He soon regretted his tolerance for ex-mutineers who were lauded by their colonel as being admirable and obedient. Their conduct proved so outrageous that Burnside sent them back to Annapolis. Serious charges were then brought against the commanding officer of the regiment, who hotly denied having had any part in the mutiny.

Disgusted officials of the War Department refused to convene a court-martial. This course of action was not necessary, they pointed out. Conduct of D'Epineuil and his men had been so outrageous that no hearing was needed in order to determine whether or not they were loyal and effective fighting men. In a rare gesture during an acute shortage of manpower, officials ordered the mutinous 53rd to be mustered out after only four months of service despite the fact that "three years or the duration" had become standard. [D, 3, 1424; OR I, 9, 361–62]

23

1862–From Adams Run to Peralta

January 1—1st Kentucky

Pvt. Richard Gatewood of the 1st Kentucky didn't get into the OR. Were it not for a vigilant newspaper correspondent, his name might have been forgotten. Since Kentucky was officially neutral, the regiment to which he belonged was organized at Pendleton, Ohio. While on duty somewhere in the valley of the Kanawha River, Gatewood went berserk.

Probably without benefit of a court-martial he was found guilty of "desertion, mutinous conduct, and a murderous assault of a sentinel while on duty." As a result the mutineer was executed on the first day of the new year. He died a few miles from Harpers Ferry at Charles Town, Virginia—where John Brown was tried and sent to the scaffold a trifle more than two years earlier. [D, 3, 1197; *Cincinnati Gazette,* January 1, 1862]

February 2—4th Missouri

Asst. Adj. Gen. N. H. McLean issued General Order No. 26, at Saint Louis in order to deal with disobedience and mutiny. Several companies of the 4th Missouri had been disarmed and were confined at Benton Barracks. He directed that privates and non-commissioned officers be sent to Cairo, Illinois, to work on the fortification there under guard. Commissioned officers had not "joined in this mutinous demonstration," McLean ruled. But they had failed to enforce "order, obedience, and military discipline." As a result, he directed that they be mustered out and discharged. [OR I, 8, 542]

February 15—Lyles Rifles, C.S.

Men who made up Co. B. of the 7th South Carolina were a proud lot—some owned plantations, others were tradesmen and farmers. Most of them were not accustomed to taking orders from anyone, and they showed absolutely no respect for a high-ranking officer's gold sleeve markings that they ridiculed as "chicken guts."

C.S. Gen. Nathan G. ("Shanks") Evans got nowhere when he tried to force leaders of the Rifles to do as they were told. As a result, on February 15 he directed a dispatch to Asst. Adj. Gen. W. H. Taylor from otherwise unknown Adams Run, South Carolina. In it he said:

> Inclosed please find charges and specifications against Capt. J. H. Rion, Lieutenants [John R.] Harrison, [John L.] Kennedy, and [H. L.] Isbell, of the Lyles Rifles. These officers have positively refused to obey my order. I have arrested them, and placed an officer of another company in command of the Lyles Rifles.
>
> I would respectfully request that a court-martial be ordered as soon as possible for their trial, and that the court consist of as many officers of experience as the good of the service will admit. [OR I, 6, 382–83]

If a court-martial was convened, records of its findings were lost. The only other significant surviving mention of any of these mutinous officers was made more than six months earlier. Late in July, 1861, Rion—then a colonel in state service—"declined to muster into Confederate service" somewhere near Manassas Junction, Virginia. [OR I, 6, 382–83; OR II, 1, 413]

February 17—93rd New York

Numerous men who signed up for a New York regiment were under the impression that it would become a special services body. At Albany, they found that it had been transferred into the infantry as part of the 93rd New York. While in transit to Washington, Enfield rifles were offered to the entire regiment, but Co. B. refused to receive them. "Maintaining their attitude as independent citizen soldiers," they marched into the capital unarmed.

While encamped near the city these men reluctantly accepted Remington rifles that were equipped with saber bayonets. These were sufficiently different from Enfields to make their holders easily spotted. Men of Co. B agreed to take them, however, only after having been promised that within 60 days they'd be issued Sharps rifles in order to serve as a skirmish company.

Early in May the 60-day period ended. Meanwhile both Col. John S. Crocker and Maj. Ambrose L. Cassidy had been captured. "After dress parade," according to Lt. Elwood S. Corser, "Company B, or all of its members on parade who insisted on observance of the pledge made, marched to the Quartermaster's tent, stacked their guns," and the weapons were turned over to their captain. Soon men of Co. B were placed under guard and Corser was escorted to the headquarters of Gen. Innis N. Palmer.

Palmer questioned the New Yorker in some detail, spoke of "a drum head court martial," and put him in a nearby tent. He heard instructions given to his guards: "Shoot the prisoner if he attempts to escape." During the night leaders decided to move toward Rebel positions at Yorktown, Virginia. Needing every man available for an expected assault, they released all members of the mutinous company except Lt. Col. Benjamin C. Butler, who rode toward the enemy under guard at the rear of the regiment. No additional punitive action was taken, but men of Co. B issued no more demands. Men who were thoroughly subdued as a result of spending a single night under guard fought valiantly throughout the war in the 93rd New York and were present at Appomattox Court House. [Corser, 368-69; D, 3, 1441-42]

February 19—1st California

A dispatch from Lt. Col. J. R. West gives all known details about mutiny in his regiment. Except for its non-commissioned officers and one private, men of Co. A refused the order to "drill with knapsacks on." By the time 12 men had been thrown into the guardhouse, half of the regiment was "in a state of mutiny." West raged that the "scepter of authority being once cast down, no dependence can be placed upon any order being obeyed." He would have liked to use force but only labeled the entire regiment as demoralized. Not knowing whether he had any men he could rely upon, he reluctantly decided to suspend drills entirely. Though he asked for "early instructions from district headquarters," he seems to have been left to handle the mutiny as best he could without outside help. [OR I, 50, 880]

March 21—4th Iowa Cavalry

Records concerning disaffection among troops stationed at Rolla, Missouri, were not preserved. On March 21, however, Gen. Henry W. Halleck sent a blunt directive to Col. S. H. Boyd: "If any of the Fourth Iowa Cavalry there refuse to go forward immediately arrest them for mutiny and place them in confinement." [OR I, 8, 632]

May 22—1st Maryland, C.S.

Numerous bodies of troops from Virginia were made up of men who had enlisted for 12 months of service. Eagerness of men in infantry regiments to transfer into the cavalry or go home spread into ranks of the 1st Maryland. This regiment was made up largely of men who had crossed state boundaries in order to sign up at Richmond, Harpers Ferry, and the Point of Rocks. Its members were "nearly in a state of mutiny" as they marched toward Federal forces.

The muster at Harpers Ferry expired on May 22. That day, most men of the 1st Maryland stacked their arms and refused to do duty. These actions constituted mutiny, so their colonel had their weapons packed in wagons and put the men under guard. An emotional appeal was made to them by a color-sergeant, and about half of the mutineers agreed to move toward Front Royal as fighting men. Their comrades went along under arrest.

At a point about five miles from Front Royal, orders came from Gen. Thomas J. Jackson. It being considered a high honor to lead an assault, he had given this privilege to the 1st Maryland—not knowing of the mutiny. Their colonel read Jackson's dispatch, then voiced his own feelings by saying:

> You are the sole hope of Maryland. You carry with you her honor and her pride. Shame on you—shame on you. I shall return this order to General Jackson with the endorsement, "The First Maryland refuses to face the enemy," for I will not trust the honor of the glorious old State to discontented, dissatisfied men. I won't lead men who have no heart. . . . If I can get ten good men, I'll take the Maryland colors with them and will stand for home and honor, but never again call yourselves Marylanders. . . .

According to a Confederate account, men under arrest "pleaded with tears to be allowed to return to duty." When given permission to do so, they "ran back miles to the wagons, got their guns and rejoined their regiment by the time it attacked at Front Royal." This may have been the only instance in which an emotional appeal just prior to a battle brought a mutiny to a screeching halt. Inside Front Royal, the regiment was given an opportunity to take a large building and once-mutinous men "went at it like a charge of canister." [CMH, 2, 68–71]

May 31—6th South Carolina, C.S.

During heavy fighting at Seven Pines, Gen. John Bratton took a direct hit. He fell to the ground and was too weak to get up when men under his command came under heavy artillery fire and were forced to retreat. Lying on the ground, Bratton ordered those wounded men who could walk to go to the rear instead of waiting for ambulances or litter-bearers.

According to his first-person account, "All who could obeyed the order except W. Boyce Simonton of Company G, and Gandy of Company E. They mutinied and refused to leave me." Probably given

Chapter 23

a surge of fresh strength by one of the most unusual incidents to be branded as mutiny, Bratton managed to hobble to the rear with the help of the pair of mutineers. There he was captured and taken to a Federal field hospital. [Bratton, 126-27]

April 15—Confederate Army of New Mexico

U.S. Col. Edward R. S. Canby had his hands more than full. As commander of the Department of New Mexico, he represented the Union in the vast and largely untamed region. Early in April his scouts reported that a Confederate force of some size had left Albuquerque and was moving east and south. Other troops had joined his at Tijeras, so he pushed the entire command 36 miles to a camp near Peralta. Men in blue arrived at their destination before the enemy knew that they were on the move.

According to Canby, Rebel troops held one of the strongest points in the state. Hence he moved cautiously, waiting until his men had rested and eaten before undertaking a reconnaissance that led to a desultory skirmish that lasted for much of the day. Early the next morning, he was surprised to find that the enemy had given up his strong position and had pulled out. Sick and wounded Confederates were left behind, he said, "without attendance, without medicines, and almost without food." [OR I, 9, 550-51]

Confederates led by Gen. Henry H. Sibley were believed to have numbered about three thousand men a few weeks earlier. Intelligence reports soon indicated that the Rebel force had shrunk to not more than 1,200. U.S. Col. Benjamin S. Roberts of the 5th New Mexico boasted that the short engagement at Peralta had put the enemy's forces "in utter rout." [OR I, 9, 553]

Reports filed by Canby and his officers suggest that they did not know why the brief clash at Peralta had such significant results. A summary drawn up by Sibley in May said of Peralta only that a day was spent "in ineffectual fighting on both sides."

The real story of the clash that had little or no military significance is found only in letters by men who were there. According to them, an estimated 250 Rebels who had no intention of taking part in a full-fledged battle mutinied during the night of April 15. They reportedly warned officers that if necessary they'd kill them in order to avoid full-scale combat. Not knowing how many more men would refuse orders to go into battle, Sibley pulled out under cover of darkness.

With his plans having been radically altered by mutiny, Sibley took his force on a roundabout 10-day journey with rations for only a week. Inspired by actions of mutineers, hundreds of their comrades deserted while marching about one hundred miles through canyons and dense patches of small trees as well as crossing several mountains. By the

John Brown's execution spurred enrollment into Virginia units, some of whose members soon became rebellious.

The Popular History of the Civil War

time Rebels reached Fort Bliss, the Confederate Army of New Mexico was in shambles. [OR I, 9, 510-12, 553; Josephy, 33-36]

April 16—3rd Virginia, C.S. (Portsmouth National Grays)

Most of its 104 members had been recruited in the aftermath of John Brown's raid upon Harpers Ferry. Earlier a unit of the state militia, this company was about six years old when it was mustered into Confederate service for a one-year term. Its commissioned officers were transferred when the transition took place and Gov. John Letcher named Roger A. Pryor as new commander of the regiment in which it was included.

Men of the 3rd heartily despised Colonel Pryor and counted the days until they would be out from under him and free to go home. Soon after Federals launched the Peninsula Campaign, soldiers calculated that their year of service under Richmond had come to an end. They seem to have let it be known to Pryor that they'd fight under any officer except him, but preferred to have Maj. Joseph V. Scott as their commander.

Pryor formed rebellious men into ranks and told those who wished to serve under Scott to step forward four paces. Practically all of them quickly moved forward. Incensed, their colonel put the mutineers under arrest and sent them to Gen. D. H. Hill for safe keeping. Hill put them into an improvised pen for a short period, then ordered them to help build earthworks with which to resist men in blue. Other officers of the regiment intervened and persuaded Pryor to treat the incident as "disobedience due to misunderstanding."

Soon given permission to reorganize, men of Co. B chose all new officers before indicating willingness to remain in uniform. By then, Pryor was on the way to becoming a brigadier, but they were never re-assigned to him. Fighting in most subsequent major battles, including Gettysburg, less than a dozen one-time mutineers made up what was left of the company at the time of Lee's surrender. [*Virginia Cavalcade*, Autumn, 1974]

April 18—Col. E. C. Brabble, 32nd N.C., C.S.

Having received an order to send a company to protect the mouth of a canal during the Peninsula Campaign, Col. E. C. Brabble tartly responded:

> The order has not been obeyed, as I cannot get a company there without marching it 7 miles, whereas a company can be sent from the other side by marching one-third of that distance. . . . I must say, though with all respect for the general, that I would prefer to suffer the consequences of disobedience, even should the penalty be death, rather than execute it. While engaged in a war for what I claim to be my rights I cannot submit to what I believe to be unjust discrimination. [OR I, 11, III, 473]

His letter caused him to be taken to Gen. Benjamin Huger under charges. Gen. A. G. Blanchard wanted him dismissed immediately, saying that if orders were not obeyed "we have no army." Huger, who had left the U.S. Army as a major, referred the matter to the secretary of war in Richmond, recommending that Col. Edmund C. Brabble be dismissed "for positive and wilful disobedience of orders."

In less than 90 days Huger was relieved of command in order to take over inspection of artillery and ordnance. Possibly because this change prevented him for keeping up with his recommendations to Richmond, the defiant Brabble—now a colonel—was soon in command of 3,300 men in the army of Gen. Arnold Elzey. [OR I, 11, III, 472]

May—8th, 12th, 14th, and 16th Iowa

Numerous members of four Iowa regiments were captured at Shiloh and subsequently released on parole. Headed to Chicago from Cairo, Illinois, an estimated six hundred to eight hundred of them were ordered to relieve the 23rd Missouri. This caused them to be

Cairo, Illinois, was a major point where troops were transshipped.

Henry Lovie in *The Soldier in Our Civil War*

"put on service which they deemed inconsistent with their parole." As a result, military authorities decided to treat this body of men as mutineers.

N. B. Baker, adjutant general of Iowa, tried to intervene on their behalf early in July. His action led Gen. Henry W. Halleck to issue a terse ruling according to which paroled prisoners who refused "guard, police and fatigue duty" were mutineers. A long and acrimonious debate between state and federal authorities followed in which the central topic was what could and could not be required of men on parole who had not been exchanged.

Gen. Benjamin Huger took charge of a rebellious colonel.

Battles & Leaders

On November 1, Halleck responded to pressure from Gov. Samuel J. Kirkwood and took steps that led to exchange of the Iowa parolees in December. Though these men had flatly refused to obey orders, talk of treating them as mutineers was dropped and plans were made for reorganization of the four regiments from which they came. [OR II, 4, 242, 260, 298–300, 598, 626, 638–39, 672; OR II, 5, 47]

May—The Fort Sumter Garrison, C.S.

James Chestnut, Jr., head of South Carolina's military department, became alarmed at news sent to him by "several most worthy and distinguished" residents of Charleston. Hence he notified Gen. J. C. Pemberton that "disaffection prevails in a large portion of the garrison of Fort Sumter, extending to threats of mutiny and refusal to fire against the enemy if he should appear."

Within days, Gov. Francis W. Pickens referred matters to Gen. Robert E. Lee with a suggestion about handling the incipient mutiny. "Let two native-born artillery companies from Charleston be immediately ordered into Fort Sumter as a guard upon the enlisted men, who are strangers," he proposed. Citing the mutiny in the garrison at Fort Jackson (see chapter 5), the chief executive of the state wanted no repetition of that disaster. A battalion of "native infantry" should go to Fort Moultrie to serve as a guard against mutiny, he urged.

Col. James Chestnut, who notified state leaders about a possible mutiny at Fort Sumter

South Carolina State Archives

Lee, who had his hands full dealing with Federal forces in Virginia, took prompt and decisive action. On May 29 Gen. Roswell S. Ripley was removed from command and plans were under way to select a replacement for him. Though the uproar at Sumter kept the entire state of South Carolina in turmoil for weeks, there is no substantial evidence that military "strangers" from other states were more prone to insubordination that were "native-born" men whose roots were in the Palmetto State. [OR I, 14, 515, 517, 523–24, 527, 563–65, 770]

May—Contrabands at New Orleans

Upon the fall of New Orleans, U.S. Gen. Benjamin F. Butler named Gen. George F. Shepley military commander of the port city. One of Shepley's immediate problems was the state of the levees, many of which had caved into the Mississippi River at spots. Shepley designated Capt. Charles B. Childe of the 8th Vermont to supervise "a large number of the able-bodied negroes" whose task was to rebuild levees.

Childe didn't know it when he took charge, but white foremen were stealing rations provided for the black laborers. This caused a rebellion among them that the Federal officer labeled a mutiny. At his insistence, Shepley assigned 160 paroled Union prisoners to serve as unarmed guards. Hence the thefts stopped and the mutiny among civilians who were not yet citizens came to an end. [Childe, 194–95]

June—Sigel's Division

U.S. Gen. Franz Sigel, a graduate of the German Military Academy who settled in St. Louis, led his division into the Shenandoah Valley on June 6. Soon he and his men were pelted with heavy rain that marked the start of a six-day storm of great intensity. Despite an incessant downpour, he forced his men to march 32 miles in 40 hours. By the time he permitted them to stop his troops were "in almost dissolution and some in open mutiny."

Gen. John Fremont, commander of the Shenandoah Valley expedition, intimated that he used a very strong hand to put down demoralization. He said that this spirit was "induced by privations" that led men to the brink of open mutiny. In their reports, neither Fremont nor Sigel mentioned the real cause of disaffection in Federal ranks. Men in blue who were forced to march in heavy rain for days had lost their spirit due to rebuffs and defeats suffered at the hand of Rebels led by "Stonewall" Jackson. [OR I, 12, I, 11; OR I, 12, III, 346]

June—Foreign Mercenaries

During and after the war, large numbers of Southerners were convinced that Union victories stemmed partly from widespread use of foreign mercenaries. An incident involving several hundred such persons was described by C.S. Accredited Commissioner A. Dudley Mann. There is no positive proof, however, that these foreigners had been offered U.S. citizenship in return for their enlistment in Federal forces.

According to Mann, the steamer *Bellona* reached Antwerp with "something like 500 able-bodied men, designated as 'workmen'" and headed to New York. The reputed appearance at Antwerp of the warship USS *Niagara* was taken by Mann to mean that it would escort the transport vessel loaded with soldiers-to-be. These reportedly represented about ten percent of a force recruited for Federal military service by an unidentified Polish national.

Mann said that Belgians were unwilling to cross the Atlantic in order to fight in blue uniforms. According to him, however, "Germany has been scoured by the meanest of mercenaries." Men so secured were described by him as among the worst specimens of humanity ever seen in the streets of Antwerp. Apparently they converged upon the port in order to wait for arrival of their transport.

Just before the departure of the *Bellona*, William Grayson Mann reportedly spent two or three days in Antwerp. Fluent in German, he spent that period telling mercenaries what they could expect upon reaching New York and "influenced 40 or 50 to desert." Many who sailed had been affected by what they heard

U.S. Gen. Franz Sigel triggered mutiny by a long forced march in bad weather.

Smith Engraving

Men under U.S. Gen. John Fremont in the Shenandoah Valley were worn out and thoroughly demoralized.

The Soldier in Our Civil War

from him and as a result there was "well-nigh a mutiny upon the *Bellona* before she departed to sea." [NOR I, 2, 3, 1158–59, 1166]

June—10th Illinois Cavalry, 1st Missouri, 14th Missouri State Militia

Officers in command of Federal troops stationed in Missouri had an unusually difficult time during this month. From Springfield Gen. E. B. Brown reported to Gen. John M. Schofield at St. Louis about trouble in the ranks. He said that he found 103 horses unfit for use "in a regiment that has done no service." According to him, animals belonging to the 10th Illinois Cavalry had been sold or traded. He had reason to believe that 40 members of the regiment had deserted, "taking their horses, equipments and arms." Rebellion in the ranks had led Col. James A. Barret to resign, and Brown believed him guilty of having stirred up desertion and mutiny. Conditions in the 14th Missouri State Militia were said to be equally bad.

Almost simultaneously, a full-blown mutiny took place in the 1st Missouri, commanded by Col. Robert J. Rombauer. Gen. William S. Ketchum became involved and ordered the arrest of mutineers in this regiment. Gen. Samuel R. Curtis, who outranked other command-ers in the region, was informed about the situation by Schofield. From Batesville, Arkansas, on June 30 Curtis sent a dispatch to Ketchum. In it he said:

> Your dispatch informing me that General Schofield ordered Rombauer's mutineers to be disarmed and turned over to me as prisoners is received. Excuse me. I want troops, not prisoners. I had trouble enough with those U.S. Reserve Corps at Rolla when I ordered them back, because they were worse than no troops.

Curtis suggested that the rebellious troops should be left at West Plains. A plan proposed by a major general was unlikely to be taken lightly. Hence it is probably that many mutineers were taken to a re-mote outpost and there vanished from the record. [OR I, 13, 455–57]

June—Members of the Crew of the USS Patroon

During this troubled month, Lt. J. W. A. Nicholson had his hands more than full in Florida. Aboard the USS *Patroon* members of the crew were in the habit of stealing whiskey "from the spirit room" where liquid refreshments for officers were stored. Using false keys, they entered this supply room several times, after which they be-came drunk and mutinous and fought among themselves.

Aboard the USS *Isaac Smith*, Nicholson was incensed when he learned of what was taking place on the smaller vessel. He went aboard the *Patroon*, mustered all hands, and issued a stern warning to crew members plus the executive officer whom he termed "disobedient and mutinous." He warned that if the ship's whisky was touched again, he'd invoke a congressional edict and "stop the liquor portion of the ration" issued to men.

Though commissioned officers on land could have all the whisky they could down, alcohol was forbidden to enlisted men. Aboard ship, things were different during early months of the war. A long-traditional grog ration was regularly issued to seamen—but aboard the *Patroon* this seemed simply to augment thirst that led to theft and mutiny. [NOR I, 13, 109]

July 19—Cherokee Unionists

A military incident all but overlooked by one officer might be labeled mutiny by another officer. Loose usage and lack of uniformity in designations was dramatized at a camp on the Rio Grande River, probably in southwestern Colorado. For reasons unknown, the commander of the camp was arrested and units made up of white soldiers were withdrawn. U.S. Indian Agent E. H. Carruth informed Gen. James G. Blunt that the arrest of Col. William Weer was "considered a mutiny" by tribesmen whom Weer had led.

On behalf of that portion of the Cherokee Nation professing fidelity to the Union instead of the Confederacy, Carruth begged for protection. In the aftermath of the action that tribesmen saw as threatening to them, he was sure that many families faced the danger of murder. Unionists of a vast region had been left with only three Indian regiments "to fight the enemy's forces, amounting to from 3,000 to 10,000 men."

C.S. Col. Henry Benning was violently opposed to conscription.
Fort Benning, Georgia

Blunt, who commanded the military Department of Kansas, was known for his ardent abolitionist views. He was among a handful of military officers who had earlier been associated with John Brown. Perhaps slaves meant more to him than did native Americans, for there is no record that he responded to the plea sparked by what Cherokees regarded as a mutiny. [OR I, 13, 458, 478]

July—C.S. Col. Henry L. ("Rock") Benning

From the start of discussion about enacting a conscription law, Benning had been bitterly opposed to such action. During a conversation with Robert E. Lee and Secretary of War George W. Randolph, he became heated. Denouncing the law as unconstitutional and knowing that he had the strong support of Georgia Gov. Joseph E. Brown, he said he'd refuse to obey orders based upon it. Lee or Randolph or both were at the point of placing the future general under arrest. Benning's men, who knew of the controversy, were prepared to mutiny. In this critical situation, the colonel who was ready to break the law came to jurist/Gen. Thomas R. R. Cobb "for advice and counsel." Cobb paid a call upon Randolph, poured oil on troubled waters, and as mediator secured mutual concessions that warded off "a bitter war" then brewing in Richmond. [Cobb, 294]

July—Col. William A. Hoskins, 12th Kentucky

At or near the end of the month, Col. William A. Hoskins withdrew his resignation, offered a bit earlier. By this time, the Union's second confiscation act had gone into force in the North. Under its terms Rebels who did not surrender within 60 days were to be punished by having their slaves emancipated. Ex-slaves were given no assurances concerning their future, but were to be offered transportation to a colony in a tropical country. Hoskins was as bitterly opposed to the Union edict as was Henry L. Benning to Rebel statutes concerning conscription. Precisely what aspect of the measure aroused the Federal officer's ire is unknown, however.

Gen. Don Carlos Buell, then stationed at Huntsville, Alabama, was so concerned about the fate of Hoskins that he sent a special dispatch to Gen. George H. Thomas. After reporting that the colonel had changed his stance, he said:

> I wish you to talk with him and be well assured that he understands now the nature of his step, and that he has sincerely repented of it. He should know that it is treason as well as mutiny. It is not sufficient that he should have been mistaken in regard to the confiscation act. He must understand that it was not for him to pronounce on its constitutionality. I do not desire to treat his folly harshly, but it is necessary that he should appreciate the matter fully. [OR I, 16, II, 297]

Thomas may or may not have spent some time with the military officer whose objection to a congressional edict was branded as both treason and mutiny. Whatever the case, once he withdrew his resignation Hoskins was soon back in command of the 12th Kentucky. [OR I, 16, II, 591–94]

July—Five Federal Officers

When the month ended, two colonels, a major, and two captains were under arrest and were waiting to appear before a court-martial.

Their status stemmed from a charge made by their commander, Gen. Thomas Williams. According to him each member of the quintet had been guilty of refusing to obey orders and of "exciting a mutiny among officers and men."

About ten days after their arrest, the five accused officers were escorted to the New Orleans headquarters of Gen. Benjamin F. Butler. With obvious relish that displayed his personal dislike of Williams, Butler told them that a battle had taken place at Baton Rouge on August 5. Heavy fire was exchanged between ground troops in gray and Union battleships on the Mississippi River plus infantry and artillerymen in blue.

Without telling the accused officers that their comrades had scored a significant victory the day before, Butler informed them that their arrest was terminated. Waiting until they had registered surprise and delight, he then explained that this change of circumstances was due to the death of Williams in battle. C.S. Gen. Earl Van Dorn notified Richmond that the martinet was no more, and Butler issued General Order No. 56. In this document Williams was lavishly praised as "a chivalric American gentleman" and a "patriot hero" who "received the death-shot leading his men."

During the Baton Rouge conflict, Williams' head had literally been taken off by a cannonball. Even bystanders were not sure whether it came from a Confederate or a Union gun—but Williams never knew what hit him. A single cannon ball caused the most unusual of all dismissals of mutiny charges against commissioned officers. [OR I, 15, 14, 41; CWT, 7/75, 5]

July 16—Officers of Weer's Indian Brigade

Summer saw a great deal of action in what was then known simply as Cherokee country. Late in June or early in July Federal forces crushed the resistance of two hundred to three hundred braves who served as guards of 71-year-old John Ross. As soon as the mixed-blood leader left his Park Hill home near Tahlequah in a carriage, hundreds of Confederate Cherokees began switching their allegiance.

Col. William Weer, whose men had effected the capture of the most notable Cherokee of the region, formed at least one regiment from former followers of Ross. To celebrate his success, Weer swigged alcohol day and night at his camp. When a Confederate force made up of whites plus Choctaws and Chickasaws appeared across the river, Weer was too drunk to take action. He may not have known that the enemy body was under the command of Gen. Thomas C. Hindman, whose immediate attention was devoted to Arkansas.

Admittedly frightened by the prospect of facing the enemy without a leader, officers of the Indian Brigade got their heads together.

Mixed-blood Cherokee leader John Ross, whose capture was soon followed by a mutiny
Dictionary of American Portraits

To a man, they decided that their only reasonable course of action was to mutiny and get rid of Weer. These men reasoned that it would be easy to demonstrate, if necessary, that Weer had shown indecision and vacillation. He had also exploded in fits of rage well before he became hopelessly drunk.

Mutineers seem to have been aided by Col. Frederick Salomon of the 9th Wisconsin, who immediately assumed command of Weer's force. U.S. Indian Agent E. H. Carruth later claimed credit for the arrest of the drunken colonel, but is likely that he simply persuaded Salomon to cooperate with him. With the entire Cherokee country having been thrown into chaos, Federal officers who outranked Salomon seem to have been too busy to investigate. As a result, the Prussian-born colonel who was earlier a brigadier in the Kansas Army was never punished or officially reprimanded for having taken advantage of a mutiny to boost his own power. [Duncan, 241–43; WWW, 555; OR I, 13, 458, 478]

September—Army of Tennessee, C.S.

Theoretically and officially neutral, Kentucky was invaded late in August, 1862, by Rebels under the command of Gen. Braxton Bragg. His poorly planned foray ended at Perryville on October 8. Weeks before that Confederate debacle, Bragg and his actions began to be hotly debated in Richmond.

Some members of the C.S. Congress believed reports that Bragg had announced plans to execute a Kentucky soldier who committed a minor offense. Gen. John C. Breckinridge had said that the execution would constitute "military murder" and his remarks probably triggered mutiny in "company after company of Kentucky troops" whose members "rushed from their tents to stack arms." After the mutiny, the offender was shot as ordered.

On September 12 a member of the C.S. Committee on Military Affairs called for a formal investigation of Bragg, the execution, and the mutiny. Numerous colleagues objected on the grounds that if news of congressional debate should reach Bragg's army, it "might incite to disaffection and mutiny." Fear of new uprisings among enlisted men prevented a congressional investigation that might have led to Bragg's censure and removal.

After his performances at Chickamauga and Chattanooga only his intimate friendship with Jefferson Davis prevented his military career from screeching to an ignominious halt. Hundreds of men who had earlier mutinied to protest his leadership must have rejoiced when they learned that he had been relieved by Gen. Joseph E. Johnston. [JSHS, 46, 113-17, 127; Frankfort, Kentucky, *Commonwealth*, February 9-12, 1863]

September—Lt. William B. Hardy, Middlesex Artillery, C.S.

Six months after having been made a brigadier and taking command of Robert E. Lee's artillery, William N. Pendleton launched a program of reorganization. The tenth battery he inspected during the fall of 1862, originally led by Capt. W. C. Fleet of the Middlesex Artillery, had been sent to Leesburg because it was not in condition to move forward. Under orders from "Stonewall" Jackson, 11 of its best horses were detached and sent to other batteries.

When Lt. William B. Hardy appeared in order to report the condition of the unit, Pendleton noticed his body language. As described by the artillery chief, the young officer "bore himself with strangely improper violence." Willing to ignore this matter, on the following day Pendleton sent an order to Hardy. Under its terms, a detail of men and horses were to be delivered to other batteries about to head toward Maryland. Hardy ignored the directive, so Pendleton rode to his camp and asked if he refused to obey. According to the general's first-person account:

> He promptly replied that he did refuse. It [the order] was then presented to each of the other lieutenants with the same result. They were immediately placed under arrest, and the refusal in the presence of the men being really mutinous, they were sent under guard to a distant part of the camp.

On September 23 Gen. A. P. Hill sent word that he would like to have this battery restored to full size and sent into action. Pendleton promptly made plans to bring back animals and men who had been temporarily assigned to other units. He sent written word to the rebellious junior officers, saying that he hoped they would make proper acknowledgment that they had violated discipline. By doing so, he could order them released and restored to duty.

Hardy and his comrades made no admission of having done wrong; instead, they defended their actions. Pendleton gave them a second opportunity to change their attitude but they again "maintained that their disobedience was a necessity." For the third time, he offered them a chance to make amends. According to his terse notes made at the time, "Further answer they decline. The case, therefore, must await a court-martial. Charges shall be immediately submitted [to Jackson]."

Pendleton probably did not know that the Army of the Potomac was being made ready for the invasion of the North that led to the battle of Antietam. He relieved all officers of the battery and ordered that temporary assignments of men to other units should become permanent. He then effectively dissolved the unit by assigning its remaining men to Capt. Marmaduke Johnson's battery. In the aftermath of the bloodiest day of the war, Hardy and his fellow mutinous lieutenants dropped from records. [OR I, 19, II, 623, 650–54]

October 3—6th Kentucky, C.S.

At Knoxville while en route to Kentucky, the famous "Orphan Brigade" from the Blue Grass State camped near the city. A great deal of paper work had to be done, since this had been neglected for several weeks. In the process of making sure that organization was up to date, the enlistment of men who made up the 6th Kentucky expired. Once the magic date at which they expected release was reached, they refused to do duty.

According to Pvt. John S. Jackman, an officer had the entire brigade drawn up. He then "made a little speech to the boys" in which he referred to the stacking of arms as a form of protest. Such action constituted the crime of mutiny, he warned. Rebellious men of the 6th were given one-quarter of an hour to return to duty. Without exception, Jackson wrote, they did so "before the time expired." [Quoted, Denney, *Years,* 221]

October 8—Gen. Robert B. Mitchell

Trouble was not limited to ranks of Confederates. U.S. Gen. Don Carlos Buell was widely criticized for his leadership at Perryville, Kentucky, and was relieved soon afterward. During a post-battle inquiry Gen. Robert G. Mitchell was called as a witness for the government. He testified that at the time of the battle, Buell was lame due to a fall from his horse.

Mitchell and his men fell back about 5:00 P.M. on October 8. He then sent an aide to his commander, Gen. C. C. Gilbert, but the aide failed to make contact. "I was unable to get any orders," Mitchell said, except through one of Gilbert's aides-de-camp. "I refused to obey them, because they had deceived me before."

Members of the court of inquiry paid little attention to the fact that Mitchell had deliberately refused to obey orders. They spent days digging into the reason only nine Federal brigades were engaged at Perryville, while an additional 15 brigades within supporting distance were not called into action. Though the court sat for six months, it adjourned without making a recommendation concerning Buell. In its brief summary, the court said nothing at all about actions by Mitchell that would have constituted mutiny had he been an enlisted men. [OR I, 16, I, 96-97]

October—1st Maryland

This regiment, easily confused with the Confederate body of the same designation, was made up of eastern shore volunteers. It's doubtful that any other Federal unit included more slave owners. Organized in Cambridge County, its first commander was Col. James Wallace who owned nine slaves. One of his captains, John R. Keene of Company C, was a member of a family that held 60 slaves. Wallace, Keene, and numerous other officers of the outfit brought some of their slaves with them when they entered Federal service.

Ordered to go outside their own state, the Marylanders in blue rebelled. Hundreds of men—variously said to make up two or four regiments—who had been put aboard the river transport *Belvidere* "mutinied and refused to leave the boat" in order to land at Pungoteague.

Gen. H. H. Lockwood sent an urgent request for a gunboat with which to force the mutineers to obey orders. Actg. Rear Adm. S. P. Lee of the North Atlantic Blockading Squadron was reluctant to comply with the request. He told Lockwood not to use force unless absolutely necessary and said that Gen. John A. Dix "had plenty of troops and transports."

Dix didn't learn of the rebellion, however, until it had been resolved by a decision to use these men in their own state, only, for the time being. They later fought with distinction at Gettysburg—but service there was a response to the Rebel invasion of Union territory. [OR I, 4, 449; CV, 7, 408; NOR I, 8, 150, 169-70]

October—Kentucky Regiments, C.S.

Lt. Junius B. Holloway of the U.S. Army's 5th Cavalry was captured in September, 1862. He went into an enemy camp as a prisoner of war, where he made careful observations about Rebel activities. He was surprised to find an acquaintance on the staff of C.S. Gen. John C. Breckinridge. Through this unidentified Confederate, he was permitted to pass through enemy lines. Reaching Bowling Green, he was interviewed by Gen. William S. Rosecrans and provided a detailed written account of his observations.

According to the U.S. Army officer, Rebel regiments made up of men from Kentucky had completed their terms of enlistment.

Instead of being permitted to go home, they were ordered to remain in uniform for two more years. As a result, wrote Holloway, they were "in a state of mutiny" that led large numbers of them to desert. His undocumented account gains credibility from the fact that during the same time period U.S. Gen. Jacob D. Cox reported that many of C.S. Gen. John Hunt Morgan's men were "almost in mutiny." [OR I, 19, II, 474-75; OR I, 20, II, 25-26]

November 8-9—Federal Regiments

On November 5, Washington learned with alarm that some Rebels had moved past the line of advance of forces under Gen. George B. McClellan. Lincoln had long been impatient with the leader who was lauded by many of his men as The Young Napoleon. Confederate moves gave him a new motive to act, so on November 5 the President instructed Halleck to relieve McClellan and put Gen. Ambrose Burnside at the head of the Army of the Potomac. Halleck's order was delivered by Burnside himself during the evening of November 7.

Even his harshest critics have nearly always conceded that regardless of what the President thought of him, most of McClellan's men revered him. C.S. Lt. Col. Robert P. Blount, then a prisoner of war in the capital, managed soon to get a report to Jefferson Davis. According to it, men of several regiments laid down their arms "when the news of General McClellan's dismissal came. Others were ordered to arrest and march them off and refused to obey." This crisis, according to Blount, caused Halleck to visit the Federal camp in person in order to quell what could have become a general mutiny. [OR II, 4, 949-50; McClellan, 650-53; Sears, 338-43]

November 28—Crew of the USS Hussar

Joint military/naval operations of Federal forces took place many times. In most or all instances, a military officer held the top command. That was the case at New Berne, North Carolina, when trouble erupted aboard the USS *Hussar.*

Gen. J. G. Foster immediately requested help from the commander of naval forces in the sounds of North Carolina. The crew of the ship "having refused to do duty," Foster wanted seamen to "haul alongside" the *Hussar* in order to put all who refused duty into irons.

Cmdr. H. K. Davenport responded promptly, simultaneously notifying Foster of naval actions. Since vessels under his command were short of coal and wood, he had permitted men to let fires in boilers go out. Lacking steam power to send a gunboat to the point of the mutiny, he resorted to the use of four small boats. Under the command of an acting lieutenant, they were rowed to the *Hussar.* Officers of Foster's staff, reported Davenport, were satisfied with

Contrabands thronged the North Carolina river port of New Berne, where a mutiny broke out aboard a vessel of the U.S. Navy.

J. H. Schell in *The Soldier in Our Civil War*

the fashion in which "the duty has been performed." Since no more was heard of rebellious members of the ship's crew, they either submitted and returned to duty or were shipped off to prison. [NOR I, 8, 238]

November 29—2nd Missouri Artillery

Far to the west of North Carolina sounds, members of the 2nd Missouri Artillery let it be known that they expected to go home because their term of enlistment had expired. At St. Louis, Gen. Samuel Curtis issued General Order No. 21, in order to deal with the situation.

Men involved had first enrolled as Home Guards, he pointed out. Later, with their own consent, they were mustered in as three-year volunteers and the change of status was "fully explained in German and English." Having set the status of the 2nd Artillery straight, Curtis minced no words. He stressed the importance of "quiet obedience to duty," then warned bluntly that circulation of petitions to be mustered out or threats of mutiny would lead to arrest and punishment by a military commission. [OR I, 32, 794-95]

U.S. Gen. John G. Foster called upon seamen to help subdue rebellious members of a ship's crew.
Library of Congress

Late November—C.S. Gen. Daniel N. McIntosh

Reporting to U.S. Gen. James G. Blunt from near Fort Gibson in the Cherokee Nation, Col. William A. Phelps summarized some earlier events with which Blunt may not have been familiar. He noted that C.S. Gen. David N. McIntosh (who should have been identified as Daniel N.) was up the Arkansas River about 20 miles from the fort with his regiment plus two hundred Osages. Then he referred to earlier events, remarking that before the battle of Prairie Grove McIntosh "refused to obey Gen. [Samuel] Cooper's orders to join him on the march."

It is unlikely that any brigadier in gray or in blue who refused obedience would have been severely punished—unless he was serving under "Stonewall" Jackson. The casual manner in which Phelps mentioned the case of McIntosh strongly suggests that no disciplinary action was attempted or even suggested. Stars on his shoulders protected the general who balked, but he might have gotten away with disobedience even if he had not displayed these symbols of rank. McIntosh was a mixed-blood chieftain of the Creeks who received his commission from Richmond in the aftermath of Bull Run. After the battle of Pea Ridge, he spent much of the rest of the war in the Indian Territory. [OR I, 22, I, 874; WWW, 417]

December—26 Officers of the 20th North Carolina, C.S.

Col. Alfred Iverson of the 20th North Carolina, C.S., was promoted on November 1. Duties of his new rank were such that he did not immediately turn his attention to the matter of a new commander for his old regiment. After it went into winter camp, he decided to give his former post to a long-time friend. Lt. Col. William S. DeVane was a native of the Tar Heel State, but to men of the 20th that was not nearly enough. He had not fought in their ranks. Instead he was in the 26th North Carolina, which belonged to a different brigade.

Officers of the 20th became more and more angry as they discussed their former colonel's effrontery in trying to put a man from another brigade at their head. Soon a written protest was framed; signed by 26 officers, it was addressed to Gen. Samuel Cooper in Richmond. Iverson learned of what was going on and refused to sanction transmission of the document. According to Capt. William Brooks, men who had served under the former colonel went around him and managed to get their protest to Cooper.

This action made Iverson furious, so he put all insurgents under arrest. Writing to his father on December 20, Lt. O. E. Mercer said that charges had been preferred and that a court-martial would be held. Mercer was wrong. Probably under pressure from the War Department, during January Iverson withdrew his charges and all officers who were under arrest were set free. Though they had been wilfully disobedient, the likelihood that they would have been charged with mutiny is remote. Even had a court-martial convicted them of Iverson's charges, the worst a commissioned officer could expect from such a course of events was surrender of his commission. [B&G, 2/95, 24; B, 429]

November—Marine Artillery at Roanoke Island, North Carolina

Records concerning a mutiny at Roanoke Island, North Carolina, are sparse. They do not indicate the date of the insurrection and do not identify the units to which mutineers belonged. From New Berne, Asst. Adj. Gen. Southard Hoffman simply dispatched an urgent request to Cmdr. H. K. Davenport of the U.S. Navy.

Writing for Col. Thomas C. Amory, he requested that the steamer *Delaware* be immediately sent "to assist, if necessary, in sustaining the authority of a court of investigation." Davenport promptly told Lt. Amos P. Foster to take the *Delaware* to the island. She sailed at once "for the purpose of assisting in quelling an anticipated mutiny" among members of the marine artillery.

Under the terms of General Order No. 64, an unspecified number of these men faced serious charges triggered by "their disgraceful and mutinous conduct in refusing work." In addition, they had threatened to abandon their post and to seize an armed vessel. On December 4 they were ordered to go into land-based artillery units where they would be subject to army rather than navy regulations.

News of their impending sentence probably caused about two hundred rebellious men to make threats of such nature that authorities thought they needed help. Since the *Delaware* returned to New Berne on December 5, the show of naval force made by her seems to have been sufficient to put a stop to talk of additional mutinous actions. [NOR I, 8, 250-51, 301; OR I, 18, 471-72]

24

1863–Unidentified Sailors, Generals Galore, One Hundred Deserters

January 2—Gen. Roger W. Hanson, C.S.

On the Stones River battlefield, C.S. Gen. Braxton Bragg realized that things were going badly, but refused to admit it even to himself. Some of his officers who knew him well took the initiative in trying to find a soft spot at which to hit the enemy. Gen. John C. Breckinridge stumbled upon information that led him to take a look at a pair of fords, but he quickly discovered that the ridge on the east bank of the river held several batteries of Federal artillery.

When summoned to headquarters by Bragg, the native of Kentucky was dumbfounded to be ordered to attack the position he had personally investigated earlier in the day. A vehement verbal protest by Breckinridge proved to be breath wasted; Bragg wanted the attack to start late in the afternoon so that night would fall before the enemy could launch a counter-attack.

"I have given an order to attack the enemy and I expect it to be obeyed," Bragg stormed at the former Vice President of the United States. Though his subordinate realized that obedience would mean certain death to a large number of his 4,500 men, he indicated readiness to get them deployed.

Another native of Kentucky was not so pliant when he learned what plans were afoot. Probably muttering something about permissible mutiny under unusual circumstances, he considered gathering friends and staging a revolt. He went so far as to suggest that he might go to headquarters, personally kill Bragg, and cause the command to devolve upon the officer next in rank.

Breckinridge refused to have any part in conduct that would be considered mutinous, so at 4:00 P.M. shouted: "Up, my men, and charge!" Some Rebels managed to reach the crest of the little slope, where savage hand-to-hand fighting took place. Against all odds, they demonstrated that the Bragg's order leading to near mutiny could be carried out. Soon they went too far, however; following fleeing foes in blue they came under heavy fire from Federal artillery at other nearby points and were cut to pieces.

With the sun setting at 4:45, it was all over. Back across the river, Rebel units re-formed their ragged ranks. With tears in his eyes, Breckinridge raged that he had failed to follow the path suggested by Hanson, who had died on the field. Too late, he realized that mutiny by high-ranking officers would have been preferable to sense-less slaughter that accounted for many of the 12,000 casualties suf-fered by Confederates at Stones River. [OR I, 20, I, 674-82, 702, 779-81, 789-92, 796-98, 827-36, 840; OR I, 52, I, 356-57; *Battle of Stones River*, 35-43; Cozzens, 177-86]

January 9—Civilian Sailors Aboard the Sparkling Sea

At Turtle Harbor, East Florida, Lieutenant Cavendy was in com-mand of the U.S. bark *Gemsbok* early in 1863. On the afternoon of January 7 he saw a large transport run upon a reef about 13 miles away. A launch was quickly sent to her assistance, and men from the naval vessel managed to kedge the *Lucinda* into deeper water. That gave her a safe haven in which to wait for a change of wind.

Early on the morning of January 9 another transport hit the reef at a point about three miles south of the spot at which the *Lucinda* was anchored. Fortunately the launch from the *Gemsbok* had not yet returned, so officers and men from the warship again went to the rescue. They found the second damaged vessel to be the *Sparkling Sea* out of Hampton Roads, Virginia. She carried Federal troops plus horses and forage and had beat so heavily against the reef that her hold was already full of water.

Cavendy got word to Rear Adm. Theodorus Bailey at Key West that government property was in danger. Bailey sent the steam-pow-ered USS *Sagamore* to the site of the shipwrecks, and the *Lucinda* proceeded on her way when pulled out into the sea. Soldiers aboard the *Sparkling Sea* were taken to Key West.

Soon after this sailing vessel hit the reef, her crew mutinied and refused to do duty. An officer plus a boat's crew from the naval vessel went aboard "to preserve discipline and secure Government property." Subsequent movements of the mutineers during a period of several months were not recorded. On June 13, however, the USS *Sonoma* of the West India Squadron made New York after a seven-day voyage from Key West.

Cmdr. Thomas H. Stevens immediately prepared a report in which he said he had brought to the North seven members of the crew of the *Sparkling Sea*. These men, he said, came as prisoners who were to go to "the penitentiary at Washington" after having been found guilty of mutiny. Since the *Sparkling Sea* and the *Lucinda* were not vessels of the U.S. Navy, data concerning their tonnage and speed do not appear in official records. [NOR, I, II, 51]

January—6th Kansas Cavalry

Early in January, U.S. Col. Albert L. Lee and his command reached Tennessee from Mississippi. In addition to the 7th Kansas Cavalry, he was in charge of 10 companies of the 4th Illinois Cavalry. After two days of rest the entire command was ordered to move north in an effort to find and defeat Rebels led by Col. R. V. Richardson. They had barely managed to get across Wolf River when new orders arrived from U. S. Grant. He directed Lee and his men to seize "horses, mules, saddles, and bridles" from the countryside in order to "mount as many infantry as possible." [OR I, 24, III, 141]

Following orders, Lee detached some companies from the Federal column and instructed men in these companies to bring in "all horses, mules, saddles, and bridles fit for use." After dark the Federal body bivouacked at a plantation a few miles from Somerville, Tennessee. Lee's men were soaked from a severe storm and since he would not permit fires to be lighted they went without supper.

Very early on January 6 they moved into Somerville, where they found no trace of Rebel troops. Learning that Richardson and his Confederates were believed to be only about 12 miles north of the town, Lee sent scouts to try to find them. Simultaneously, he named Lt. Col. Thomas P. Herrick of the 7th as provost marshal of Somerville and assigned six companies to him.

To the surprise of Herrick and Lee, residents of the town showed no animosity toward the force of occupation. They even provided soldiers with a "singular profusion of wines and liquors of all kinds." Lee found in one warehouse 14 barrels of whisky that belonged to Rebel forces, so described the town as being "full of intoxicating liquors."

Herrick had stationed Co. B of the 7th Kansas at the southern edge of Somerville, in order to serve as pickets. Their leader, Capt. Fred Swoyer, ate breakfast in the home of residents and was plied with enough alcohol to become "somewhat exhilarated." While he was eating and drinking a pair of his men tried without success to get into the house where the barrels of whisky were stored.

Back in the saddle, Swoyer directed the men of Co. B to fall in and ordered the would-be whisky thieves to surrender their weapons and submit to arrest. A private who was affected by this directive protested and tried to offer an explanation of what had been done. Swoyer drew his pistol and told the fellow he'd shoot him if he said another word. When the unidentified cavalryman again tried to protest, Swoyer fired at so close a range that his pistol ball passed through the body of the man who wanted to talk.

Within seconds another unidentified member of the company committed flagrant mutiny by shooting at his captain, whom he missed. Swoyer turned his horse toward the fellow, who spurred his horse into quick retreat. He was soon overtaken and the two riders shot simultaneously. A ball "passed through the body of the captain," but his shot went through the head of the mutineer. Dodging a hail of bullets from men he commanded, Swoyer raced into Somerville and died there the next morning.

Lee was at the court house, about half a mile away from the scene of the mutiny. When he learned of what had taken place he sent one of his officers and an entire company "to quell the mutiny," which was readily accomplished. Withdrawing from Somerville with about three hundred captured horses and mules, the Federal body camped south of Wolf River at a spot not far from Moscow. Lee established regimental courts-martial in which all men accused of drunkenness were tried and more than two hundred were sentenced to lose a month's pay.

Inquiry was then made into details of the mutiny and the two deaths associated with it. No verdicts had been handed down when Lee filed a lengthy March 5 report that went to his commander, Gen. Stephen A. Hurlbut. He, in turn, forwarded it up the chain of command to by way of Gen. Charles S. Hamilton. [OR I, 24, III, 141–43]

Handling of the Somerville mutiny seems to have been the lightwood that caused an already simmering feud between the two general officers suddenly to flare with great intensity. Hurlbut was not satisfied with Hamilton's investigation of the 7th Kansas Cavalry so he recommended to Washington that his colleague "should be assigned to duty elsewhere." In early March, Hurlbut reported to Washington that Hamilton seemed to be trying to provoke him, so he said he probably would have to place him under arrest.

Before the day ended, Hurlbut notified Hamilton that he was in danger of being arrested and sent to Vicksburg. Hamilton retorted that he was confirmed as a major general on September 19, 1862, and demanded to know from his star-bedecked opponent when he was confirmed. Hurlbut refused to respond to the question and pointed out that Lincoln had put him in command of the XVI Corps.

Hamilton stormed that he had no notion of trying to strip Hurlbut of the XVI Corps. He added, however, that if he was the senior officer it became his duty "to assume command of the District of

West Tennessee." Hurlbut referred his colleague to Army Regulations plus special orders sent to the Department of the Tennessee early in February. "No question of seniority can arise until commissions come," he wrote. Then he warned that if Hamilton tried to "exercise independent authority" he'd be placed under arrest and sent to Vicksburg.

In a separate dispatch Hamilton told Hurlbut that his messages seemed "unnecessarily harsh and peremptory as coming from a junior to a senior officer." He then pointed out what every general officer knew quite well—that commissions not confirmed before the adjournment of Congress expired. This factor, he chortled, left both of them as brigadiers "and as such I am your senior." [OR I, 24, III, 138-41]

Records indicate that Hamilton became a brigadier on May 17, 1861, and was promoted on September 19, 1862. Hurlbut, the only native of South Carolina who became a Federal general officer, was made a brigadier on June 14, 1861. His commission, however, ranked from May 17. He was named as major general two days before Hamilton, so outranked him at that level. If Hamilton was correct in believing that neither of the pair of later commissions had been approved by Congress, the question of seniority rested upon the hours at which the two men had been made brigadiers on the same day. [WWW, 277, 329]

At this point in the quarrel that came to the surface as a result of mutiny in which three men died but only one was named, U. S. Grant interposed his authority. He had earlier come to the conclusion that Hamilton was "making indirect efforts to get General McPherson removed from the command of his army corps, and to get the command himself." Since Grant was extremely fond of McPherson, the possibility that intrigue was directed against him caused his bile to rise.

With correspondence about the mutiny in the 7th Kansas Cavalry before him, Grant used the quarrel between two of his generals as an excuse to order Hamilton to the front. He considered the matter to be of such grave importance that he requested Halleck to lay it before Lincoln. Disgruntled, Hamilton submitted his resignation and it was accepted on April 13. If Lee's court-martial convened to try mutineers reached verdicts about them, its findings other than those dealing with drunkenness were not preserved. [OR I, 24, III, 137]

January 13—96th New York (McComb's Plattsburg Regiment)

Organization having been completed at Plattsburg on March 7, 1862, this regiment left the state four days later. It was stationed near Washington and in Virginia until December, and experienced plenty of action. McComb's men were in the Peninsula march and

Seven Pines (or Fair Oaks) saw the 96th New York in action.
U.S. Army Military History Institute

the siege of Yorktown before their first real experience of combat at Williamsburg. They soon fought at Seven Pines, in the seven days before Richmond, White Oak Swamp, Malvern Hill, and Harrison's Landing. [D, 3, 1443]

After a period of inactivity, they were ordered to North Carolina on December 4. Almost as soon as they landed and made camp, they went with Gen. John G. Foster's other regiments on the *Goldsborough* before being given semi-permanent quarters at New Berne.

Barracks life included much more free time than they were accustomed to having. In the relatively relaxed atmosphere at New Berne, they began to grumble and then to complain about having to wait so long for pay. Nothing happened, so on the night of January 13 they went on a rampage.

Two days later Foster's General Order No. 22 dealt only with the conduct of the 96th, whose actions were labeled as mutinous "and such as all good soldiers should be ashamed to have shared in." Foster then wrote:

> The only effect can be to lay the men open to trial for mutiny, and consequent punishment, and cannot hasten, certainly, their desires. . . . The officers of the Ninety-sixth and those regiments to which the mutineers went lamentably failed in their duties as commanders, or the breach of discipline referred to would have been promptly punished.

Foster's lengthy scolding ended with warning: "Another offense will surely meet its punishment." This suggests that rebellious men and their tolerant officers got off scot-free because Foster didn't have the facilities to put hundreds of men into the guard-house. [OR I, 18, 518]

January 24—Indiana and Ohio regiments

Humphrey Marshall, an 1842 graduate of West Point, led the 1st Kentucky Cavalry during the Mexican War. He later served in Congress and was U.S. Minister to China. His name was prominent among those of Blue Grass State leaders who moved heaven and earth in a futile attempt to keep it in a neutral position after Bull Run.

When he sensed that it would be impossible to keep Kentucky out of the war, Marshall accepted a commission as a Confederate brigadier on October 30, 1861. During the next eight months he and his men did not win a single victory. Their only clash of any significance took place at remote Princeton, Virginia (now West Virginia). [GG, 212-13]

With ample time on his hands to do as he wished, Marshall bombarded Richmond with dispatches. During a period of a few months he sent a great deal of second-hand information plus lengthy advice to Jefferson Davis, whom he addressed as a close friend. [OR I, 52, III, 283-86, 345, 419-20, 424-25, 433]

Writing to the C.S. President from Jonesville, Virginia, on February 7 he passed along news picked up by two of his men who had been in Pendleton County, Kentucky, for a period. According to these informants, a mutiny took place among Federal troops at Elizabethtown and other points on January 24. Marshall said that "600 Indianians laid down their arms and refused to participate any further in the contest. The Ohioans (one regiment) ordered to Richmond, Ky., from Lexington refused to march."

His men also reported that Frank Wolford—evidently known to both Marshall and Davis—"certainly said he would not take up arms any more." Though this report from Rebel spies cannot be taken at face value, it suggests that Federal commanders in Kentucky had their hands more than full early in 1863. [OR I, 52, III, 419]

February—Members of the Crew of the CSS Selma

James Carr, a native of Brooklyn, New York, deserted from the CSS *Selma* on February 19. He and two comrades managed to get away from the Rebel gunboat when an officer sent them to Heron Bay, Alabama, for oysters. It took them four days to reach the USS *Clifton* in waters not far from Mobile Bay.

Carr's story was typical of many that could have been told. At age 17 he was working on a Mississippi River steamboat, and was arrested in New Orleans as a suspected spy for the Union. He was confined in the Parish Prison of the big Southern port while awaiting trial. William L. Bradford, who was a lieutenant on a Confederate gunboat, became acquainted with him and expressed personal interest.

Bradford persuaded the youthful prisoner to sign papers indicating his willingness to serve on the gunboat *Ivy*. This gained his release, so he went on board the little vessel. Soon transferred to the gunboat *McRae*, he was close to Fort Jackson at the time its Confederate garrison mutinied. An injury sustained in the fight that led to the fall of New Orleans incapacitated him briefly. While on shore recuperating he was cared for by Bradford's mother at Jackson, Mississippi.

As soon as his arm healed, Carr joined his benefactor aboard the CSS *Selma*, where Bradford was a first lieutenant. For about a year he served as wardroom steward on the Rebel vessel that was commanded by Lt. Peter U. Murphey. Because Bradford had great confidence in him, he was sent with two other members of the crew to harvest oysters at a point not far from Mobile Bay. This night expedition enabled him to escape from the Confederate craft.

Carr correctly described the *Selma* as having a battery of two 9-inch Dahlgrens, one 8-inch and one 6-inch rifled gun. All four guns were mounted in pivot, he told Com. H. H. Bell of the West Gulf Blockading Squadron. He accurately described the vessel's single engine as being of the low pressure type, with an inclined cylinder. This wooden sidewheel steamer was capable of making nine knots, he said.

All of his information was of importance to U.S. naval officers likely to come in contact with the vessel. His most significant and interesting revelation about her, however, centered in the makeup and actions of her crew. Carr said that of the estimated 65 men aboard the Rebel gunboat, only about half a dozen were of Southern birth.

Slightly more than a dozen members of the crew were English and French nationals, the youngster from Brooklyn said. According to him, the majority of men aboard the little ship were "Northerners, who had been pressed." That is, they had been seized and forcibly taken aboard the ship—or impressed. Carr didn't say whether or not the men responsible for manning the Confederate vessel had given alcohol or drugs to the fellows they seized. Impressment was so common a practice that persons living in port cities took it for granted, however.

Men who made up the polyglot crew of the *Selma*, said the Northerner who had been aboard under duress for months, were at the point of mutiny. They would "take the vessel from the officers at the first opportunity," he predicted. That estimate was plausible, for Carr was sure that eight of them were "already in irons for drawing a cutlass on an officer and for mutinous conduct."

Had officers of the U.S. Navy not taken down the deserter's story in minute detail, nothing would be known of the mutiny aboard the *Selma*. His account must be judged as accurate, since it corresponds with detailed Confederate records. Carr's name even appears on the muster roll of the ship from which he deserted the C.S. Navy. To official records, however, he added a description of the makeup of the crew plus a summary of the mutiny that had already taken place aboard the *Selma*. [NOR I, 19, 626–29; NOR I, 20, 590, 705; NOR I, 21, 266]

February—87th Illinois Regiment

Shawneetown, Illinois, was regionally noted only as being the spot at which a ferry took passengers across the Ohio River. Isolated and tiny though it was, the hamlet was the center at which a regiment was mustered into service on October 3, 1862. [D, 3, 1083]

In mid February, Washington got word that two of the companies commanded by Col. John E. Whiting were "in a state of mutiny." News from Shawneetown took a long time to reach the outside world, so trouble in the 87th may have stemmed from word that the regiment would soon be moved to Memphis.

Gen. Henry W. Halleck handled the report promptly and decisively. He passed the problem along to Gen. Horatio G. Wright at Cincinnati—far up the Ohio River from the trouble spot. "You will immediately take measures to suppress any such mutiny," he directed, "and to have this regiment sent into the field." [OR I, 23, II, 61]

February—109th Illinois State Guard

Often the coldest month of the year in Illinois, February took its toll upon men of the State Guard as well as some who had been mustered into Federal service. At Holly Springs, men of the 109th lived and trained in the middle of a hotbed of secessionists. Had a poll been taken, it is probable that more than half of the residents of Union County would have acknowledged allegiance to the pro-Southern secret society known as the Knights of the Golden Circle.

When guardsmen mutinied some time in February, civilians who would have preferred to be living in Confederate country were thrown into "a fever of excitement." Numerous enlisted men and some officers of the regiment were arrested. Gov. Richard Yates took the matter so seriously that he notified Washington he was sitting on a powder keg. At least four regiments should be sent to the state "ready for instant hostilities," he said.

When Gen. U. S. Grant learned of the mutiny, he took it casually. Instead of endorsing the governor's call for troops with which to quell it, he simply disbanded the 109th and stripped insurgents of their weapons. [OR I, 24, 68]

February—Maj. Gen. John G. Foster and Staff

Few if any high-ranking officers who wore blue uniforms were involved in more frequent or more momentous controversies than was Gen. David Hunter. While in Missouri very early in the war, he was an observer when Gen. John C. Fremont issued an emancipation proclamation that rocked the North. Hunter saw the President act quickly and decisively to nullify Fremont's actions and then to make things difficult for him. The Republican famous as "The Pathfinder" was relieved for the second time while trying to pin down "Stonewall" Jackson in the Shenandoah Valley, so he held no other command after June, 1862. [WWW, 226, 228-29, 327-28]

Fremont's one-time subordinate had become a major general on August 13, 1861. Shunted from Missouri into Kansas, he devoted much of his time and energy to complaints. In spite of his record, he was given command of the Department of the South and later of the X Corps as well. His troops plus warships of the U.S. Navy besieged Fort Pulaski in Georgia and forced its Rebel garrison to surrender on April 11.

One day later he repeated Fremont's move in Missouri by declaring all slaves held within Union lines to be free. On May 9 he issued another emancipation proclamation by which he decreed that all slaves within the department were liberated. As he had done with Fremont, the President soon annulled Hunter's emancipation orders. [WWW, 327; B, 418-19; GB, 243-44]

With so much controversy on the record, Hunter's high-profile quarrel with Gen. John G. Foster in February, 1863, would appear to have resulted in military oblivion like that of Fremont, but it did not. More than two years later he presided over the trial of those accused of having assassinated the chief executive with whom he had sparred.

From his Hilton Head, South Carolina, headquarters on February 11 Hunter labeled the conduct of Foster as "disrespectful, insubordinate, and tending to excite mutiny." One day later he lashed out at one of Foster's subordinates, Gen. H. M. Naglee. Hunter demanded from the brigadier "a certified copy or report of all the secret instructions, verbal or written, received by you from Major General Foster." Troops sent from North Carolina to the Hilton Head as reenforcements constituted another bone of contention. The two generals were at odds over whether these men should serve in Hunter's X Corps or Foster's XVIII Corps. [OR I, 14, 402-3, 417, 419, 423-24, 428]

By February 19 Hunter had concluded that "many, if not all, the members of General Foster's staff have indulged in statements and remarks of a character tending to create disaffection, insubordination, and mutiny." This sweeping indictment was made in his Special Order No. 97. At about the same time it was issued, the man accustomed to controversy directed Foster and all members of his staff to "quit this department by the first steamer going North."

Foster had until this time commanded the Department of North Carolina, which was within and subsidiary to the Department of the South. He wore the same insignia of rank that Hunter displayed, but his commission was dated October 23. Hunter outranked him by more than two months, hence was his superior. The code of military discipline demanded that he obey Hunter or resign, so he chose to obey after a fashion and took a detachment of his XVIII Corps to St. Helena Island instead of boarding the first steamer headed North. [OR I, 14, 396, 405, 409-10; WWW, 226; GB, 157-58]

In Washington, Halleck got into the fray and dispatched a mild rebuke to Hunter. From Hilton Head, a curt rejoinder went to the general in chief on February 19. In it, Foster and his staff were accused of "repeated acts of insubordination." Collectively, charged Hunter, these constituted "a deliberate and systematic course directly tending to create a general disaffection, if not an organized mutiny, amongst the re-enforcements brought from North Carolina." [OR I, 14, 400-401, 409]

An attempt by Foster to gain the support of the secretary of war was unsuccessful. Halleck reported that a bundle of papers was sent to Edwin M. Stanton "for such instructions as he might deem proper to order." Lincoln was deeply involved in the dispute behind the scenes, and may have felt that the North wouldn't tolerate disciplinary action against the general who had tried to free slaves of southern states. This complicated power struggle ended when Halleck reported that Stanton had given him no instructions. [OR I, 14, 427]

Immune from severe punishment even if he had gone before a court of inquiry and been found guilty, Foster may have been the officer of highest rank whose commander accused him of fostering mutiny. He was not relieved and did not resign—but his resistance to Hunter's directives sent him into virtual oblivion for a period.

May 1—2nd Regiment, Arizona Brigade, C.S.

Most men included in the six undersize battalions of the C.S. Arizona Brigade were Texans who reluctantly agreed to fight even though they could not take Lone Star emblems into battle. Gen. J. Bankhead Magruder consolidated these small units into "three good regiments and a small surplus battalion." Under the leadership of Virginia-born Col. Joseph Phillips the third regiment started on a long journey to Louisiana.

Near the town of Anderson in Grimes County, many of its members and at least two of its officers held an unauthorized meeting. They didn't like the notion of going out of Texas, and were openly dissatisfied that they had not been permitted to elect their own officers. Phillips learned of what had taken place, so he called two officers to his tent the following evening. After reading the 7th and 8th Articles of War to them, he warned that a repetition of events on May 1 would lead him to have them arrested and charged with mutiny.

His intervention brought relative tranquility to the regiment until it came close to the Sabine River, boundary between Texas and Louisiana. A week after the first meeting in which there was talk of rebellion, disaffected men met again. This time, Phillips had informants present. They reported to him that there was great dissatisfaction in the ranks and that it had been encouraged by Capt. George W. Durant and Lt. A. W. Noble.

Knowing that Phillips would make a personal report to the staff of Gen. E. Kirby Smith, Durant requested permission to go along. He was told that he could do so, but when they reached Smith's headquarters the colonel went straight to Insp. Gen. Benjamin Allston. Allston listened to an account of what had taken place in the regiment, then called in Durant and informed he that he was guilty of mutiny.

In a report to Smith, Allston described his meeting with Durant, who seems to have carried with him the orders under which the regiment was formed by Magruder. If the general exceeded his authority, said Allston to Durant, he was responsible to the War Department. The business of Durant and his fellows was to obey orders, he stressed. Durant indicated satisfaction with the explanation provided by Smith's inspector general, and promised he'd abide by it. Hence he returned to his regiment in a quite different spirit from that of the week beginning May 2.

Allston suggested to Phillips that it would unwise to arrest the two mutinous officers until the regiment reached Natchitoches. Armed troops at that point could be used to support him, if necessary. Hence the colonel kept a close eye on both officers as the march proceeded. Soon he decided that they were repentant, so decided not to arrest them, after all. He expected quickly to go into combat and needed all of his officers, he explained in a detailed report of the matter that went to Smith's assistant adjutant general from a camp near Simsport, Louisiana.

There was an additional consideration, the colonel pointed out. He was extremely reluctant to "having a public exhibition of this mutinous conduct as long as the general good the service would not suffer." He expressed great pride in his regiment and admitted that he would be mortified for events of early May to be made public. Changed attitudes on the part of officers who had been called mutineers plus pride of their colonel brought an end to the matter without a court of inquiry.

Magruder was almost as lenient as Phillips. Near the Sabine River about one hundred of his men deserted and an estimated seven hundred members of the 32nd Texas held meetings in order to voice protests about being sent out of their state. Magruder said he'd arrest the commanding officers if they could not give satisfactory explanations of their conduct, but believed that the mutiny had not yet "ripened." He was of the opinion that news of a Federal retirement would postpone talk of rebellion or bring it to an end. [OR I, 26, II, 45-47, 57-65, 66-67, 529-31]

May—Unidentified Rebels

In the field near Vicksburg, Mississippi, U.S. Gen. John A. McClernand reported to U. S. Grant concerning destruction of an important bridge over the Big Black River. He then informed his commander:

> Major Henry P. Hawkins has just reported that there is no rebel force in the rear, except one brigade in the neighborhood of Raymond. That force is so demoralized that many threw away their arms, swearing they would fight no more. The last seen of them they were 12 or 13 miles east of Big Black, on their way to Jackson. [OR I, 24, III, 336]

June 9—Tennessee and Georgia Regiments, C.S.

Charles A. Dana, a former managing editor of Horace Greeley's noted *New York Tribune*, was in the Western Theatre as a civilian observer during many months. On June 1 he was given a commission as a major but declined to accept it. Reporting to Edwin M. Stanton from near Vicksburg on June 10, he said that men under Gen. William T. Sherman reached a point only 50 feet from the Rebel front during the early evening of June 9. His detailed report then moved into the realm of supposition, saying:

> A violent fire of musketry was heard within Vicksburg yesterday afternoon. No doubt it was mutiny, as we know that disaffection has long existed among their troops, and that on the day of our

attack [May 22] both Tennessee and Georgia regiments refused to participate in the fight. [OR I, 24, I, 95]

Dana's report gains credence from a document marked simply "Appeal for help." Found among the papers of C.S. Gen. John C. Pemberton, it was signed "Many Soldiers."

According to the appeal, rations of fighting men had been reduced to "one biscuit and one small bit of bacon per day." Many soldiers remained in the trenches day and night. It was useless for them to try to forage in the city, since civilians had even less food than they did.

Unidentified men in gray challenged the commander of the port city: "If you can't feed us, you'd better surrender us, horrible as the idea is, than suffer this noble army to disgrace themselves by desertion." The document continued that "You'd better heed a warning voice . . . This army is now ripe for mutiny."

Men who prepared this appeal didn't attach their names to it. Had they done so, they almost certainly would have suffered reprisals for their insubordination. Some of them and their comrades may have been responsible for the volleys of musket fire heard at a distance by Dana. [OR I, 24, III, 982-83]

June 13—Officers of the 1st New York Cavalry

During early June, Rebel and Union forces in and around Winchester, Virginia, skirmished almost continuously. Retreating from Berryville, men of the 1st New York Cavalry were spotted by a body of Confederate riders estimated to number two thousand. Near Opequon Creek one battalion of men in gray charged the Federal force. Attackers under Maj. James W. Sweeney were slowed and then thrown into confusion by fire of carbines from the well-equipped New York unit. Maj. Alonzo W. Adams sensed victory within his grasp, so ordered his force to charge. Capt. Lambert J. Simons and Lt. Frank Passegger ignored the command, so Adams reported them for "disobedience of orders in front of the enemy."

Falling back to the opposite side of the Opequon, the 1st New York Cavalry was reformed at a spot where a turn in the road offered them concealment. Supported by an artillery battery commanded by Capt. Frederic W. Alexander of the Maryland Light Artillery, the New Yorkers scored what they considered to be a victory.

At what Adams called his "moment of victory over the enemy," two of his officers who had been sent on an errand appeared. Maj. Timothy Quinn and Lt. Erwin C. Watkins declared that they came to assist, upon orders from Col. Andrew T. McReynolds.

Quinn, said by Adams to show "unmistakable signs of jealousy and envy," interviewed some men of the regiment. Though official casualty figures showed only two men killed and about 10 wounded, Quinn concluded that these had been suffered "by risking a battle at that place." As a result, he said, officers and men of the 1st Cavalry were dissatisfied and wanted him to take command.

Charles A. Dana heard musket fire at a distance and believed it meant Rebel soldiers had mutinied.
Harper's Monthly

Adams retorted that he'd permit no such talk in front of members of the regiment since it "was well calculated to excite mutiny with officers and men." Quinn then sent Watkins to McReynolds with a message to the effect that Adams had sacrificed "a large number of men unnecessarily by giving battle to the enemy at the wrong place." Soon Watkins returned, saying that McReyolds had ordered Adams to be placed under arrest and Quinn to take command.

Though Adams considered resistance to the order, he submitted and remained under arrest until Federal forces reached Winchester. There he was released and restored to command. His official report, forwarded to Gen. Joseph Hooker through Asst. Adj. Gen. John O. Cravens used extremely strong language concerning the two officers who had raised questions about his actions.

Neither Quinn nor Watkins was in what Adams called a battle, he wrote, but arrived after his victory over the enemy. Their envy, jealousy, and malice, he charged, led them to try "by word and act to produce discontent, insubordination, and mutiny." In many instances, such charges against officers would have resulted in a court of inquiry or an informal investigation by the commanding general. Had such a course of action been followed, the ax might have fallen upon the two charged with malice, but it could also have led to serious charges against their accuser. As it was, nothing at all was done. Hooker, soon to be replaced by George G. Meade, was too busy with his own affairs to bother with a "mutinous" squabble over leadership of a single regiment. [OR I, 27, II, 81–86]

June—Gen. Beverly H. Robertson, C.S.

A Virginia native and graduate of West Point in the class of 1849, Beverly H. Robertson was dismissed and later relieved. Having

accepted an appointment as a Confederate captain without resign-
ing from the U.S. Army, he was dismissed on August 8, 1861, on
grounds of "proof of disloyalty." Nearly two years later he was with
Gen. J. E. B. Stuart in the still-controversial ride around much of the
Army of the Potomac on the eve of Gettysburg. Considered by Stuart
to have been "troublesome" during the famous ride, he was reputedly relieved of his command in the aftermath of making "mutinous
remarks to his brigade." [GG, 259-60; B, 702-3; WWW, 547]

June—Mississippi State Troops, C.S.

Virginia native James R. Chalmers helped to take Mississippi
out of the Union. He entered military service before Rebels fired upon
Fort Sumter and despite lack of experience was made a brigadier in
February, 1862. Much of his subsequent service was in his adopted
state. [WWW, 112]

While stationed at Payola in June, 1863, he was directed by Gen.
Joseph E. Johnston to guard a steamboat at Greenwood. He ordered
nearby companies of state troops to take this responsibility, and
officers of a unit from Bolivar County refused to obey. Chalmers
accordingly sent 10 men plus one of his officers to place them under
arrest and bring them to his headquarters under guard.

Benjamin S. Ewell, then a colonel, promptly sent a telegram ordering that the rebellious com-
pany be left in its home county.
Men were needed there, according to Ewell, "to get out supplies
and keep the negroes in subjection." Reporting about the matter to Maj. A. P. Mason, who was
Johnston's assistant adjutant
general, Chalmers indicated he
would do as requested by Ewell
"unless the commanding general
shall otherwise order."

There is no record that
Johnston became involved in the
issue of disobedience by members of a body of state troops. He
had abundant opportunity to do
so, however, for Chalmers was
greatly agitated about the incident. He warned that unless the
offending officers were punished,
their refusal would "result in
evil."

Gen. George G. Meade assumed
command of the Army of the Potomac
a few days before Gettysburg.
Harper's History of the Great Rebellion

What's more, he went on record as planning to prefer charges "against the officers who refused to obey orders" and send them to Mason. Johnston's aide, he suggested, couldn't fully appreciate the importance of discipline until he became familiar with what was going on in the 5th Military District of the Department of Mississippi and Louisiana. Until he took command there, he pointed out, men had been "permitted to do just what they pleased." Their disregard of discipline was fostered by the fact that their geographical location made it easy for them to "go into the enemy's lines and avoid service whenever they choose to desert."

Despite the vehemence of the report in which Chalmers said he would take action against mutinous officers of state troops, there is no record that any of them ever went before a court of inquiry. [OR I, 24, III, 980-81]

July 20—50th Massachusetts

Gen. Charles P. Stone spent 189 days in prison in the aftermath of the Federal disaster at Ball's Bluff without charges having been brought against him but was never stripped of his rank. When released from confinement, he went to the Department of the Gulf and became chief of staff on July 25. [WWW, 626]

Shortly before assuming that post he was in command at Port Hudson, Louisiana. There he made a routine inspection of "the camps, hospitals, kitchens, &c." of the brigade led by Gen. Daniel Elman. In spite of "large mortality from dysentery and measles he found these facilities reasonably well policed, or cleaned up.

He was concerned, however, when he discovered that among men of some regiments that had enlisted for nine months of service there was "very considerable disaffection." While Stone was making his inspection, a company of the 50th Massachusetts "mutinied and refused to do duty."

Organized at Oxford in November, 1862, these men without combat experience had sailed directly for New Orleans on the steamer *Jersey Blue*. Transferred to the *Guerrilla* at Hilton Head, they reached Louisiana on January 20. Several companies spent more weeks on the water than on land, going from New Orleans to Philadelphia to Fort Monroe and then back to New Orleans and Baton Rouge. In July the regiment was assigned to the Department of the Gulf, commanded by Gen. Nathaniel P. Banks. [D, 3, 1265]

After taking part in bitter fighting at Port Hudson, Louisiana, they were put in garrison duty. The regiment had served only eight of the nine months it owed to the Federal government. Despite this fact with lots of time on their hands, Stone found that "Most of them think of nothing but getting home, without regard to want of transportation."

The 50th Massachusetts was in the thick of the fight at Port Hudson, Louisiana.

Harper's History of the Great Rebellion

Stone wanted it known that he'd permit no insubordination, so he put the mutineers under guard. He planned to send them to Ship Island, where they would be put at hard labor for the duration of the conflict. This plan was of course subject to the approval of Banks, he acknowledged.

Within hours after having decided how best to punish mutineers whose term of enlistment would expire in one month, Stone was notified that they had "made their submission." As a result, Gen. George L. Andrews had promptly restored them to duty. Stone didn't approve of what Andrews had done, but didn't think it proper to modify his order. As a result, mutineers who faced the possibility of hard labor until April, 1865, remained on garrison duty for nine days more. They were then moved to Boston by way of Cairo, Illinois, and were mustered out on August 24.

Rebellious members of the 50th were aware that they stayed in uniform four days longer than required by the terms of their enlistment. Still, they must have rejoiced without constraint that their capitulation saved them from hard labor on Ship Island until April, 1865. [OR I, 26, 648; D, 3, 1265]

July—50th Pennsylvania

Organized at Harrisburg, the 50th Pennsylvania left for Washington on October 2, 1861, under the command of Col. Ellen Franklin. Within days the regiment was ordered to take part in what proved to be the earliest important Federal success in the Deep South—the November capture of Port Royal and Hilton Head, South Carolina. Their vessel, the *Infield Scott,* wrecked off the coast of North Carolina, depriving them of playing any role in the great victory. In December they proceeded to their destination, where they were in the army of occupation for more than six months.

Sent back to the Eastern Theatre, the 50th was at Sulphur Springs, Graviton, Second Bull Run, Chantilly, South Mountain, Antietam and Fredericksburg before getting respite from combat for any length of time. Passing through part of Kentucky to Cairo, Illinois, from that port they went down the Mississippi River to Vicksburg in time to take part in the siege of the city. [D, 3, 1590-91]

Soon afterward, an unspecified number of men in the 50th were found by Gen. Darius N. Couch to be in a "mutinous state." He informed Gen. William F. Smith of this state of affairs, warning that everything possible must be done to avoid a general mutiny. Smith, meanwhile, received directly from Franklin a report that was not preserved. He said that his men were dissatisfied at being in detention but indicated he was not sure that any other regiment would act "to force the refractory one to do its duty." By July 31, Franklin was in command of the 2nd Brigade of Smith's 1st Division and leadership of the rebellious 50th had devolved upon Col. Thaddeus Stevens, Jr. Since men of the regiment reenlisted en masse on January 1, 1864, by then their mutinous spirit had presumably given way to unquestioning obedience to orders. [OR I, 27, III, 758, 764; D, 3, 1591]

July 20—Deserters Aboard the Steamer Detroit

In Civil War usage, the term mutiny was sometimes applied to persons not actively engaged in the service of a military or naval unit. Civilians who engaged in riotous behavior were occasionally called mutineers. So were rebellious prisoners of war, and on at least one occasion the label was given to captured deserters who were on the way to prison.

Aboard the U.S. schooner *Sophronia,* Acting Master James Taylor received July 20 word of serious trouble on the transport *Detroit.* A band of one hundred prisoners on the ship were described to him as being troublesome and "making some show of revolt." As a result, he immediately ordered the USS *Primrose* to act as overnight convoy to the vessel that was upbound on the Potomac River.

Except for the log of the *Primrose* nothing else is known about this unusual "mutiny." According to records made by Acting Master James Taylor, his vessel stood out at 9:30 P.M. "and proceeded up the river as convoy to the transport steamer *Detroit*, she having deserters on board in a state of mutiny." [NOR I, 5, 308, 607]

September—11th Missouri Militia

Facing what he considered to be an emergency, U.S. Gen. John M. Schofield hurriedly called out a number of companies of Missouri Militia. None of these men had experienced combat, and most of them had received little or no formal training. These raw troops proved worse than useless, for the men who made up some of them had no respect at all for military discipline.

By the middle of the month, eight men of Company G were in the guard house at Rolla, under arrest for mutiny. They were soon joined by an unspecified number of mutineers from the 11th Militia. Leaders of the insurrection, who were not named in Schofield's Special Orders, No. 255, were ordered confined in the military prison to wait for a general court-martial. Their followers were sent under guard to Rolla, having been sentenced to confinement at hard labor "until further orders." [OR I, 22, I, 616–17; OR I, 22, II, 542–43]

September 8—Crew and Soldiers on the USS Sachem

At least as early as the last of July, U.S. Rear Adm. David G. Farragut gave tacit approval to a plan developed by Acting Lt. Frederick Crocker of the U.S. Navy. Many Federal leaders were desperately eager to get a foothold in eastern Texas, expecting that from such a point they could rapidly move toward the interior of the vast state. Crocker proposed a joint army/navy expedition aimed at the reduction of tiny Fort Griffin on the bank of the Sabine Pass. Once this installation was silenced, he urged, warships and transports could proceed up the Sabine River.

Elaborate preparations having been completed, an expedition was launched with the approval of Gen. Nathaniel P. Banks. Plans called for four warships and seven transport vessels to leave the Gulf of Mexico, move rapidly up the river and quickly reduce the Confederate fort. Most of the 1,200 soldiers who headed toward Sabine Pass were aboard transports, but at least 26 of them were passengers on the USS *Sachem.*

The enemy consisted of 43 members of the Davis Guards who were named in honor of Jefferson Davis. Though Capt. F. H. Odium was their commander, he was not present on the momentous day, so command had devolved upon Irish-born Houston saloon keeper Lt. Richard ("Dick") Dowling. He and his men had two 32-pounder guns, two 24-pounders, and two small howitzers—none of which could be moved on their travel bars. Gen. J. Bankhead Magruder, who had learned of the impending invasion, considered the fort to be indefensible against a force of any size. He therefore ordered it abandoned, but Dowling and his men decided to stay and fight. [OR I, 26, I, 296-98; E, 650; JSHS, 29, 314-15]

Members of the attacking force did not know that Dowling and his men, who had helped to build Fort Griffin, had a great deal of time and abundant ammunition on their hands. During a period of several weeks they spent part of their days placing range markers in the river and then firing at them with their half dozen small guns. A blockading gunboat, the USS *Owasco*, was stationed too far from the fort to be in danger of fire from it.

Plans called for the *Owasco* to serve as the point of reference for gunboats. When it ran out of coal, however, the Federal vessel steamed to Galveston for fuel on September 6—depriving oncoming forces of their sole geographical guide. Early the next day the USS *Granite City* came up one side of the immense oyster bed that divided the river into two channels. Three other gunboats and all of the transports trailed behind. When no sign of the *Owasco* could be found, the flotilla turned around and headed back toward the Gulf. After having made about 30 miles, lookouts recognized Calcasieu Pass and masters of vessels then knew where they were.

They turned back toward the west and leaders assembled to make plans for the attack. Acting Lt. Frederick Crocker headed the naval expedition, whose distinguished passengers included Gens. W. B. Franklin and Godfrey Weitzel. Franklin took along a dozen guns— twice as many as were mounted in Fort Griffin—plus 50 wagons and great numbers of horses and mules. [CV, 36, 453-54; OR I, 26, 297]

Only seven miles long, the Sabine River linked Sabine Lake with the Gulf of Mexico. About one mile wide, its depth ranged from 20 to 40 feet. The tiny Confederate fort was located about five miles from the Gulf on the west or Texas side of the river. Earlier, it had formed one of the boundaries between the United States and Mexico. [JSHS, 29, 314-15]

With action scheduled to begin at 6:30 A.M. on September 8, the USS *Clifton* hove to about a mile from Fort Griffin in order to give stability to the vessel. Her gunners fired 26 shots, only two of which hit the ramparts of the installation. Gunfire was heard in Beaumont, where the commander of the Marine Department of Texas jumped on a horse and galloped toward the scene of the action. Before he arrived the gunboat withdrew and leaders of the expedition came together in order to hold another conference.

. They decided that the *Clifton* would lead the attack, moving through the Texas channel on the port or western side of the river in front of the *Granite City*. The *Sachem* was to follow along the Louisiana shore, with the *Arizona* close behind. Each of the transports— *Suffolk, St. Charles, Landis, Exact, Laurel Hill, Thomas,* and *Gen. Banks* was assigned an exact position in the flotilla. A reconnaissance by the Confederate gunboat *Uncle Ben* drew three 30-pounder Parrott shots from the powerful *Sachem* but men on both sides knew that the fight had not really started.

Precisely at 3:00 P.M. all 11 Federal vessels weighed anchor and started up the river with precise distances between them. Dowling restrained his gunners until the *Sachem* came abreast of the Confederate installation at a distance of about 1,200 yards. Armed with a 20-pounder Parrott rifle plus four 32-pounders, the gunboat had gained fame earlier. It had escorted the USS *Monitor* to Hampton Roads, Virginia, so that the Federal ironclad could take place in the battle that changed naval warfare forever.

All six of Dowling's guns fired at the *Sachem* simultaneously. A ball from one of them went directly through the steam drum of the gunboat. According to Crocker's report, the vessel was instantly disabled and steam quickly drove sharpshooters from her upper deck. He wrote:

> Many, thinking the vessel was about to blow up, jumped overboard. At the same time the enemy got our range, and their fire began to tell severely. The vessel twice caught fire, and the men were falling fast. . . . I was met by two of my officers, and informed by one of them that he had hauled down the flag, and that we could not fight any more. With great indignation, I ordered it hoisted again, and all to stand to their guns; but the example had become contagious; with few exceptions the men had left their guns and were taking to the water. . . . The conduct of the commanders of the Arizona or the Granite City, or of my officer who hauled down the flag I am not now called upon to characterize; nor that of General Franklin in failing so utterly to cooperate; but I trust my Government will soon place me in a position to ask an inquiry into the facts.

Orders given under fire had been disobeyed by gunners plus other members of the crew, officers of the gunboat and all of the soldiers who were aboard. Some of them managed to make it to the *Arizona* or another Federal craft and comparative safety. In direct violation of orders, Acting Lt. Amos Johnson formally surrendered the gunboat soon after men guilty of mutiny in combat had left it. [OR I, 26, I, 301–2; NOR I, 2, 1, 195; Butts, 235]

Participants said that the rudder rope of the *Clifton* was severed by a shot within seconds after the *Sachem* was disabled. Since the *Clifton* did not respond to movements of her helm, the tide soon swung her at a spot where she lay directly between the *Arizona* and the *Granite City*. Her new position made it impossible for either of the two relatively undamaged gunboats to take part in the action. Men aboard the *Clifton* fired three of her guns for about half an hour, then a shot went through her boilers and machinery and rendered her helpless.

In Fort Griffin, Asst. Surg. George H. Bailey helped to serve the guns. Long before the 45-minute fight came to an end, Dowling had begun joking about Bailey's role. As a tribute to Magruder, who commanded the District of Texas, New Mexico, and Arizona, some of the balls sent hurtling toward the enemy were called "Magruder pills." Fame of the brief but decisive struggle was such that this nickname for cannon balls came into widespread use. [CV, 36, 454]

With the *Sachem* out of the fight, the *Clifton* hopelessly disabled and the *Arizona* plus the *Crescent* temporarily aground, all of the transports and those gunboats still navigable began their withdrawal to the Southwest Pass of the Mississippi River. They left an estimated four hundred prisoners behind, and two hundred thousand rations thrown overboard from the *Crescent* dotted the surface of the big river. Smokestacks of the transport *Laurel Hill* had been blown away, so she lightened her load by dumping two hundred mules into the water. [NOR I, 2, 1, 195; OR I, 26, I, 297, 299]

Weitzel filed a hopelessly inaccurate report. In it he listed his casualties as two officers and 69 men of the 75th New York plus one officer and 25 men of the 161st New York who were aboard gunboats as sharpshooters. After enumerating these, he admitted that "How many were killed and wounded I do not know." [OR I, 26, I, 298–99]

In Richmond, the Confederate Congress passed a resolution of thanks to officers and men of the Davis Guard. Language of the measure incorrectly listed the defeated Federal force as having consisted of "a fleet of five gunboats and twenty-two steam transports, carrying a land force of fifteen thousand men." Despite this gross error, language of the resolution was accurate and appropriate when it described the brief battle punctuated by mutiny under fire as "one of the most brilliant and heroic achievements in the history of this war." [NOR I, 2, 3, 161]

October—24th Georgia Cavalry, C.S.

As was the case with men who made up many Federal units, members of the 24th Georgia Cavalry pondered evidence and concluded that they had been deceived when they enlisted. Recruitment officers, they said, had made promises to them that were not kept. Their discontent simmered for months and finally boiled over not far south of Savannah. Anger at having been duped when they donned uniforms was almost certainly augmented by their hopeless attempts to weaken the armies of U.S. Gen. William T. Sherman who were on their famous March to the Sea.

The insurrection in Rebel forces was of sufficient gravity to lead G. B. Lamar to call it to the attention of Gen. Samuel Cooper in Richmond. According to him, men in uniform were "every day spreading a most injurious sentiment of disaffection for the war." He was positive that many men in Anderson's command were ready to surrender. Partly due to their influence, at least 1,000 draft dodgers were said to be "concentrated in the Okeefinokee Swamp." *[Spelling as in original]*

Alarmed, C.S. Secretary of War James A. Seddon requested an explanation of the matter from Gen. Hugh W. Mercer, commander of the Military District of Georgia. From Savannah—not yet reached by Sherman's forces—Mercer protested that the "disaffection" in the 24th Georgia Cavalry was against its officers "and not the cause [of the Confederacy]." According to him, former officers really had been engaged in intrigue designed "to gratify private malice and produce certain political effects."

According to Mercer, most of Anderson's men who had turned their backs upon the war returned to his command after short absences. Whether anyone involved was telling the truth is unknown since the March to the Sea soon severed communications between Richmond and Rebel forces of the region. [OR I, 28, II, 411-12]

October—Members of the Army of Tennessee, C.S.

Charles T. Dana heard from a distance the sounds of small arms fire inside besieged Vicksburg and guessed, perhaps correctly, that weapons of this size would have been fired only by mutineers. Three months later from a distance he heard the boom of big guns at Missionary Ridge plus Ringgold, Georgia.

From Col. Daniel McCook, he learned that the struggle on Missionary Ridge had lasted for many hours, but he had no sure word about its outcome. Confederate guns were believed by Dana to have been brought down from Lookout Mountain, and their entire camps were said to be in motion. Reporting to Edwin M. Stanton, he surmised that the actions about which he had second-hand information stemmed either from "a conflict with Burnside's flanking column or a mutiny." [OR I, 30, I, 210]

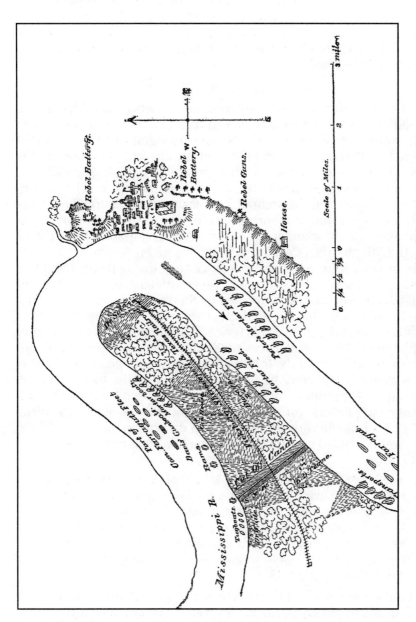

Vicksburg, Mississippi, was located at a bend of the Mississippi River.

Official Records

Though huge quantities of Confederate records were destroyed or lost, a mutiny at Lookout Mountain would almost certainly have been described in letters and diaries. Since no such supporting evidence exists, it appears that this time the future assistant secretary of war of the United States was indulging in wishful thinking about mutiny in Rebel ranks.

November—Col. Joseph O. Shelby, C.S.

During a period of six week starting on September 22, C.S. Col. Joseph O. Shelby led cavalrymen in a little-known raid that cut a wide swath through much of Missouri. Its significance is indicated by the fact that reports from him and his officers plus those of his foes fill more than 50 pages of fine print. [OR I, 22, II, 593-665]

A wealthy pre-war planter and rope manufacturer, he had investments scattered throughout Kentucky and Missouri. Shelby was both combative and stubborn in his loyalty to the secession movement and as a commander. After service in the Missouri State Guard and the 5th Missouri Cavalry, C.S., he was given command of a brigade in Gen. John S. Marmaduke's cavalry division. He fought at Carthage, Wilson's Creek, Elkhorn Tavern, Helena, and Camden and took part in two Missouri raids led by Sterling Price. [GG, 273-74]

By July, 1863, he admitted that there was "great dissatisfaction existing among the men at this time." That did not prevent him from continuing to hit Federal forces suddenly and hard or to race through the countryside on raids. In the aftermath of his great raid that is not widely remembered, he figuratively trod on the toes of Gen. E. Kirby Smith. Ignoring clear regulations, he refused to forward to division headquarters "an official communication of one of the officers" of his brigade with whom he had a disagreement.

Smith scolded him at length, telling him what he already knew—that is:

> You have violated the indisputable right of the officers and men under you to make known their complaints through their intermediate officers, and you have refused to do that which military law and every principle of justice requires you to do, and I do not hesitate to say that before any intelligent military court it would be impossible for you to escape conviction. [OR I, 22, II, 1099-1100; WWW, 522-24, 585]

Nothing is known about the nature of the quarrel among officers of the brigade, or Shelby's reasons for wanton violation of regulations. Smith's tongue-lashing apparently had no effect, for Shelby was promoted on December 15.

The colonel who probably destroyed official communications from his dissident officers became a brigadier too late to have a significant impact upon fighting in the Western Theatre during closing months of the war. When he heard of Lee's surrender, however, he vowed that he'd never follow suit. True to his word, he led part of his men to the Rio Grande and buried their battle flag in the river. Crossing into war-torn Mexico, he offered their services to both Gen. Benito Pablo Juarez and the Emperor Maximilian. Since the names of officers upon whose rights he trampled are not known, it is impossible to determine whether or not some of them went with him to Mexico. [O'Flaherty, 242–57; GG, 274; WWW, 585]

November 28—Mutineers in Action

Capt. A. L. Vidal, with his entire company of Partisan Rangers, mutinied and deserted from Confederate forces in Texas on November 28 (see chapter 15). He successfully recruited about 250 more Mexicans, bringing the size of his command to four hundred men. Of these, 89 were mustered into Federal service during November but one was immediately killed in a brawl. By December the Confederate mutineers were under the command of Gen. Nathaniel B. Banks. According to Gen. N. J. T. Dana, they served primarily as scouts. Despite extensive records concerning Vidal and his band, there is no record that they ever played a significant role in combat after having changed uniforms. [OR I, 26, I, 439, 477, 830, 877; OR I, 26, II, 408; OR I, 34, II, 890]

December 9—The Garrison of Fort Jackson

One of the understatements of the war was made by U.S. Gen. Nathaniel P. Banks in a December 11 report. He said simply that "An unpleasant affair occurred at Fort Jackson on the evening of the 9th instant." Explaining that it was brought about by Lt. Col. Augustus W. Benedict, he admitted that the officer had "struck and punished two soldiers with a whip" at about 6:30 P.M.

Except for officers, all members of the garrison were blacks who belonged to the 4th Regiment of the Corps d'Afrique. Before enlisting they had been solemnly promised that "under no circumstances whatever were they to be subjected to the degrading punishment of flogging." Yet two drummers had been beaten mercilessly in public by Benedict. [OR I, 26, I, 458–58, 861]

A hurried investigation left officers who made it somewhat bewildered. Members of the garrison who had been engaged in mutiny shortly before didn't want to talk about it and when questioned said they didn't remember. Gen. William Dwight, who took command after the outbreak, termed this attitude "passive mutiny" on the heels of active mutiny. On December 20 he reported to Gen. Charles P. Stone that he had made no progress in dealing with the mutiny despite the fact that a military commission had begun hearings more than a week earlier. [OR I, 26, I, 860, 867–68]

Massive Fort Jefferson was located in Florida's Dry Tortugas.
Library of Congress

A partial transcript of the hearings, 19 pages in length, deals with the principal participants in the military drama. Men who were questioned in detail said that except for the fact that members of the garrison had not been paid for some time, the only other cause for discontent was the floggings administered by Benedict. Earlier stationed at Baton Rouge and at Fort St. Philip directly across the Mississippi River, he had displayed extreme cruelty well before the mutiny. Shoeless, two men who were being disciplined were tied flat on the ground and then liberally smeared with molasses designed to draw ants and other insects to them. Their punishment lasted for more than a day.

Col. Charles Drew, who commanded the 4th Regiment, said that when the disturbance broke out he ordered Benedict to his quarters because he thought his presence might "exasperate the men." Quite a few shots were fired into the air by mutineers, but they did not cause any injuries. Drew did hear men shout "Kill Colonel Benedict; shoot him," he testified. According to the colonel a member of the garrison attempted to use his bayonet on Capt. James Miller, but failed to hit him with it and was soon put under arrest.

After days of hearings and deliberation, members of the court of inquiry reported that Benedict's whipping had started the mutiny. The court found that Drew had tried to stop the uprising by telling the men that "Benedict had done wrong, but that they were doing a greater wrong." The uprising was spontaneous rather than planned, said members of the court.

Musician Edward B. Smith was found guilty of mutiny and was sentenced to one year of imprisonment at hard labor. Pvt. Frank Williams, also convicted on the charge of mutiny, was sentenced "to be shot to death with musketry." Also ruled guilty of mutiny, Cpl. Lewis Cady was given two years of confinement at hard labor. Though accused, Cpl. Henry Green plus Pvts. Jacob Kennedy and Charles Taylor were acquitted.

Pvt. Abraham Victoria, the seventh man held accountable for the mutiny, was told he'd go before a firing squad. Pvt. Abram Singleton drew 10 years at hard labor, but Pvt. Willis Curtis got only three years. His sentence was dramatically light by comparison with that of a comrade, Pvt. Julius Bondro, who was given 20 years. Pvt. Volser Verrett was acquitted of all charges, as was Pvt. James Hagan. Pvt. James H. Moore got only "one month at hard labor, under guard."

Men sentenced to die learned that their executions would take place at Fort Jefferson, Florida. The sentences imposed upon Williams and Victoria were suspended and they were directed to be sent to Fort Jefferson and kept in close confinement until further orders. Four accused men who were acquitted were ordered released and returned to duty. Evidence concerning Moore having been "conflicting and unsatisfactory," his conviction was overruled and he was told to return to duty.

When all of the men accused of mutiny had learned their final verdicts, a clerk droned that Lt. Col. Augustus W. Benedict, accused of "inflicting cruel and usual punishment, to the prejudice of good order and military discipline," had pled "Not Guilty."

Since the verdict concerning each man charged with mutiny was rendered separately after a preliminary finding had been made, it was only proper that Benedict should get the same treatment. Two sentences almost at the end of the long transcript revealed the punishment he received for having used a whip on the backs of men and thereby starting a mutiny:

> In the case of Lieut. Col. Augustus W. Benedict, the proceedings, findings, and sentence are confirmed. He ceases from this date to be an officer in the military service of the United States. [OR I, 26, I, 476-79]

25

1864-Ship's Engineers, Union Partisans, Black Volunteers

January—Disaffected Rebels

At Mt. Pleasant, S.C., on January 12 C.S. Gen. R. S. Ripley expressed great concern about a threatened mutiny. His interest, at least for the moment, centered in the 22nd S.C., then stationed on Sullivan's Island. Serious problems were not confined to that body, however. Officers who didn't want to use the formal term "mutiny" didn't hesitate to write freely about what they called "disaffection" among troops.

The 22nd had plenty of reasons to cause trouble. Eight months earlier, its colonel went on trial for mutiny and still had not returned to his command. Its lieutenant colonel had been suspended for a month "for utter incompetency." Its major had been absent without leave for nearly a year. Maj. James Rion, placed in temporary command, was absent because of sickness.

Small wonder that "a rebellious state of feeling" was displayed by the six hundred to seven hundred members of the regiment. Col. H. L. Benbow ordered an investigation of the unit's "mutinous disaffection." He filed a report in which he admitted that results of his inquiry were "by no means satisfactory." The situation could be brought under control, he urged, only by "a thorough reorganization of the line officers, and the appointment of competent field officers."

Gen. P. G. T. Beauregard immediately sent an urgent message to Richmond. He pointed out that the serious shortage of officers in the 22nd was called to the attention of the War Department on December 9. Nothing had been done, however. Hence he made what he called an earnest request "that steps may be taken to supply this regiment with competent field officers." Several members of the 1st

South Carolina were already in confinement for "mutinous conduct." Ripley urged that they should be sent into Charleston under guard. There is no record that steps were taken to restore morale, but on February 21 the 21st regiment that may still have been without essential officers relieved the 18th at Cumming's Point. [OR I, 35, I, 26, 194, 200, 204, 518-19]

Before the month ended, most of the 4th South Carolina plus most members of three companies of the 3rd displayed "disgraceful and mortifying conduct." According to Gen. J. H. Trapier, their actions grew out of their belief that their enlistments had expired and that they were "no longer amendable to military authority." Even the officers of the units affected adopted this point of view, causing "the demoralization of their commands" to be complete. Since the units involved were state troops, authorities eventually ruled that their term of service really did end six months from the first of August. [OR I, 35, I, 560-62]

At Beaulieu near Savannah, men in gray dubbed "conspirators" rather than mutineers made plans to march away in a body. They planned to take their weapons with them and go into hiding in the interior of the state. Gen. Hugh W. Mercer appointed a board of officers to make a quick investigation and to have guilty men arrested "and placed in close confinement for trial and punishment." [OR I, 35, I, 529-30]

Things were at least as bad in parts of Florida as in South Carolina and Georgia. Both civilians and soldiers were going over to the enemy, partly because many men had received no pay or clothing for six months. The situation was so perilous that Gov. John Milton suggested suspension of habeas corpus and imposition of martial law. [OR I, 35, I, 563-65]

January—Engineers Aboard the Steamer Home

Acting Rear Adm. David D. Porter, commander of the Mississippi Squadron, was held responsible for everything that took place on the river—not naval affairs, only. Illicit commerce was a constant problem, because trade between the warring sections could be extremely profitable. Masters of vessels engaged in such activity were prone to ignore the revenue laws, as well.

On January 26 Porter ordered Fleet Capt. Alexander M. Pennock to take stern measures with men aboard the steamer *Home.* There seemed to be clear evidence that its master had paid little if any attention to revenue laws. Part of its cargo was owned by the U.S. government, but some items were aboard for trade. These included six barrels of whisky and 18 barrels of salt. Their presence on the river steamer, said Porter, endangered the property of the government.

He also ordered Pennock to try to get to the bottom of charges and counter-charges that emanated from those aboard the vessel. Its engineers had indicated a willingness to testify against their captain. He, in turn, had lodged an accusation of mutiny against the engineers. By this time, the North was in turmoil as a result of publication of the Emancipation Proclamation. There was no certainty that it would be possible to prove that mutiny had taken place and or to punish civilian engineers who were accused of it. [NOR I, 24, 200-201]

January—The Confederate Garrison of Fort Morgan

At New Orleans, three men who debarked from the steamer *Jackson* on January 18 reported to Com. H. H. Bell that "a mutiny exists in the rebel forts on Mobile Bay." Eager to get confirmation, Bell ordered Lieutenant Commander Greene to get all the information he could and forward it to Bell aboard the USS *Pensacola*. Three days after word reached New Orleans, Cmdr. Robert Townsend relayed Bell's report to Rear Adm. David D. Porter. [NOR I, 21, 42-44; NOR I, 25, 706-7]

No mention of this report is found among surviving Confederate documents. Though this throws some doubt upon the account, it does not prove it to have been a rumor planted by some Rebel officer. Many an officer did his best to suppress news about an insurrection in his command, and reason suggests that such efforts were successful at least part of the time.

January—Clanton's Brigade, C.S.

Georgia native James H. Clanton entered military service as colonel of the 1st Alabama Cavalry. He was made a brigadier on November 16, 1863 after having recruited men enough to form two infantry regiments plus one company of artillery and 24 companies of cavalry.

Residents of northern Alabama are believed to have founded The Peace Society very early, but its existence was not known to Confederate authorities until 1862. By that time it had branches in Alabama, Tennessee, Mississippi, and Georgia. Members of the society scored several successes when they set about trying to influence elections in August, 1863. Emboldened, some of them who were in uniform under Clanton formulated plans to lay down their arms at Pollard and quit the service on Christmas Day of that year.

This mutiny in the making was detected and its leaders were severely punished, but the sting of having it come close to maturity under his nose was humiliating to Clanton. Early in January he contacted Alabama Gov. T. H. Watts more than once, asking his help in diverting official attention from the near mutiny. Watts and other prominent civilians sent lengthy letters to Gen. Leonidas Polk in which they urged that Clanton's entire command should be sent into Alabama's segment of the Tennessee Valley.

Possibly because Polk knew that this was a hotbed of Peace Society members and leaders, he decided to bring Clanton to his side as an aide. This relationship prevailed until Polk was killed near Atlanta. While on Polk's staff, Clanton secured from the military court at Mobile a detailed statement absolving him from blame in the Pollard incident. Later sent to the Department of the Gulf, the general from Alabama was wounded and captured. Upon his release he resumed his career as an attorney and office holder.

Six years after the regional conflict ended, the man who did everything he could to erase from his record the stains made by Peace Society members became one of the last casualties of the war. At Knoxville, Tennessee, he was shot and killed by a drunken son of one of the leaders of the mountainous region's powerful Unionist movement. [OR I, 26, II, 554-56, 588-90; GG, 50-51; WWW, 122; E, 564-65]

February—11th Missouri Cavalry

A detachment of men under the command of a sergeant was sent from Springfield to Buffalo by U.S. Gen. John B. Sanborn on February 15th. Their task seemed simple enough; they were under orders to arrest some members of a battalion of the 11th Missouri Cavalry and send them to headquarters.

Upon arrival at the camp, Maj. Lyman W. Brown was informed about what was to take place. He explained that before his men could leave under guard they'd have to exchange public horses that were owned by the military for "private horses." While this was supposed to be taking place, comrades of the men facing charges pulled their revolvers and said they'd shoot anyone who tried to take these men away. When this situation was reported to Brown, he exclaimed: "I can't help that; I can't help that."

There was great confusion in the camp. Many of its men and at least one officer were heard to swear that the prisoners would not reach their destination. They were laughing and jeering at the detachment from headquarters as its members plus their prisoners rode away. Incensed when he heard what had happened, Sanborn recorded his judgment that "no officer of the battalion is really suited to or fit for the service if he stood by and silently allowed such an occurrence."

That verdict was rendered before it became known that the prisoners were rescued and released, presumably by other members of their command. Asst. Adj. Gen. O. D. Greene, who notified Sanborn of this development, was furious. He reminded his commander that he had recently spoken of "steady and great improvement in the discipline" of Brown's battalion. "What, in God's name, must it have been before you got hold of it, if this rescue occurrence be a fair sample of its discipline now?" he demanded. One man was placed under arrest, but there seems to have been no punishment for the unit as a whole. [OR I, 34, II, 346–47, 386]

Probably in a move designed to disperse dissidents, Capt. Albert B. Kauffman and 40 men were soon assigned to the 1st Nebraska and a detachment of one hundred men was ordered to Pocahontas on the Black River. If high-ranking officers thought that these actions would quickly end troubles with the 11th Cavalry, they soon found themselves to be wrong.

Six squadrons were ordered to Batesville, Arkansas, on February 26. Partly because they were escorting a wagon train, real anxiety was registered when not a word had been heard from them on March 1. Col. William D. Wood, his men, and the wagon train finally reached Batesville on March 10, many days late. As a fresh gesture of defiance, these riders may have deliberately wandered from their course. Again, they may have camped for several days in some nice spot—knowing that their failure to appear would lead officers at Batesville and Springfield to gnaw their fingernails very short. [OR I, 34, II, 425, 475, 548, 616]

February 16—Crew of the Bark Powhatan

At 1:00 P.M. that afternoon men of the USS *Augusta Dinsmore* became about as active as it was possible to be, short of combat. Patrolling near the mouth of the Rio Grande River, the 834-ton two-master schooner equipped with a steam engine came in sight of a craft that looked to be a blockade runner. The naval vessel carried a light battery consisting of one 20-pounder Parrott rifle, one 12-pounder rifle, and two 24-pounder smoothbores.

At the risk of running into trouble if the stranger should outgun their vessel, Acting Ensign H. M. Pierce and a crew of only three men boarded it and met no resistance. Finding it to be English-owned and having come to these waters from Barbados, they seized it as a prize. That meant officers and crew members of the gunboat would later divide between themselves according to well-established formulas the value of the *Scio* and its cargo.

While still rejoicing at their good luck an hour later, someone on the *Dinsmore* noticed that another nearby bark was flying the American flag upside down—using the emblem as a distress signal. A boat was sent alongside, and the ship was found to be the *Powhatan*, out of New York. As soon as she was boarded, it was discovered that the crew was in a state of mutiny. At the request of the captain, two seamen whom he identified as leaders of the outbreak were taken aboard the *Dinsmore* and confined in single irons. Though no prize money was involved, it made members of the U.S. Navy hold their heads higher to know that they had quelled a mutiny. [NOR I, 21, 90]

February 20—A Scantily-Clothed Rebel Officer

Mutiny, whether or not formally designated as such, was one of the gravest matters in which soldiers and sailors were involved. A truly humorous incident in which the label was used—perhaps the only one of its kind in 1861-65—took place in coastal North Carolina.

Aboard the USS *Monticello*, Lt. W. B. Cushing devised a plan whose goal was to embarrass the enemy and bring fame to his crew. As his name hints, C.S. Gen. Louis Hebert was a native of Louisiana. A West Pointer, he spent a dozen pre-war years superintending his father's sugar interests. He entered Confederate service and was soon made a brigadier. After the fall of Vicksburg he was put in charge of the heavy artillery at Wilmington's Fort Fisher. Possibly because he preferred rural life, he made his headquarters at tiny Smithville instead of at Wilmington. The village was best known for its salt works, and had none of the big guns that guarded the nearby port.

Known to house a barracks for one thousand men, Smithville was lightly defended. A very small party of seamen, moving through the place long after dark, were not likely to be noticed. Hence Cushing put Acting Ensign J. E. Jones at the head of a party whose goal was the capture of Hebert.

According to the log of the *Monticello*, two small boats left the warship at 8:40 P.M. on Saturday night, March 5. Cushing was in the gig, accompanied by Acting Master's Mate W. L. Howorth. Jones, who had charge of the cutter, took along a second assistant engineer and a single seaman. They moved up a small river and moored as close as possible to Hebert's headquarters.

Cushing and the trio of other men from the warship quickly identified the building in which the general worked and slept, just across the street from the barracks. They found it easy to enter and within minutes captured a Captain Kelly *[no given name]* who identified himself as chief engineer of Smithville's defenses. From him they learned to their chagrin that Hebert was not at hand, having gone to Wilmington.

Having decided to settle for whatever officers they could easily take, the intruders turned their attention to Hebert's adjutant general. In the darkness and confusion, William D. Hardeman jumped to the conclusion that a mutiny was in progress. Believing that he might be a target of mutineers, the officer "took to the woods with a great scarcity of clothing" without pausing to turn out the garrison.

Probably laughing until their sides were sore at the way
Hardeman had raced into the woods nearly naked, men from the
Federal warship returned to it with Kelly as a trophy. A few hours
later Cushing described the adventure in a dispatch to Acting Rear
Adm. S. P. Lee. He ended the account by saying that "I send Captain
Kelly, C.S. Army, to you, deeply regretting that the general was not in
which I called." [NOR I, 9, 511–12; GG, 130–31]

March 25—Officers of Six Regiments

Joseph Hooker, a West Point graduate in the class of 1837, had
a distinguished record during the Mexican War. He remained in uniform until 1853, then became a farmer in California. His failure after
leaving the army was almost as complete as was that of U. S. Grant.

Like Grant, he tried to return to the U.S. Army very early in the
conflict, but was ignored because he had earlier testified against Gen.
Winfield Scott before a court of inquiry. He was a civilian observer at
Bull Run, and was made a brigadier on August 3. He soon put regiments together in order to form a brigade named for him that won
lasting renown.

The Hooker Brigade fought with distinction in battles that in-
cluded Fair Oaks, White Oak Swamp, Harrison's Landing, Bristoe
Station, Second Bull Run, Fredericksburg, Chancellorsville,
Gettysburg, Kelly's Ford, and Mine Run. Combat-weary officers and

At Seven Pines (or Fair Oaks) Hooker's Brigade was in the thick of the action.
Popular History of the Civil War

men rejoiced when they learned that they'd be put on duty at Brandy Station during the late winter of 1863-64. They stayed there much of the time for several months. [D, 3, 1248, 1251-53, 1257, 1361, 1585, 1602; GB, 233-34]

While encamped, numerous officers turned to a different kind of warfare. They devoted much of their time and energy to fighting the military establishment. Gen. George G. Meade had announced a reorganization of the Army of the Potomac, dissolving its I Corps and III Corps on March 23 and sending constituent units into the three remaining corps. This action sent the six regiments of the Hooker Brigade into the II Corps, where their brigade commander was Gen. Joseph B. Carr.

Men and officers of the 11th and 16th Massachusetts, 11th New Jersey, 26th and 84th Pennsylvania regiments bristled at the thought of again being led by Carr, who had earlier been their commander for months. Many of them positively despised Carr but others praised him.

Conflicting attitudes concerning Carr were magnified in importance by his unusual status. He was a brigadier by virtue of rank conferred upon him by the War Department, but the U.S. Senate refused to confirm him as of the recommended date. Gen. George G. Meade pointed out to Stanton on April 30 that this made him junior to Gen. Gershom Mott. The mood of the big encampment was also significantly affected by rivalry between Cols. Robert McAllister of the 11th New Jersey—who had seniority—and William Blaisdell of the 11th Massachusetts.

Formal announcement of drastic changes in the structure of the Army of the Potomac led to a protest meeting by junior officers. They came together on March 25, but since no records were preserved the number of commissioned men involved is unknown. At least 30 officers are thought to have been involved, and their number could have been more than 50. They are believed to have discussed possible strategy by which it might be possible to air their feelings to Meade, the secretary of war, or even to Abraham Lincoln.

What was said is unknown, but informants believed to have belonged to the 11th New Jersey reported about the session to Carr. He immediately had Capt. E. C. Thomas of the 26th Pennsylvania arrested. Capts. Walter Smith and James R. Bigelow plus Lts. Henry Blake and George Forrest of the 11th Massachusetts went into the guard house. All five were held on charges of mutiny and incitement to violation of discipline.

Gen. Winfield Scott, who knew no details of the incident, gave routine approval to Carr's request for a court-martial. Gen. Alexander

B. Hays and seven other officers interrogated all of the accused, nearly a dozen witnesses for the defense, and numerous other officers and men of the Hooker Brigade. From the beginning it was clear that the protest meeting would have been considered a mutiny only by an extremely legalistic or partisan commander.

After nearly a month the court ignored the death penalty and cashiered Bigelow, who had been praised for his leadership at Williamsburg a year earlier. Capts. Walter N. Smith and Edward C. Thomas plus Lt. Henry N. Blake received light punishments. All five officers were consistently termed mutineers during interrogations. Yet Smith, Thomas and Blake were merely fined three months' pay and reprimanded.

Members of the court could not have failed to realize that neither physical nor verbal mutiny had taken place. More than a century later the resolution adopted during the protest meeting seems innocuous and unoffending. It expressed regret at the reorganization, but pledged obedience to orders from Meade and willingness to serve faithfully in the future.

Small wonder, therefore, that no account of the court-martial was included in the OR. Yet the mild protest by an unorganized body of line officers has no counterpart among Civil War actions that were treated as mutinous. No other mutiny has been the subject of two full-length books. This somewhat strange state of affairs is probably due to the fact that letters, diaries, and recollections about "the mutiny at Brandy Station" provide unusual insight into jealousy and rivalry among comrades plus military politics at high levels. [Arner, 27-33, 41-44, 45-80; OR I, 33, 1025; WWW, 317-18; E, 172-76; B, 187-91]

April 1—Loudoun (Virginia) Rangers

Under authorization of the U.S. Secretary of War Samuel C. Means succeeded in organizing pro-Union civilians of Loudoun County, Virginia, as a body of partisan rangers. The region from which they came was widely known as "Mosby's Confederacy" because it was largely controlled by Confederate partisans led by John S. Mosby. Serving as captain of the Unionists, Means mustered them into Federal service on June 20, 1862. He and his men were initially lauded by citizens who delighted that a body of this sort had sprung up in "Mosby's Confederacy."

Much of the action seen by the heavily German Loudoun Rangers was directed against Mosby's 43rd Battalion of Virginia Partisan Rangers. During the late winter of 1863-64 it became evident, however, that men who made up this body of virtually independent Unionists were more interested in lining their pockets than in saving the Union.

Repeated refusals to obey orders brought them to the attention of German-born Gen. Franz Sigel.

In his role as commander of the Department of West Virginia, Sigel issued special orders on April 1, 1864. Under their terms Col. R. F. Taylor was directed to select a reliable officer and put him in charge of a detail of 200 men. Their mission was to go to Point of Rocks, Maryland, "to arrest and bring to these headquarters Captain Means and his battalion." Use of whatever force might be necessary to execute the order was authorized.

The birds had flown the coop when soldiers arrived to seize them. Ostensibly by authority of the secretary of war, the Loudoun Rangers had again crossed the border that separated Maryland from Virginia. During their foray into the region where they lived earlier they succeeded in killing one Rebel and taking one prisoner. According to Gen. Max Weber, the "unattached" body suffered no casualties during the protracted raid and returned to Point of Rocks on April 19.

Weber, who may not have been aware that men of another unit had been sent to arrest Means and his men, ordered them to Charles Town, Virginia. When they refused to obey, he took prompt steps to quell the mutiny. Without indicating precisely what those steps were, he reported on April 15 that after having taken "measures to enforce the command," they did as they were told. In each of three subsequent clashes with Rebel rangers they suffered humiliating defeats and most remaining men of the unit surrendered to Mosby on April 5, 1865. If the arrest ordered by Sigel was ever accomplished, records concerning it and its aftermath vanished in the confusion of partisan warfare on the Virginia/Maryland border. [OR I, 33, 480, 789, 912, 1129; E, 449]

April—6th Pennsylvania Reserves

Enrollment dates, often crucial to determination of whether or not the time of a man or a unit had expired, were usually kept by both state and federal agencies that often found themselves in disagreement. According to records maintained in Harrisburg, the 6th Pennsylvania Reserves—later designated as the 35th regiment of volunteers—was organized at the capital in June, 1861. By the spring of 1864 members of the regiment were convinced that they were due for discharge.

They cited several factors that they considered to buttress their position. The time of comrades who re-enlisted as veterans was calculated from the date of enrollment, they said. The Pension Bureau of the War Department relied upon the same date and granted pensions to some men who had not yet served two years. Finally, they argued, comrades who transferred to the Federal volunteers in the fall of 1862 were discharged three years after their enrollment for state service.

When these arguments failed to win a promise of an early discharge, members of the reserve regiment became so surly and rebellious that seven of its members were arrested and charged with mutiny. Gen. George G. Meade, who became involved in the controversy that was spreading into other regiments, sent a special dispatch to the War Department. In it he pointed out that the Pennsylvania Reserves was "a peculiar organization." Some of its regiments were mustered into state service, only, and were never officially transferred into federal service. He knew that to be the case with the 1st Pennsylvania Rifles, he wrote. Because "symptoms of disorder and mutiny" were appearing in the Army of the Potomac, Meade said:

> My experience is decided that it is inexpedient and impolitic to retain men beyond the period which they honestly believe they are entitled to a discharge, and I would therefore recommend the Reserves be discharged from the date of enrollment or muster into the State service. It is of the utmost importance that a speedy decision thereon be made.

According to Col. William McCandless, who called the attention of high-ranking officials to the dilemma, the charge of mutiny would be dropped if the seven men under arrest were found entitled to be discharged.

Meade's unequivocal directive settled the matter, not only for the 6th but for all other regiments included in the reserves of Pennsylvania. On April 30 he forwarded to McCandless a War Department dispatch that had been sent to him. It was of great significance to men of numerous Pennsylvania regiments, for it told the commander of the Army of the Potomac:

> Your recommendation that the regiments of the Pennsylvania Reserve Corps be discharged from their respective dates of muster into the service of the State has been approved by the Secretary of War. A list showing the aforesaid dates of muster will be sent you by mail.

In accordance with this decision, men of the 6th—including those who earlier were about to be tried for mutiny—were mustered out on June 11. [OR I, 33, I, 924-25, 1032; D, 3, 1578]

April—54th and 55th Massachusetts

As soon as sectional differences erupted into a shooting war, abolitionists of the northeast began agitating for the use of blacks as soldiers. This move was forcefully resisted by the Lincoln administration from fear that border states in general and Kentucky in particular might be tipped into the column of secessionists. Early in his tenure, the President strongly emphasized his willingness to leave slavery alone where it existed. He went so far to give strong public endorsement to the Fugitive Slave Law that was widely hated in the North.

Emancipation proclamations of Gens. John C. Fremont and David Hunter in Missouri and the Department of the South, respectively, were quickly repudiated in Washington. Had skilled attorney Benjamin F. Butler not coined and used the term "contraband," there is no assurance that Federal commanders would have ceased to try to enforce the Fugitive Slave Law.

Even the widespread and fast-growing use of contrabands as laborers did not satisfy abolitionists, who wanted to see large numbers of blacks in blue uniforms. Lincoln's attitude concerning the use of blacks in Union forces began to soften somewhat when the war was about a year old, but he made no public change of stance. His preliminary Emancipation Proclamation was framed during the summer and shared with some of his top advisors in the aftermath of Antietam. Release of the controversial proclamation on September 24, 1862, was linked with Antietam because Lincoln insisted upon

Gen. David Hunter *(seated, left)* presided over the trial of the Lincoln conspirators.

National Archives

labeling it as a Union victory, despite the fact that most military experts regarded it as a drawn battle.

To the consternation of many abolitionists, the preliminary document included a major component of the President's personal plan for dealing with the slavery issue. In it he noted that "the effort to colonize persons of African descent, with their consent, upon this continent or elsewhere . . . will be continued." Signed at Washington on September 22, the document did not mention the question of putting ex-slaves and other blacks into uniform. Even the revised final proclamation that has led Lincoln to be known as "The Great Emancipator" bypassed the matter of military service for blacks. [OR I, 33, 1213, 584–85]

Once slaves outside of states and regions controlled by the Union and its military forces were proclaimed emancipated, the issue of military service moved front and center. Especially in Massachusetts, where there were large numbers of free blacks, agitation for their use in uniform could not be ignored. The first black regiment of the North, whose officers were white, was organized at Readville, Massachusetts, and mustered into service on May 13, 1863. Also at Readville, the black 55th Massachusetts left the state two months later. Soon the state had the distinction of having fielded four additional regiments that were labeled as Negro: the 56th, 58th, 66th, and 80th. All of these units fought at Ocean Pond, where some members of each regiment were captured. [D, 3, 1256–57; OR I, 35, II, 66, 339]

According to Gen. Alexander Schimmelfennig, both the 54th and 55th Massachusetts reached Folly Island, near Charleston, on April 18, 1864. By that time, they had been in uniform for a year without pay. "As a consequence," warned Schimmelfennig, "the greatest discontent prevails, and in several instances a spirit of mutiny has developed." At that time the officer in command of land forces besieging Charleston may not have known that many black soldiers had refused to accept what they contemptuously dubbed "half pay."

Col. A. S. Hartwell of the 55th was so incensed over failure to pay his men that he called the issue to the attention of Gen. John G. Foster in June. By no means sure he'd get what he wanted, the leader of black troops also wrote to Washington at the same time. Foster chided him for the latter action, calling it "ill-timed."

As though Hartwell did not know it, Foster pointed out that Col. Edward N. Hallowell of the 54th had been given permission to go to the North to try to get action concerning pay. The colonel was not only concerned that it was very late; he was angry that his men were still being paid $8 per month in cash plus $3 in clothing, while white soldiers were getting $13 per month and the same clothing allowance.

Hartwell's letter to Foster was forwarded to Washington, but he was warned that he had exhibited "an inclination to make trouble." In what almost seemed a move designed to get trouble-makers out of the Department of the South, one thousand men were ordered to Long Island on June 30 instead of the five hundred who initially expected to go to the North. The thousand-man contingent was to be formed from ranks of the 55th Massachusetts, 33rd U.S. Colored Troops, and 103rd New York.

By early July, Foster had changed his mind about Hallowell's trip to New York that the colonel hoped might make it possible for him to visit Washington.

U.S. Gen. John G. Foster had trouble deciding how to deal with the issue of pay for black soldiers.
Nicolay & Hay, *Lincoln*

He ordered Hallowell immediately to return to his regiment, pointing out that military officers were prohibited from going to the capital.

Two weeks later, however, there was a dramatic change in the situation. Schimmelfennig notified officers involved that the 54th and 55th Massachusetts were "soon to be paid at the rate of $13 a month, from the 1st of January, 1864." At the same time, he suggested that clothing accounts should be deducted from their 1863 pay. Such action, he was aware, would cause many black soldiers to be due only a small balance. Though many aspects of the move toward equal pay for black and white fighting men still had to be resolved, the decision to boost the level of pay for the two Massachusetts regiments dispelled all threats of mutiny in such units in and around Charleston during 1864. [OR I, 35, II, 60, 69, 139, 159, 168, 179]

April 10—Gen. A. J. Smith

Driving into Louisiana, troops under U.S. Gen. Nathaniel P. Banks were hit suddenly and very hard during the late afternoon of April 9. Rebels under Gen. Richard Taylor "appeared out of nowhere" and at Pleasant Hill Landing threw ranks of men in blue into confusion. Forces under the command of A. J. Smith turned the tide, however, and cost the enemy heavily in terms of casualties.

Smith rejoiced at having scored what he considered a victory. As a result he was furious when Banks consulted other generals and decided to abandon his offensive move. Knowing that his dead and wounded men still lay on the battlefield, he ordered a retreat to Grand Encore.

When he learned what was about to take place, Smith rode to Gen. William B. Franklin, second in command of the expedition. Virtually frothing at the mouth, he demanded that Franklin arrest Banks, take command and resume the offensive.

Astonished at such a proposal, Franklin said nothing but shook his head. Eventually he broke the silence by warning: "You are proposing mutiny; I will have nothing to do with it."

U.S. Gen. William B. Franklin wanted no part in actions that could be considered mutinous.
National Archives

Abashed at having had to be reminded of what he knew perfectly well, Smith gave up the idea of having a subordinate seize control of the force led by Banks. [OR I, 34, I, 192-94, 261-62, 303-4, 379; Josephy, 59-63]

April 19—Officers of the 25th U.S. Colored Troops

At New Berne, North Carolina, U.S. Gen. John J. Peck received word that led him to believe the enemy was about to mount a general attack. Under these circumstances he needed all the help he could get. A battalion of the 25th U.S. Colored Troops was known to be at Morehead City on the state's coast, waiting for transportation to New Orleans. In this emergency, he sent orders plus a ship to headquarters at Beaufort, South Carolina, in order to bring the regiment to his river port.

To the surprise of Peck, Col. G. A. Scroggs and an unidentified major refused to obey orders. Consequently, he sent word to Morehead City that the unit probably wouldn't be needed more than two or three days. Both the colonel and the major still refused to obey, so Peck ordered their immediate arrest. Reporting about the affair to Gen. Lorenzo Thomas in Washington, he ended by saying that "The regiment shortly after arrived in command of the senior captain." [OR I, 33, 282-83]

April 18—Chaplain James Findley, C.S.

In the mountains of northern Georgia the weather was unusually cold for the season. Despite this factor, C.S. Gen. Joseph E. Johnston scheduled a grand review of his Army of Tennessee, camped about 30 miles north of Dalton. Officers began getting ready for the review on April 14. Many enlisted men and some officers were far less interested in the upcoming display than in the fate of one of their number, however.

Chaplain James Findley, age 53, had been charged with and convicted of encouraging mutiny. In addition, he was believed to have been guilty of engaging in secret correspondence with the enemy. As a result, he was sentenced to die at Tunnel Hill on April 18. Some of his partisans clung to hope that he would win a last-minute reprieve, but he did not. Instead he made a full confession about an hour before he became the only chaplain in gray or in blue known to have been executed as a mutineer. [WWW, 346; *The Atlanta Century*, April 24, 1864]

May 10—A Federal Engineer

Col. H. M. Plaisted of the 11th Maine assumed command of a post at Bermuda Hundred, Virginia, on May 9. A quick look convinced him that its defenses need to be greatly strengthened at once. Cols. George B. Dandy and Jeremiah C. Drake, both of whom commanded brigades, promptly put their men to work. During the morning Capt. John Walker of the Corps of Engineers, U.S. Army, refused to obey Plaisted's orders concerning the construction of platforms for six guns.

Later in the day the new commander of the installation repeated his earlier order "with some emphasis." This time, the captain retorted that Plaisted wished to damage him professionally by putting him to such rough work. Frustrated, Plaisted turned to artillery officers and at his request they saw to it that the platforms were built before night.

As this job neared completion, Walker was asked to supervise the building of a defensive work at the right. He refused, saying that "he would not obey any but a superior [officer] of his own corps." Plaisted, who had lost his patience, snapped that Gen. Quincy Gillmore had placed him in command. On the heels of this reminder, he gave Walker another order to which he paid no more attention than earlier ones. Hence Plaisted placed him under arrest and told Dandy to put him in close confinement unless he should choose to leave the place at once.

On the following morning Plaisted received a memorandum from Col. G. Moxley Sorrel, the assistant adjutant general. "I have released Captain Walker from arrest," he wrote.

Walker soon turned up, saying that he was reporting for duty. Plaisted ignored him, so the stubborn captain soon returned saying that Gen. Benjamin F. Butler wanted him to take command of three regiments. He had no written authorization for such a move, so Plaisted ignored it, planning to forward to headquarters "charges and specifications against the captain."

If Plaisted followed through with his plans, his charges were ignored. The U.S. Army captain apparently knew that there were clear-cut lines of demarcation between regulars and volunteers and that an officer of the latter service would have little or no influence with the army. [OR I, 36, II, 76]

May 14—U.S. Navy Recruits

Following orders of Gideon Welles, U.S. secretary of the navy, Cmdr. Daniel Ammen and Boatswain T. G. Bell went to New York to take charge of men who were about to begin their service in the navy. They took passage on the *Ocean Queen,* which sailed for Philadelphia on May 13. There the vessel took aboard 220 former soldiers who had just donned naval uniforms. Three of them managed to change into civilian clothing and make their escape.

Because the *Ocean Queen* was a passenger vessel whose steerage was already full, men over whom Ammen had charge were directed to spaces so crowded that most of them had to sleep on deck. He was roused at midnight by a messenger who said that some of his men wanted to see him. After dressing hurriedly, he found seamen John Kelly and Alfred Bussell to be spokesmen for an undetermined number of malcontents. They complained that they were very uncomfortable and wanted whisky, but Ammen refused to give it to them.

At breakfast the next day a gang of about a dozen men complained loudly about the food. When the next meal was served, these fellows "beat the servants belonging to the *Ocean Queen,* drove them away from the tables, and threw pots and pans overboard." Visibly troubled, Capt. Edward L. Tinklepaugh broached the idea of putting in to Hampton Roads, Virginia, and getting rid of the malcontents. In spite of the fact that he found the conduct of these men "mutinous in expression," Ammen demurred and persuaded the ship's captain to proceed.

The following morning, the two men who had called Ammen from his bunk again demanded whisky, then threatened to break into the spirit room to get it. Ammen warned them not to try such a course of action, saying that it could get both of them shot. Tinklepaugh, now thoroughly alarmed, expressed willingness to resort to force. Ammen persuaded him that "if their conduct rendered it necessary to use firearms" he would give the order.

Soon Bussell, Kelly, and three of their comrades became violent when Tinklepaugh and a few others tried to keep them from going toward the spirit room. Ammen pulled his pistol and fired immediately, then Tinklepaugh or other officers of the ship followed suit. Both Bussell and Kelly received mortal wounds and died on the spot.

Knowing that the trouble probably was not over, Ammen had the men in his charge to assemble on the spar deck. There he selected landsman Thomas Riley and four sailors whose conduct he judged to have been "most disorderly and mutinous." When he ordered the quintet to the hurricane deck they obeyed and were soon put in irons. After reaching port ten of the men who made up what Ammen consistently styled "the draft" deserted and escaped. As a result, he delivered only 202 to the gunboat *Cyane.*

On his way back to Philadelphia the naval commander urged that charges be preferred against him so that a court-martial would be held. If tried before a court of inquiry and exonerated, he pointed out, he would still be subject to civil suit.

With the court-martial scheduled, before reaching the port still aboard the *Ocean Queen*, he and Bell and Tinklepaugh gave sworn statements to Stephen J. Field, an associate justice of the U.S. Supreme Court. Surgeon E. H. Gibbs, chief engineer, gave a deposition. So did E. R. Phelps, and three passengers and selected members of the crew.

Their testimony plus other evidence was given to members of a court-martial that convened in New York. After pondering evidence and hearing witnesses, the court acquitted the commander of wrongdoing. The death of Kelly and Bussell, the court ruled, was a result of Ammen's actions taken "to suppress an attempted mutiny, and in the opinion of the court the same was justifiable homicide." [NOR I, 3, 28–36]

June 17—Members of the Crew of the CSS Atlanta

Lt. Joel S. Kennard of the C.S. Navy filed a detailed report of a brief but significant struggle that took place very early on the morning of June 17. His wooden *Isondiga*, anchored near Savannah, Georgia, was believed to be potentially useful if wooden vessels of the U.S. Navy should be met during a daring foray by the warship CSS *Atlanta.*

This vessel was earlier the Scottish-built *Fingal.* Her involvement in the war began when she ran the blockade with a huge cargo of essential goods. As soon as she made it into Savannah, Georgia, however, she was bottled up by vessels of the Federal blockade. A firm in the port city took advantage of her long idleness and converted her into an ironclad ram. When ready to go into action the re-named and converted vessel carried four powerful Brooke rifles plus a spar torpedo.

Though the improvised warship was commissioned in November, 1862, she ventured only a short distance from Savannah until June 17. Capt. William A. Webb then put into action a daring plan that, if successful, would make his vessel famous. Though two Union monitors were on constant guard near the mouth of Wassaw Sound, he believed he could use his spar torpedo on one of them, then blow holes in the other with his Brooke rifles. He would then speed toward nearby Port Royal, South Carolina, and do a great deal of damage while Yankees were still wondering how he got there.

With the little *Isondiga* following close behind, the ironclad Rebel vessel got into Wassaw Sound but when within a few hundred yards of her first target at about 5:00 A.M. she became grounded. Webb's gunners quickly opened fire and those aboard her target did the same, making enough noise to cause the second Federal ironclad to begin moving toward the scene of action.

Kennard thought that the *Atlanta* quickly managed to get afloat again and to head toward the second monitor. She again grounded, and the enemy vessel fired what he described as "a raking shot." Almost immediately, men aboard the *Isondiga* were astonished to see a white flag race up the mast of the *Atlanta*.

Kennard, who immediately turned his little vessel around and headed back to Savannah and safety, was dumbfounded at the chain of events. Only 35 minutes had elapsed between the first and the last shot of the encounter, he reported. He knew that most members of the warship's crew had been recruited in the hills of northern Georgia. Few of them had ever been to sea and presumably none had been in a naval battle before. To him, the only logical explanation for the sudden surrender of the *Atlanta* was mutiny of Webb's inexperienced crew. He voiced that verdict in his official report to Stephen R. Mallory in Richmond.

Webb's report, which was not penned until October 9, confirmed much of Kennard's but said that gunfire began at 4:55 A.M. and lasted until 7:30. He said he fired seven shots and was the target of six that came from the mighty USS *Weehawken*. According to Webb, a 15-inch gun on the Federal vessel scored a direct hit and tore a three-foot hole in the side of the *Atlanta*.

This exchange took place after the Confederate vessel had become "hard and fast aground." Webb's powerful torpedo was useless, since the enemy was two hundrd yards away. By this time the USS *Nahant* had reached the scene of action, making the *Atlanta* the target of two warships rather than one. Webb could not bring his own guns to bear upon the enemy vessels, he explained, so in order to save lives he surrendered.

There was no mutiny, despite the fact that news of it reached Richmond long before Webb's report arrived. What's more, 13 shots were fired from big guns but Kennard counted them as eight. This trained observer thought the action lasted only one-third as long as did Webb. All of which strongly suggests that many a first-hand account of combat or another fast-moving set of events may be permeated with errors. [NOR I, 14, 286–92; E, 28]

July—First Iowa Cavalry

U.S. Gen. Frederic S. Salomon, a native of Prussia, had been put in command of a division of the Federal VII Corps on May 11. Stationed at Little Rock, he was at his wit's end six weeks later. About 300 members of the 1st Iowa Cavalry were claiming that their enlistments had expired and were threatening mutiny unless they were immediately discharged.

Talk about mutiny and possible plans to implement that talk came to nothing. Men of the 1st Iowa Cavalry—who may have been punished for their attempt to go home—were not discharged until March 16, 1866. [OR I, 41, II, 474; D, 3, 1158]

July—1st Arkansas Cavalry

Attorney John B. Sanborn had no military training or experience. After organizing five infantry regiments, a cavalry battalion and two artillery battalions in Minnesota he became a colonel on December 23, 1861. He was made a brigadier in August, 1863, and took command of the District of Southwest Missouri a few weeks later.

On July 23, 1864, he admitted to Lt. Col. Hugh Cameron, commander of the post at Cassville, that he was "very much chagrined." Writing from Springfield in response to news from Cassville, he said that open mutiny in a regiment under his command was a new experience for him. Referring to the 1st Arkansas Cavalry, he said that he was sure that all efforts to restore discipline had been made "in the wrong direction."

Sanborn said he was positive that "so disgraceful a manifestation of the want of all discipline as open mutiny" wouldn't have occurred had officers taken proper steps. Noting his certainty that there had been "a want of all discipline" in the regiment, he promised Cameron that he'd be backed in all efforts "to enforce discipline and order."

Without knowing what his commander regarded as "proper steps," Cameron was clearly expected to take them immediately. This meant that, like many another commander, he received a scolding but got no guidance concerning the handling of mutiny. [OR I, 41, II, 361-62]

August—Rebels in Western Virginia

Virginia attorney John Echols became a brigadier on April 16, 1862, after his regiment gained fame as a member of the Stonewall Brigade. With more than two years of experience as a commander behind him, he was named head of the Confederate Department of Western Virginia and East Tennessee. His first report to Richmond, dispatched early in September, painted a dismal picture.

After only a week in command he had found that the department was "in the worst possible condition." At least six hundred soldiers had no weapons, so he dismissed them as "valueless." Many of his regiments and battalions had lost so many men in combat and to disease that he considered them to be fragments, only. About two weeks before he arrived at his new headquarters men of one regiment had "refused to obey an order to move from their then location, and mutinied."

This disaffection gave numerous men plus an unidentified captain an opportunity to turn their backs upon those members of the regiment who remained loyal. Echols had issued orders for an active manhunt for the absentee captain and had taken what he considered suitable steps to "insure a better state of discipline."

He said it was imperative that he have immediate help in order to thoroughly organize scattered units whose members knew that some of their comrades had staged a successful mutiny. He requested Gen. Samuel Cooper in Richmond quickly to send him "one or two rigid and experienced inspectors." Until he could bring about "better organization and discipline," he warned, the enemy was likely to take advantage of the confusion in the department. His extremely long dispatch ended with a repetition of the plea voiced earlier. The inspector he needed should be sent as soon as possible, he said.

Though there is no record that he sent a copy of his appeal to Robert E. Lee, he must have done so. On September 10 the commander of the Army of Northern Virginia knew of the emergency because he told Richmond he hoped that an experienced officer with whom he was acquainted could be sent to the troubled department immediately. "The importance of having an able and experienced inspector with General Echols is very great and the necessity urgent," he said.

Since he was a native of Virginia, Echols may have known that even when supported by Lee his appeal would be futile. Richmond did not have the resources with which to respond quickly—if at all—

to emergencies in the field, even in the aftermath of mutiny. Throughout much of the South as well as the North, the pervasive judgment that the Confederacy was in its death throes would soon prove to be correct. [OR I, 43, II, 864-66]

August—The Mississippi Marine Brigade

No other unit in blue or in gray was quite like the Mississippi Marine Brigade. High-ranking military and naval officers plus members of Lincoln's cabinet were deeply involved in nearly two years of jealousy and intrigue concerning the unique body of fighting men commanded by Gen. Alfred W. Ellett. Formally organized on November 1, 1862, the brigade of more than 1,000 men operated a fleet of rams designed and built by Col. Charles Ellett. Activities of Ellett and his men fill scores of pages in both the OR (volumes 10, 19, 21, 24-24, 32-38, 50-59, 72-79, 83-85, 109-10, 118, 1123-25) and the NOR (volumes 20, 23-26)].

Treated as an amphibious force within the army, the brigade was nominally under the control of Acting Rear Adm. David D. Porter. Partly due to astute work by the Ellett, partly because secretaries of the army and of the navy were perpetually at odds, the Marine Brigade actually operated in near autonomy. Ellett reported, not to Porter, but to Stanton in Washington. This despite the fact that Gideon Welles and the Department of the Navy were responsible for routine care of the fleet of rams and their operations.

Built near St. Louis with what was widely regarded as incredible speed, the Ellett rams took to the Mississippi and other rivers in March, 1861, before they were owned by the U.S. government. Squabbling between army and navy officials over control of the river fleet began before the first of the vessels hit the water. By November Washington insiders tried to avoid mention of these craft, fearing that they might be drawn into the bitter conflict at the cabinet level. Lincoln tried to end the inter-service quarrel by personally naming General Ellett to take charge of the craft and the men who would make up the brand-new Marine Brigade for river service. [E, 238; Welles, 1, 180]

The rams were already in use, but in order to put the brigade into action Ellett needed men—lots of them. Early efforts to find 1,500 volunteers proved futile. Since the new unit was not attached to any state, no bounty was offered for enlistment in it. Initially baffled by the fact that increasingly large bounties paid to military recruits made his own recruitment efforts useless, Ellett had what he and others considered to be a splendid idea.

Thousands of military veterans were convalescing in hospitals of the Western Theater. All of them belonged to established

Some of the Ellett rams, whose operation required a large number of men
Harper's Weekly

regiments, so they were not eligible for bounties under any circumstances. Ellett therefore decided to offer inducements in lieu of cash. He promised that men who agreed to fight under him would have none of the unpleasant duties associated with life in the field. Instead of facing the possibility of sleeping in severe weather without cover, men would find themselves in "sturdy and comfortable bunks" every night. [Abel, 54–56]

Men aboard an Ellett ram would have no trenches to dig, no long marches in pouring rain, and absolutely no picket duty. By enlisting in the marines, its commander promised, a veteran could simultaneously serve his country and look after his personal comfort. Inducements that collectively added up to what Ellett termed "soldiering made easy" brought a flood of volunteers to St. Louis and by March, 1863, the brigade was ready to go into action.

Very soon, friction between Ellett and Porter reached a lofty level. The naval officer thought he had solved many of the difficulties when he relieved the ship-based brigadier from command. His directive was soon countermanded in Washington, however, where Ellett was restored to command by order of the War Department.

U. S. Grant became general in chief with the rank of lieutenant general in March, 1864. At that time he knew little if anything about the Marine Brigade and it role in minor conflicts with Rebels. Acting upon the advice of Porter, he decided to appropriate the rams for his own use and to send men of the brigade into regiments on land. In Washington, Stanton gave conditional approval to this plan but noted that enlistment contracts of the marines were unique. This factor might lead to wholesale dismissal of marines from military service if transfers of men to land were not handled with great care and accuracy, he warned.

Gen. Edward Canby, who was in command of the Division of West Mississippi, eventually received instructions to send the marines back to the military units they left upon joining the new brigade. Before acting on this order he thought it wise to examine typical enlistment contracts into which marines had entered. A single reading left him stunned by the realization that every marine had been formally discharged from his former regiments before entering the new river service. Believing that this factor left him no other alternative, he decided to turn the entire Mississippi Marine Brigade into a new military regiment under the command of Col. F. A. Starring of the 2nd Illinois, then leading the First Brigade.

This impending action triggered mutiny on the part of 45 to 60 marines. Defying orders, they let it be known that they intended to stay aboard a ram anchored at Vicksburg and that they had no intention of returning to service on land. Realizing that he faced what amounted to an insurrection, Canby acted decisively to restore order. He called for and quickly got an infantry and a cavalry regiment with which to face down the mutineers. Subdued, they and their comrades called "equally mutinous" walked down gangplanks and marched to a nearby camp.

About 48 mutineers were placed under guard and confined in a prison. Along with their comrades, they formed a new regiment that Starring characterized as "demoralized, insubordinate, undisciplined, and grossly ignorant." In doing so, however, he conceded that its members who came from "every state in the Union" had received no bounties. He registered doubt that as a unit the new regiment would "ever be of any benefit or service whatever." Consequently he recommended that its members be mustered out and permitted to reenlist in infantry or cavalry regiments as they chose. [OR I, 39, II, 320]

Starring's recommendation was not heeded; formation of the new regiment was completed and some who had rebelled against authority were included in it from the start. Though these and other mutineers were unwilling to risk death from rifles and carbines of soldiers, they were not ready to give unquestioning obedience to orders. They passed the hat and collected several hundred dollars—enough to serve as a retainer for a noted attorney.

James Pursy took the unique case and after having mastered details concerning the enlistment of the marines managed to get to Washington. Pursy's name does not appear in the *Collected Works* of the President or in a day-by-day chronicle of his activities. Oral tradition insists, however, that the Mississippi attorney saw Lincoln and convinced him that the law was on the side of the marines. Whether or not that was the precise sequence of events that took place in the capital, the President signed an order on December 5 and former members of the Marine Brigade were immediately discharged. [E, 501]

September—Unidentified Rebels

Scouts and raiders on both sides typically captured enemy mail when they could. Letters seized in this fashion sometimes provided information that would not have been found otherwise. That was the case with a shipment of Rebel mail that was captured by Federals near St. Joseph, Louisiana. It was en route to Richmond from Texas, and Gen. Edward R. S. Canby identified the writer as the wife of an officer on the staff of Rebel Gen. Kirby Smith.

According to the Confederate woman, military leaders had found it impossible to obey an order from the secretary of war. In Richmond, plans had been made to send large bodies of infantry across the Mississippi River so that they could augment forces led by Gen. John B. Hood. Federal discovery of this plan was said to have led to patrolling of the river that was so constant it was impossible to send troops across.

According to the analyst of affairs in the region, the order that would have sent hosts of men into the far West "was productive of great evil" even though it was not implemented. Thousands of soldiers in gray were described as having "positively refused to leave their homes and families to go so far, and thus mutiny, disorganization and demoralization followed."

Canby took the news included in the letter very seriously. From his New Orleans headquarters, he wrote that Federal leaders had earlier considered the disaffection to which the writer referred as having been confined to Texas troops. A short time later he conceded that "it appears to have been more extensive." Despite the mutiny and demoralization produced by the order from the Rebel capital, Canby thought that "The attempt to cross will no doubt be made." [OR I, 18, 697–99; OR I, 41, III, 355; OR I, 41, IV, 232]

September 15—6th Missouri Cavalry Members on a Tear

During much of the war, St. Louis was filled with soldiers. Some were stationed in or near the city; many others stayed there a day or two when moving from one point to another. Even Gen. Thomas Ewing, Jr., a native of the river port, seldom knew what regiments and brigades were at hand.

On September 16 Charles C. Whitewalls, secretary of the state's central Democratic committee registered a strong protest with Gen. William S. Rosecrans who was in command of the Department of the Missouri. A motley band of soldiers assembled near the Lindell Hotel, the Democrat said, for the express purpose of breaking up a meeting of the McClellan Club. With the presidential election looming, backers of the former Federal general fervently hoped he'd win the White House.

Basing his verdict upon the Articles of War, Whittlesey characterized rioters in uniform as "mutinous and lawless." Accompanied by some civilians, he said, these men rushed the speaker's stand in order to take off with a flag plus a locomotive headlight. Bystanders swore that they heard some of the soldiers say that "The general cannot control us; he has tried that once before."

Numerous witnesses believed they could identify some of the rioters if given a chance to do so. Their principal accuser disparaged the men by saying that they were very brave in attacking an unarmed crowd, but "would be careful before an armed enemy."

Charged with making a formal investigation, Col. J. H. Baker of the 10th Minnesota had more than 90 men arrested and interrogated. Most were members of the 6th Missouri Cavalry, but a few came from the 10th Kansas and from a body locally familiar as Merrill's Horse.

Lt. F. W. Becker, assistant to the chief of ordnance, had been named by civilians as a leader in the riot that some who watched it termed a mutiny. Becker swore he was innocent, and persons who had been bystanders failed to recognize him. After accumulating a large body of testimony, Baker found it "extraordinary that the guilty parties cannot be identified." He ventured to guess that this situation grew out of the fact that "soldiers make it a point of honor to shield each other in matters of this kind."

Without echoing the inflammatory label "mutiny," Baker deplored what had taken place and had General Order No. 11 issued as a guideline for soldiers wishing to attend political meetings. He promised to continue his efforts "to apprehend the guilty and bring them to punishment," but did not indicate hope that he would be successful. [OR I, 41, III, 224-29]

September 20—Rebel Raiders

Virginia native John Y. Beall scored several impressive triumphs as a Rebel adventurer. Though he enrolled as an infantry private and fought briefly in that role, he soon revealed an unusual capacity to frame elaborate schemes. While recuperating from a bullet wound he persuaded men higher up to have him released from military service so he could enter the C.S. Navy and try out some of his ideas. One of them involved freeing prisoners at Johnson's Island, Ohio, from a Canadian base. He didn't get an opportunity to try this scheme when first assigned to a ship, however.

Putting the Johnson's Island plot on hold, he became an acting master in the naval service and scored several triumphs in and around Chesapeake Bay. When he was arrested and put on trial as a spy,

Rebel leaders made skillful use of Union hostages and Beall was freed on May 5, 1864. He immediately revived his plan to free thousands of imprisoned Confederate officers and this time revealed it to C.S. Comr. Jacob Thompson in Canada.

Thompson, who knew that a clause in an old treaty limited the United States to a single warship on Lake Erie, believed that Beall's idea was workable. C.S. Capt. Charles Cole was sent to Sandusky, very close to the island prison, where he posed as heir to a great Philadelphia fortune. He became intimately acquainted with officers of the USS *Michigan,* the only formidable obstacle to Beall's success. On the night set for capture of the warship, Cole planned to drug wine that he would serve to his Federal friends. This phase of the plot was abandoned when Cole was betrayed, allegedly by an ambitious Confederate officer.

Unaware of what was taking place in and near Sandusky, Beall and his men boarded the steamer *Philo Parsons* at Detroit. This 220-ton vessel made regular runs between Detroit and Sandusky, so if it could be seized the Rebel raiders could keep her on course and everything would seem normal. On her voyage of September 19, the ship carried 60 passengers in addition to the 19 Confederates who had come aboard at various small Canadian villages.

When within about five miles of their destination, the Rebels pulled out concealed weapons and took possession of the *Philo Parsons* in the name of the Confederate States of America. Soon the vessel was

The USS *Michigan,* only a warship on the Great Lakes

U.S. Naval Historical Center

cleared for action and hove in sight of the mouth of Sandusky Bay. Moving slowly, the raiders watched eagerly for the expected signal to board the 14-gun USS *Michigan*. Though the signal never came, the craft taken over by Beall reputedly advanced under the guns of the warship.

At this crucial moment, carefully picked men serving under Beall decided that in the absence of the expected signal the venture was hopeless. Seventeen of them mutinied and the plan to free the prisoners on Johnson's Island had to be abandoned. Had his men remained faithful and obedient, no one knows what the outcome of the raid would have been. Forced by the mutiny to turn the *Philo Parsons* back toward Detroit, Beall was soon in captivity. Tried by a court-martial as a spy, he was convicted and went to his execution on February 24, 1865. He died believing that had it not been for the mutiny he would somehow have managed to bring at least one boatload of Rebel officers from their prison. [CV, 20, 67; CWT, 11/61, 24; Axelrod, 239-43; JSHS, 33, 74-76; WWW 42; Miller, 8, 298]

C.S. Raider John Y. Beall, whose greatest exploit was foiled by mutiny
Popular History of the Civil War

September 22—13th Virginia, C.S.

Mutinous conduct in battle was seldom treated with the severity that followed refusal to obey orders during encampments. That was the case at Fisher's Hill, Virginia. Heavy fighting at the site named for land- and mill-owner David Fisher went on for hours without anything resembling victory by either force.

C.S. Gen. Jubal Early fretted to his aides that U.S. Gen. Philip Sheridan had something up his sleeve and could be expected to hit very hard at an unexpected point. Events soon proved that his hunch was right. Two divisions under veteran Indian fighter Gen. George Crook managed to get upon the field of battle without being seen. At a signal, men in blue dashed down a slope covered with huge boulders somewhat like those that gave Devil's Den at Gettysburg its name.

Officers and men of Crook's command easily swept over lightly manned Rebel breastworks and moved steadily forward. A series of ridges covered with shrubs and small trees lay behind this line, and

Gen. Bryan Grimes tried to make a stand on the highest of these spots. He had only three regiments of Tar Heels with which to try to stop the Yankee attack, however.

When an estimated six thousand men in blue came screaming up the ridge, members of the North Carolina units broke and ran just as Early reached the site. Furious, the Confederate leader turned to the 13th Virginia and directed its members to fire upon their comrades who were headed toward the rear as fast as they could go. To the astonishment and chagrin of Early, men from the Old Dominion disobeyed his order. Instead of firing as directed, they looked at onrushing Federal troops for an instant and then took to their heels behind the North Carolina regiments.

Had several hundred members of a regiment openly defied an order given to them under other conditions, "Old Jubal" would have had some of their heads on a platter. In view of the crisis situation in which his authority was tested, he made no attempt to punish Virginians who had refused obedience or North Carolinians who had disobeyed commands to hold the position at all costs.

September 13—Crew of the CSS Florida

Blockade running had dwindled to an occasional voyage because the Federal blockade was now extremely hard to penetrate. Commercial traffic on the seas remained at a fairly high level, however. Confederate warships and raiders were constantly on the lookout for a vessel that could be seized. When such a ship and its cargo were sold in a prize court, officers and men who captured it divided the money according to a complex formula.

As late as August, the *Electric Spark* was a U.S. mail steamer in the New York to New Orleans trade. That made her a legitimate target for Rebel seamen, and she was captured by the CSS *Florida*. The log of the warship indicates that the mail steamer carried "a valuable cargo, 42 passengers, and crew of 39." Three Federal officers who were among her passengers were sent to New York in an English schooner.

With her prize in tow, the *Florida* was presumably headed toward a Rebel port when Midshipman William B. Sinclair drowned while trying to go from one vessel to the other aboard a cutter. Benjamin Moran, secretary of the U.S. legation in London, relayed news about the two ships to Com. T. T. Craven of the U.S. Navy in early October.

An English vessel had fallen in with them on September 13, and had found the crew of the warship in a state of mutiny. Believed to be very short of supplies and ammunition, there was some evidence that war-weary members of the crew hoped to take her to a neutral port.

Whatever the intentions of mutineers may have been, the *Florida* was at Bahia, Brazil, in early November. She was seized there by the USS *Wachusett*, and almost immediately sank in port during what men of the U.S. Navy called an accident. The capture in Brazilian waters was an international incident that created considerable excitement in Europe. In the turmoil over whether or not the U.S. warship had violated Brazil's neutrality and had then scuttled the *Florida*, no attention was paid to the crew of the Confederate vessel. [NOR II, 2, 2, 764–65, 818; NOR II, 3, 345, 623, 646, 712, 1242, 1246, 1249, 1262]

November—Gen. Sterling Price

Ex-governor Sterling Price did everything in his power to take Missouri into the Confederacy. After having been in the thick of the fight at Wilson's Creek, he captured Lexington before retreating into Arkansas. After being made a major general, he fought at Iuka, Corinth, Helena, and the Red River. In September, 1864, he led cavalry into Missouri on a raid that lasted several weeks.

Forced to retreat into Kansas, Price lost two brigadiers, more than nine hundred men, and a dozen guns at Marais des Cygnes on October 25. His remaining men followed him on a lengthy journey through the Indian Territory to what they considered safety in Arkansas. Though the famous Missouri raid was a failure, Federal leaders in the state watched his movement closely.

From Springfield, an elated Gen. John B. Sanborn sent a report to Gen. William S. Rosecrans on November 12. According to it, the ex-governor would have been guilty of mutiny had he been an enlisted man who "repeatedly stated that he would not and could not be compelled to fight any more." About six months later Price fled into Mexico, but returned to Missouri "broken and impoverished" when the government of Maximilian was overthrown. [OR I, 41, IV, 545–46; GG, 247; B, 669; WWW, 523-24]

October—Col. Frank M. Tracy

Locally known as the Doniphan County Regiment, the 9th Kansas was a militia unit that was called into service at the time of Price's Missouri Raid. Reportedly headed toward Atchison from Kansas City in mid October, the regiment was needed by U.S. Gen. Samuel Curtis. When the unit was told to halt, its commander responded that he was under orders from another commander.

Curtis checked with Gen. George W. Deitzler at Independence, Missouri, and found that he did not claim responsibility for the 9th Kansas. Consequently Curtis had Special Order No. 125 issued as a directive that Col. Frank M. Tracy and his men should proceed immediately to Wyandotte. At Fort Leavenworth, Gen. Thomas A. Davies relayed the order to Tracy. From Atchison, the militia officer retorted with a question: "Am I subject to the orders of Brigadier-General [Byron] Sherry at this place?"

By this time Curtis was explosively angry and, unlike many commanders, made few distinctions between officers and men who refused to obey orders. Calling members of the entire regiment "great cowards," on October 18 he directed Davies to arrest Tracy and "place him in close confinement at the fort." In addition, instructed Curtis, "send forward the command, arresting every officer in turn who refuses to obey the order to march to the front."

Lines of command that governed state and federal forces were far from clear. In this instance, a major general's expressed intention of punishing mutineers seems to have had no effect upon leaders of the militia. On October 26, Tracy and his men were again at Leavenworth but were not under arrest. Instead, Gov. Thomas Carney informed Lt. Col. W. H. Stark that the regiment was on the way home and requested him to provide transportation to Saint Joseph. [OR I, 41, IV, 60–61, 96–98, 148, 256]

October 18—Col. James J. Neely, C.S.

Tennessee native James J. Neely donned a gray uniform in the immediate aftermath of Fort Sumter. Initially a captain in the 6th Tennessee Cavalry, C.S., he later won appointment as a first lieutenant of artillery in the permanent army. Retaining his place in the cavalry, he was disgruntled when the battalion he led was merged with other companies in order to form a new regiment.

Reorganization of units left the captain with a commission but no troops. He requested and received approval for a plan to go behind Union lines in western Tennessee in order to try to raise recruits. Though the region was heavily Unionist, he managed to find enough men to form a regiment and upon organization of the 14th Tennessee Cavalry became its colonel and commander.

Brig. Gen. Robert W. Richardson and his men served under Gen. Nathan Bedford Forrest during much of the summer of 1864. Meanwhile another Tennessee unit, the 16th Cavalry Battalion, saw a great deal of action. Led by Col. E. W. Rucker, it was sometimes identified as Rucker's Legion but was also listed as the 1st Tennessee Legion.

With the dissolution of his legion impending, was ordered to the 6th Brigade on June 13, 1864. Soon the 14th Tennessee Cavalry was incorporated into Rucker's Brigade. Consequently, Neely was relieved by Rucker in August. The officer whose command had been taken away from him twice protested with great vehemence. His attempt to keep his command became a complicated power struggle that is most clearly revealed in pages of *The Confederate Veteran.*

Before it ended, Neely was charged with disobedience and having incited a mutiny. As a result, on October 18 he became one of the few officers on either side who was cashiered for having made trouble.

Many of the officers of the 14th Tennessee Cavalry had been persuaded by Neely to join him in opposition to Rucker. They were not charged with mutiny, but the uproar they created was so great that the majority of them were arrested and suspended from command. [OR I, 4, 509; CV, 4, 178; 6, 435–36; 8, 401, 403, 405; 10, 150; 11, 112; 12, 277; 16, 562; 19, 584; 20, 473; 29, 431; 31, 278; 32, 270, 479; 34, 218–20; 36, 256; WWW, 208, 559]

December 18—3rd Missouri

U.S. Col. Chester Harding was at St. Joseph, Missouri, on December 15. He left for Kansas City with 130 officers and men of his 3rd Missouri who had been captured and later paroled. Bad weather plus repeated derailments of the train on which they were traveling made progress of the body very slow.

During a severe night Harding discovered that many of the men he was taking with him had entered into a covenant. Fearful that they were about to be made to cross the frozen Missouri River, many soldiers had vowed to mutiny if such an order was received.

The colonel, who had not anticipated such a development, had cautiously kept one totally loyal company in reserve. With this body behind them, men of only one "disaffected" unit gave silent signals that they would refuse to go forward. At Harding's signal, members of his reserve company fixed bayonets and marched down the riverbank.

Reporting about the incident, he said that the movement of men whose bayonets were at the ready "settled the matter." Many mutineers had been confined in St. Joseph and within a day or two the majority of them expressed penitence. None had yet been arraigned for trial, so their colonel requested permission to withdraw charges and bring them back into service. His lengthy dispatch to Gen. Clinton B. Fisk that ended with a request drew an eight-word reply: "Release the mutineers and order them to duty." [OR I, 41, IV, 890–91]

26

1865–Well Past Appomattox, Durham Station, and Palmito Ranch

January—"No Consolidation!"

At least five hundred thousand men in gray and in blue had now been killed in combat or had succumbed to illness. Untold numbers of others had been voluntarily or involuntarily discharged because their wounds made it impossible for them to be effective. An estimated 1,500,000 men had deserted. Large numbers of them had been captured or had returned to their ranks voluntarily, but tens of thousands were still at large.

Collectively, death plus incapacitating wounds and desertion had blown gaping holes in companies, brigades, regiments, divisions, corps, and armies. Though only a small percent of Rebel officers and men still held out hope, leaders on both sides knew that the fight to the finish was not over. Hence lawmakers in Washington and in Richmond tinkered with military structures by enacting measures designed to compel decimated units to consolidate.

This process, which appeared wholly reasonable to congressmen and senators, was aimed at filling the ranks of some units and disbanding others in the name of efficiency. Along with various forms of reorganization, it had already seen limited use by military commanders. Now it seemed sure to become all but universal.

Many commanders saw the great advantages that would accrue from consolidation and supported it in principle—but not in practice if the existence of their own units was threatened. Rank and file fighting men on both sides were bitterly opposed to these moves. Almost all regiments were state-orientated, initially made up largely of officers and men from a single state who were sure that they had much in common with their comrades.

278

C.S. Gen. James Longstreet warned Robert E. Lee that consolidation could have serious side effects.
Harper's History of the United States

During month after month of combat, men who remained in the ranks of a unit had undergone a process that might be termed "psychic welding together." Having marched, forded streams, experienced empty stomachs and cartridge boxes and dodged enemy bullets and shells together, they were bitterly opposed to being separated or being forced to accept strangers into their ranks.

A consolidation bill passed the C.S. House of Representatives on January 10. That very day, C.S. Gen. James Longstreet dispatched a lengthy warning to Lee, who supported the concept of breaking up regiments and organizing new ones. "Lee's War Horse," who often differed with his chief, predicted that every new appointment made would lead to the loss of a man.

Members of the U.S. House of Representatives passed consolidation legislation without hesitation.

Library of Congress

If that happened, he pointed out, consolidation would not result in a net increase in strength of fighting forces. At Wilmington, North Carolina, George H. Sharpe did not know Longstreet's views. Writing to Richmond, however, he pointed out that "the consolidation bill makes the officers angry and they incite the soldiers to mutiny."

Opponents of consolidation had good reason to fear it. During the final months of the war shouts of "No consolidation! No consolidation!" echoed wherever significant numbers of fighting men on either side were gathered. At least as much as any other factor, Federal and Confederate steps taken in the name of consolidation triggered bitter opposition and open mutiny during final months of the war. Since a change of officers or geographical location had many of the same subjective effects as consolidation, these changes were bitterly and often violently resisted throughout all armies. [OR I, 46, II, 132-33; OR I, 48, I, 1321]

January—16th Kansas Cavalry

From Fort Larned, Kansas, Col. James H. Ford sent a request to headquarters of the District of Kansas on January 8. Charged with keeping native American tribesmen subdued, he requested a radical change for the 16th Kansas Cavalry. He wanted officers and men of the regiment sent to him with a promise that they'd be "entirely foot loose from post duty." That would enable them, said Ford, to "live on the plains all the time, same as Indians, coming into the post only for rations." [OR I, 48, I, 461-62]

Within weeks the regiment ordered to move out of familiar territory had stopped at Council Grove, and members of Co. D were "in a partial state of mutiny." From Fort Riley, officers of the 2nd Colorado Cavalry were ordered to go to Council Grove "investigate the affair, arresting all the guilty parties, sending them to Fort Riley for trial." Having been given this special task, men of the Colorado unit were authorized "if necessary, to arrest the whole company and the captain." [OR I, 48, I, 763, 817]

Upon reaching the troubled post, the unit sent to restore order found things worse than they expected. A February dispatch included one of the understatements of the year, indicating that Kansans were "in a partial state of mutiny, having shot the lieutenant of their company (mortally wounding him)." It developed that eight enlisted men had fired on the lieutenant. Their captain knew what had taken place but did nothing about it. Men of the regiment were in the process of trying to burn down the town when the Colorado company arrived. [OR I, 48, I, 74-75, 796-97]

The fate of men who were "partially mutinous" was not recorded, but early in March 47 stragglers from the regiment were directed to escort two hundred horses to Fort Kearney. Plans for a raid upon Indians in the region of the Black Hills were changed because "for some accountable reason, not yet explained, the Sixteenth Kansas Cavalry was over two months reaching their destination." By June the number of mounted men of this regiment who were on hand for action against tribesmen had dropped to seven.

Later rejoined by about 75 stragglers, men of the unit who had been ordered to make a drastic change in location were no better satisfied than they had been early in the year. At Fort Laramie what was left of the regiment staged a July 30 mutiny that was quelled by an officer who "did his talking" with two howitzers. Four months after Appomattox, seven ringleaders of the rebellion in ranks of the 16th Kansas Cavalry were in irons waiting for trial. [OR I, 48, I, 331, 1080, 1145]

January 20—Prisoners in Castle Morgan

A report by the commandant of the Caaba, Alabama, Confederate prison known as Castle Morgan provided a detailed account of incidents that took place this day. Capt. H. A. M. Henderson said that inmate George Scholar, a civilian, led a small group of men who tried to escape some time after 3:00 A.M. Guards were overpowered, then dragged to the latrine and locked up there. Using weapons they had seized from guards, the men described as mutineers told other inmates what they had done and asked for help in rushing the gate of the prison.

"Scholar" was later found to be Capt. Hiram Hachette of the 16th Illinois Cavalry. He had been captured by Confederate cavalry late in November, 1864. Somehow he managed to exchange his Yankee uniform for nondescript civilian clothing. Apparently Hachette had concealed his identity too well; except for a handful of intimates, other prisoners did not know that he was a military officer in disguise. Suspicious of his invitation to help effect a break, most refused to have anything to do with it.

Hachette and his close colleagues didn't constitute a force powerful enough to charge the gate. Two sentinels posted there sensed trouble, however, and ran for help. Soon the mutineers found themselves facing a gun of undetermined size that they were told held a double load of canister. With the attempted break foiled, prison officials mounted an intense hunt for leaders of the foray and soon identified "Scholar." He and seven of his close associates were put in irons and thrown into a tiny dungeon below the town jail.

Eventually the matter came to the attention of Gen. John D. Imboden, who commanded all Rebel prisons of the region that lay west of the Savannah River. After a detailed inquiry into the incident, Imboden ordered seven of the mutineers to be released and returned to the general population of the prison. Fearing that Hachette still had not told the truth about his background and capture, the Rebel commander directed that he be held for trial—not as a prisoner/mutineer, but as a spy.

Soon, however, General Order No. 2 was issued from the Augusta, Georgia, headquarters of C.S. Military Prisons of the region. Under its terms, any inmate of a prison in Georgia, Alabama, or Mississippi who tried to escape was branded as a mutineer. Guards were authorized instantly to fire upon such persons or "the whole body of prisoners" they represented until "perfect order" was restored. Any prisoner found with a weapon in his hands at the time of a mutiny or forcible attempt to escape was ordered to be "instantly shot to death." [OR II, 8, 117–23; CWT, 11/82, 18]

February 11—Rebels Encamped at Asheville, North Carolina

Capt. George Tait of the 69th North Carolina was put in charge of an encampment that held men from an unidentified regiment. He reached Asheville on February 11 and was surprised to be "shown a very cold shoulder." Within hours after having taken command he found a mutiny to be in progress and tried to quell it without the use of force.

Hit in the head by a large rock, the unarmed officer was momentarily knocked senseless. Soon he recovered enough to look around and find that what he called "the insubordination" included the entire camp.

Tait fired off a detailed report to Gov. Zebulon Vance in which he said that "the cowardly manner in which the regiment acted" would prevent him for ever feeling "the love and respect" for it that he should. His complaint went to the capital in Raleigh rather than to an army commander. Were there no other record this would show that mutineers were members of a state militia force.

The colonel seems to have believed that the mutiny was directed at Vance rather than at him. "I cannot command a mob who would dare to strike you through me," he said, "for there can be no personal prejudice against me. Since five officers and 125 men of the 69th North Carolina state troops deserted at Asheville two weeks later, this regiment must have been the mutinous body over which Tait tried without success to take control. [OR I, 47, II, 1178–79; OR I, 49, I, 1034]

February—Officers Serving Under C.S. Gen. Nathan B. Forrest

Gen. Nathan B. Forrest had urgent business that required his presence in Mobile, Alabama, during the second month of the year. Just prior to leaving his men he announced that a "supernumerary officer" would be in command during his absence. This was being

Nathan B. Forrest was the only soldier who rose in rank from private to lieutenant general.

done, he explained, because Maj. Philip T. Allen was still recovering from a wound received at Moscow, Mississippi.

According to Capt. J. C. Blanton, numerous officers who served under Forrest considered the action of their commander to constitute an affront to Allen. One of them later said that "We felt it our duty to contend for the rights of our wounded brother officer." They did so by protesting the temporary arrangement and refusing to obey orders.

When Forrest rejoined his battalion, he placed all of the insurgent officers under arrest and charged them with mutiny. Almost immediately, however, he restored Allen to command. Mutineers signified readiness to obey Allen, so they were quickly released and "were ready for battle again." [CV, 3, 77–78]

March 9—Prisoners of War

Musketry and some artillery shots were heard in Federal outposts about one and one-half miles from Manchester, Virginia, at 8:00 P.M. on March 9. The sounds of firing continued for about an hour and one-half. U.S. Gen. E. O. C. Ord, reporting to U. S. Grant about the incident, said he got information from a deserter. According to this unidentified fellow, returned prisoners of war had refused to obey orders that directed them to go on duty without a furlough. As a result of this mutiny, men who had spent months in prison were said to have been fired upon by fellow Rebels who tried to compel them to obey. [OR I, 46, II, 917]

April 8—A Detachment of the U.S. XV Corps

Sporadic action took place in South Carolina during the final phase of Robert E. Lee's withdrawal from the Army of the Potomac. At Pocotaligo, a soldier allegedly fired his gun without orders. Colonel Henry reacted by having him tied hand and foot.

Cpl. Lucius W. Barber of the 15th Illinois described subsequent events in detail. His company having been organized at Marengo, Illinois, in early May, 1861, Barber had seen a great deal of action. He found, however, that four years of war had not hardened him to some of the things that a man in uniform could experience in camp.

Though he did not take part in the mutiny, Barber watched as a body of about 20 men descended upon Henry's headquarters and demanded that he release the man in bondage. Instead of doing so, the colonel ordered them to stack arms. They paid no attention to what he said, so Henry whipped out his pistol and promised to shoot the first man who didn't do as commanded.

Surprisingly, a single officer with a revolver cowed the band of mutineers, all of whom were quickly put under arrest. Great excitement prevailed throughout the encampment, and soon an estimated four hundred men were milling about Henry's headquarters. He knew that they had come to release the prisoner, so he sent a hurried request to an officer of the XVII Corps.

Barber was among the men sent in response to the call for help. He and his comrades seized their weapons and hurried to the scene of the confrontation. On the way many of them, including the Illinois sergeant, made up their minds that they'd "never shed the blood of our brother soldiers" in the XV Corps. Their arrival served to cool things down, however.

Henry ordered mutineers with the exception of the man considered to be their ringleader to be released. According to Barber the instigator was given a trial and was condemned to go before a firing squad. Subsequent military action prevented him from learning whether or not the sentence was carried out. [Quoted, Denney, *Civil War Years*, 556]

May 3—C.S. Troops Escorting Jefferson Davis

Jefferson Davis fled from Richmond when he received news of Lee's surrender at Appomattox. A number of Confederate officials accompanied him, and they took along what gold was left in the Treasury. He initially hoped to make quick contact with Rebel forces in the Deep South and personally to take command of them. When he found that this scheme was impracticable, he decided to head toward Mexico.

A few miles south of Abbeville, South Carolina, some members of his escort mutinied on May 3 and demanded immediate payment of wages due. When nothing was done to satisfy them, they reportedly broke open the chests of gold that were being carried in wagons. Gen. John C. Breckinridge, secretary of war, rode upon the scene and appealed to the mutineers by reminding them that they were still Confederate soldiers.

They paid no attention to him or to anyone else. Oral tradition says that Davis turned back and tried to restore order, but failed. Mutineers, who made no effort to divide their loot equally among themselves, quickly took off with the gold. Those members of the escort who remained loyal rode with Davis and his aides toward Washington, Georgia.

Some analysts hold that the amount of gold taken from Richmond was substantial, and that its disappearance was due to the mutineers. Others are of the opinion that a very small amount of precious metal remained in the Confederate capital at war's end and that it was largely used to pay expenses incurred by Davis and his entourage. [CWT, 5/65, 35]

May 21—1st New York Engineers

With the war over, men in blue expected to go home at once. Some commanders insisted that they needed their men and refused to release them. At Key West, Florida, Gen. J. M. Brannan received mutineers belonging to the 1st New York Engineer Regiment on May 21. He had them put into Fort Taylor as prisoners, but planned to put them to work. Any who refused to work would be made to "undergo such punishment as they may deserve," he reported to the headquarters of the Southern District at Hilton Head, South Carolina. [OR I, 14, 344]

May—Men of the XXV Corps

C.S. Gen. Joseph E. Johnston, who led the last large Confederate force, surrendered to Sherman at Durham Station, North Carolina, on April 18. A handful of Rebels were later engaged at Palmito Ranch, Texas, where the last officially recognized shot was fired on May 13.

Shortly before or after the skirmish in Texas most black soldiers still in uniform were brought together at City Point, Virginia. According to 2nd Lt. Frederick W. Browne of the 1st U.S. Colored Cavalry, this was the place at which the new XXV Corps was organized. It was not officially created until December 3, however. Semi-official word had it that the entire body of troops would soon go to Mexico in order to fight the French and the Emperor Maximilian.

Jefferson Davis and entourage, headed toward Washington, Georgia
Leslie's Illustrated Weekly

Scuttlebutt warned that the new unit whose ranks included many ex-slaves would be sent South "to work on the cotton plantations to pay the national debt."

Rumors plus fanciful tales that circulated in abundance created a great deal of ill will among these soldiers. About half of the regiment in which Browne served went aboard a small river steamer, said to be headed toward Hampton Roads. The journey down the James River had barely started when men on the lower deck began firing at objects on shore. Browne, who was on the upper deck, pulled his revolver and started down to put an end to the shooting.

According to one of the most vivid of first-person accounts of mutiny, soon after he started down the steps a dozen carbines were pressed against his head and chest. Mutineers told him that he might kill one of their comrades, but if he managed to do so that would be the last man he'd ever kill. Forced to return to the upper deck, he and the mutineers reached Hampton Roads and went aboard the *Meteor*. There the lieutenant learned that the other half of the regiment had also mutinied while moving down the river.

Aboard the *Meteor*, men swapped accounts of their exploits and then "just went wild." To Browne, it seemed that not a man in the regiment was willing to obey orders. Collectively, the cavalrymen began "raising the devil generally."

An officer managed to get a message to Gen. Nelson A. Miles who was then in command at Fort Monroe. He ordered the steamer

Durham Station, North Carolina, where the last large body of Confederate soldiers surrendered

Leslie's Illustrated Weekly

to stop at 8:00 A.M. so that men of the regiment could debark. They obeyed this order gayly, "supposing they were to have their own way and not be sent south." Men were drawn up in line about 150 feet from the water and were ordered to ground arms. Though some hesitated, all eventually obeyed. Once they had no weapons, they were sent back aboard their vessel.

Stunned and feeling betrayed, the black soldiers quickly broke into the sutler's stores aboard their vessel and many became roaring drunk. Browne then wrote:

> Just about sunset a big pock-marked mullato got on top of the pilot house near the bows of the ship and was haranguing the crowds on the deck below him when he turned, and, shaking his fist at the group of officers on the quarter deck, he said, "You damned white livered —— of ——, we will throw you overboard, at which a great howl went up from his audience, whereupon three of the officers with their revolvers in their hands forced their way through the crowd and jerked the orator off the pilot house and dragged him back to the quarterdeck where Capt. Whiteman of Xenia, Ohio, put his pistol to his breast and told him to put his thumbs together. We were going to swing him up to the rigging by his two thumbs, but the fellow simply folded his arms and looked at his captors with an air of drunken bravado. Whiteman told him three times to hold up his hands, but he made no motion to obey and Whiteman fired. I was standing at Whiteman's left and was looking the man in the face when the shot was fired, and he did not change a muscle, and I thought Whiteman had missed him, but, looking down to his breast, I saw blood reddening his shirt front, and at once his arms dropped limply at his sides and he fell in a heap at our feet on the deck.

Instead of restoring order, the peremptory execution caused men of the regiment to raise a wild yell and seize whatever weapons they could find—axes, hand spikes and pieces of lumber. Soon they began pouring aft in order to attack their officers.

Sixteen officers lined up across the quarterdeck with their revolvers in their hands but did not fire. After a long pause some of those in the front rank of mutineers dropped back to let others get ahead. Eventually the mass of angry men stopped and all glared at their officers "like wild beasts." One man dropped his axe, then a hand spike hit the deck and "we knew we had conquered."

As soon as men retreated, officers unlashed a 30-pounder Parrot gun that was lashed to the rail. Loaded with canister, it was positioned so that it could sweep the forward deck. Still holding drawn revolvers, officers sent for the band and ordered musicians to play for about an hour. By the time the music stopped, quiet prevailed.

On the following day, their transport sailed to Mobile but this proved simply to be a stopping place. They moved on to Brazos Santiago, Texas and landed there on July 3. After three months in camp, Browne wrote out his resignation. It was approved by his colonel and then by the brigade commander, but both officers told him it would never get past headquarters. Undeterred, the lieutenant went to Brownsville aboard a Rio Grande steamer and reached the headquarters of Gen. Godfrey Wetzel, who gave him his discharge.

In retrospect, Browne said he was involved in hand-to-hand fighting while in the infantry. Combat, he said however, "was a Sunday School picnic compared to the time when a howling, rushing mob of 700 half-drunken devils" rush a tiny band of officers who knew that they "must either conquer or die." Since white officers did conquer despite constituting a tiny minority of the corps, it went on to Texas and formed part of the army of occupation until it was discontinued on January 8, 1866. [Browne, 211–24; DxD, 921, 1041; D, 1, 403; B, 201]

May—Rebel Forces in Louisiana

Col. L. A. Brainier of the 7th Louisiana Cavalry, C.S., somehow managed to keep some of his men in uniform. Responding to an inquiry, Gen. Joseph L. Brent informed him through an aide that in his opinion:

> The fact can no longer be concealed that the whole army and people, with scarcely an individual exception, are resolved to fight no more and to break up the army at all hazards. All is confusion and demoralization here [at headquarters], nothing like order or discipline remains. Heavy desertions and plundering of government property of every kind is the order of the day. . . . in a word, colonel, the army is destroyed and we must look the matter square in the face and shape our actions (personally and officially) accordingly. [OR I, 48, II, 1310]

June—3rd Pennsylvania Cavalry

At Philadelphia during July and August, 1861, one of the regiments that was in process of organization was the 3rd Pennsylvania Cavalry—also known as the 50th Volunteers and Young's Kentucky Light Cavalry. The unit moved to Washington late in August and its members first "saw the elephant," or engaged in combat, at Marauder's Ferry, Virginia, on September 16. Some of its many subsequent engagements and battles included Yorktown, Seven Pines, New Market Road, Savage Station, White Oak Church, Malvern Hill, Antietam, Fredericksburg, Chancellorsville, Brandy Station,

Gettysburg, Culpeper Court House, White Sulphur Springs, New Hope Church, The Wilderness, Spotsylvania, and Petersburg.

Veterans of many battles were transferred into the 5th Pennsylvania Cavalry—also known as the Cameron Dragoons—in May, 1865. As was often the case when units were consolidated, trouble erupted almost as soon as men of the 3rd Cavalry were ordered into the 5th. They immediately began protesting against having to wear the numeral "5" on their caps and created such an uproar that many of them were sent to prison for a time.

After being pardoned and released, the mutineers stubbornly insisted on identifying themselves as members of Young's Kentucky Light Cavalry as a memorial to their service in the Blue Grass State. Back in Philadelphia, the few survivors of the original 3rd Cavalry were discharged on August 15, 1865. [D, 3, 1558-60, CWT, 11/69, 7]

July 3—Miners at Marquette, Michigan

Lt. Cmdr. F. A. Roe of the USS *Michigan* reported on operations of the vessel from the time she was hauled out of winter quarters to September 9. His warship had earlier been saved from possible capture by Rebel raiders under John Y. Beall by the mutiny of Beall's crew. Upon arriving at Marquette, Michigan, on July 3 he came upon a quite different form of mutiny.

Miners had rebelled, he learned from residents who feared that the town would be burned by them. He proceeded to ports where copper ore was loaded on cargo ships in great quantity, and there found that "disaffection" had been manifested among miners who produced it. Learning that "the mutiny had again broken out at Marquette," he returned to that port and found that miners had seized two railroads. Roe put field artillery ashore and prepared to use it against mutineers, but they gave way when they discovered that they would be fighting against sailors with heavy guns.

Though this post-Appomattox disturbance was among civilians, the veteran U.S. naval officer repeatedly labeled it as a mutiny. [NOR I, 3, 590-91]

July 6—2nd Wisconsin

Men of the 2nd Wisconsin remained in uniform long after the last shot of the war was fired. Aboard the steamer *Hillman* they reached Alexandria, Louisiana, on July 6 and came under the command of Gen. George Armstrong Custer. Like men of the XXV Corps whose officers were white but whose enlisted men were black, members of the 2nd thought they might soon be involved in an invasion of Mexico.

Sgt. Leonard Lancaster, described as "a popular officer," agreed to lead a protest whose purpose was to demand a new colonel. The unruly mob was dispersed by members of the guard, and Lancaster was soon arrested and charged with mutiny.

Custer assembled a court-martial and put Lancaster on trial. Soon found guilty, he was condemned to go before a firing squad along with an Indiana private who had deserted and been captured. Custer assembled his entire division to watch the executions and the two condemned men were led out, blindfolded. Both were pushed to their coffins, and the commands of "Ready" and "Aim" were given. Following orders of the general, the sergeant convicted of mutiny was taken aside before the command "Fire!" was given, so only the deserter died that day. [CWT, May/June, 1993, 35–37; Utley, 37]

Gen. George Armstrong Custer pardoned a mutineer when he was sitting on his coffin.
Library of Congress

July 9—11th Kansas Cavalry

Ordered to move out from Camp Collins, men of Company F of the 11th Kansas Cavalry mutinied, saying that their enlistments had expired. They eventually followed orders under compulsion from other troops. Meanwhile, Co. B of the same regiment sent an offer of assistance to the mutineers. Though the mutiny was quelled, several companies of the regiment continued to be "insubordinate and disobedient."

In a July 21 dispatch to Gen. Grenville M. Dodge, Gen. Patrick E. Connor described the regiment as "still mutinous." He then went on record as saying that he could not punish these men because they were scattered, and he could not do without their services.

At Platte Station men in blue were attacked by a body of one thousand warriors on July 25. Twenty-five enlisted men of the 11th Kansas who may have been among the mutineers were killed that day, along with a lieutenant. Dodge informed Gen. John Pope in St. Louis about the massacre, adding that bodies of dead soldiers were "scalped and horribly mutilated." A massacre accomplished what mutiny did not; members of the regiment were mustered out of service on July 26. [OR I, 48, II, 1061, 1067, 1113, 1133; D, 3, 1184]

July—1st Nebraska

Troops under Irish-born Connor were spread out over a vast area and were in a state of rebellion before he took over the District of Utah. By late July he was plagued by demands for discharge by men of the 6th Michigan and 16th Kansas, whom he characterized as showing "much dissatisfaction." They never quite reached open mutiny such as broke out in the 1st Nebraska during July, however. It subsided before the end of the month. Reported from Laramie in the Dakota Territory to Gen. Grenville M. Dodge at Fort Leavenworth, Connor blamed the mutiny on Col. Robert R. Livingston who had been in command at Fort Kearney a few months earlier.

Livingston had been mustered out, Dodge was told. This action presumably quelled the mutiny about the time Connor took command. Organized at Omaha in July, 1861, the regiment was ordered mounted in October, 1863, and it became the 1st Nebraska Cavalry. The latter designation was not, however, universally used. Veterans who had survived four years of combat and a post-war year during which they fought Indians were mustered out on July 1, 1866. [OR I, 48, II, 1122–23; D, 3, 1344–45]

August—Regiments in the Department of the Northwest

U.S. Gen. John Pope, commander of the Army of Virginia, was left out in the cold when his forces were combined with those of the Army of the Potomac in September, 1862. Since he had a commission but no command, he was sent to the Department of the Northwest and charged with putting an end to the great Sioux uprising of 1864.

At St. Louis on August 15, 1865, he was faced with what may have been the last widespread move toward mutiny by men who had volunteered to fight the Rebels. In a dispatch to Gen. W. T. Sherman of the Military Division of the Mississippi, he told the man who conceived and led the March to the Sea that most volunteer regiments within his department were "dissatisfied, not to say insubordinate and mutinous."

This state of seething rebellion in the ranks, Pope said, stemmed from the fact that soldiers believed "their terms of service to have expired with the conclusion of the war." Officers as well as enlisted men were so disaffected that "disintegration of the organized forces in the department" was threatened. Pope therefore registered a vigorous request that he be supplied with five infantry and two cavalry regiments of the U.S. Army or volunteer regiments "enlisted since the conclusion of the war."

Hoping for action in time "to prevent embarrassment and trouble," Pope wanted quickly to get rid of those who were disaffected and win Sherman's support for his request for new regiments. Many if not most volunteers then stationed in the northwest really had become eligible for discharge months earlier. Their mutinous behavior stemmed from realization that they might be forced to remain in uniform for many more months unless they made themselves undesirable. [OR I, 48, II, 1183–84; WWW, 514]

Conclusion

It is widely believed that mutiny was rare among fighting forces in both blue and gray. This erroneous idea rests in part upon the fact that the huge index volume of the *Official Records* (OR) includes only six references to "mutiny," plus a single reference to "mutineers." Only those instances of refusal to obey orders and regulations that led to formal investigations and/or courts-martial whose records have been preserved in whole or in part in the OR are indexed there, however.

Approximately two hundred separate incidents have been treated briefly or in detail here. If they had been spread out equally from start to finish of the conflict, they would have occurred at one-week intervals from Fort Sumter to Durham Station. Large numbers of other incidents that some commanders would have considered mutinous were virtually ignored or quietly settled. If all of these were included, a great many more serious breaches of discipline would be listed.

Smoothed over, quickly quelled, or treated with utmost gravity, mutiny was pervasive from the beginning of the conflict until after its end. It took place among virtually all branches of service, in every geographical region, and among fighting men of numerous national and ethnic backgrounds. Clearly, mutiny was endemic in all fighting forces of the warring regions.

On both sides, many thousands of soldiers who were involved in resistance to authority yielded under duress. Multitudes of these rebels against the system became veterans who didn't forget that they stayed in uniform or under despised officers against their will.

No single mutinous event approached the significance of a minor battle. Collectively, however, they had a profound impact. Tens of thousands of men in blue and in gray fought for months or years, not for cause and country, but to escape quick death or long imprisonment. It goes without saying that these disaffected officers and men, whether openly mutinous or not, did not have their heart in the conflict. Forced into battle against their wills, these multitudes of "disaffected" fighting men had an imponderable but significant impact upon the outcome of many a conflict.

Bibliography

Abel, Christopher A. "Marines Under Fire," CWT, 5/96, 54-61.

America's Civil War (magazine). Cited as ACW.

The Atlanta Century (newspaper), 1861-65.

Arner, Frederick B. *The Mutiny at Brandy Station.* Kensington, Md.: Bates and Blood Press, 1993.

Axelrod, Alan. *War Between the Spies, History of Espionage During the American Civil War.* Atlantic Monthly Press, 1992.

Bailey, Donald H. *The Bloodiest Day.* Alexandria: Time-Life, 1984.

———. *Forward to Richmond.* Alexandria: Time-Life, 1983.

Basler, Roy P., ed. *The Collected Works of Abraham Lincoln.* 8 vols. Brunswick, N.J.: Rutgers University Press, 1953-55. Cited as CW.

Bates, Joshua H. "Ohio's Preparations for the War," MOLLUS, 1, 128-41.

The Battle of Stones River. Yorktown, Va.: Eastern Acorn, 1991.

Battles and Leaders of the Civil War. 4 vols. Secaucus, N.J.: Castle reprint, n.d. Cited as B&L.

Berlin, Ira, et. al., eds. *Freedom: A Documentary History of Emancipation, 1861-67.* Series 2. N.Y.: Cambridge University Press, 1982.

Blue & Gray (magazine). Cited as B&G.

Boatner, Mark M., III. *The Civil War Dictionary, Revised.* N.Y.: Random Vintage, 1991.

Bowers, John. *Stonewall Jackson.* N.Y.: Morrow, 1989.

Bratton, John. "The Sixth South Carolina at Seven Pines," JSHS, 13, 119-33.

Brooks, U. R. *Stories of the Confederacy.* Columbia, S.C.: n.p., 1911.

Brother Against Brother. Alexandria: Time-Life, 1990.

Browne, Frederick W. "My Service in the U.S. Colored Cavalry," MOLLUS, 61, 211-24.

Butts, Frank. "The Monitor and the Merrimac," MOLLUS, 37, 219-67.

295

Castel, Albert. *General Sterling Price.* Baton Rouge: Louisiana State University Press, 1968.

Charleston Courier, April, 1861–May, 1865.

Charleston Mercury, April, 1861–May, 1865.

Childe, Charles B. "General Butler at New Orleans, 1862," MOLLUS, 5, 175–98.

Civil War Times Illustrated (magazine). Cited as CWT.

Cobb, T. R. R. "Extracts from Letters to Mrs. Cobb," JSHS, 28, 280–301.

Commager, Henry Steele, ed. *The Blue and The Gray.* N.Y.: The Fairfax Press, 1950.

Commonwealth (newspaper), February, 1863, Frankfort, Ky.

Confederate Military History. 19 Vols. Reprint, Wilmington, N.C.: Broadfoot Publishing Company, 1988. Cited as CMH.

Confederate Veteran Magazine, 1893-1932. Wilmington, N.C.: Broadfoot Publishing Company, 1990.

Conrad, D. B. "History of the First Battle of Manassas," JSHS, 19, 82–92.

Corser, Elwood S. "A Day With the Confederates," MOLLUS, 29, 364–78.

Cozzens, Peter. *No Better Place to Die.* Urbana: University of Illinois Press, 1990.

Current, Richard N., ed. *Encyclopedia of the Confederacy.* 4 vols. N.Y.: Simon & Schuster, 1993. Cited as EC.

Dabney, Robert Lewis. *Life and Campaigns of Lt. Gen. Thomas J. Jackson.* London, 1864–66, 2 vols. N.Y.: Blalock and Co., 1866; Harrisonburg, Va., 1976.

Davis, William C. *Jefferson Davis: the Man and his Hour.* N.Y.: Harper Collins, 1991.

Denney, Robert E. *Civil War Prisons & Escapes.* New York: Sterling, 1993.

———. *The Civil War Years.* N.Y.: Sterling, 1992. Cited as *Years.*

Duncan, Robert L. *Reluctant General.* N.Y.: Dutton, 1961.

Dyer, Frederick H. *A Compendium of the War of the Rebellion.* 3 vols. Reprint, N.Y.: Yoseloff, 1959.

Eaton, Clement. *Jefferson Davis.* N.Y.: Free Press, 1977.

Eggleston, George C. "Notes on Cold Harbor." *Battles and Leaders* 4, 23–32.

Farwell, Byron. *Stonewall.* N.Y.: Norton, 1992.

Faust, Patricia, ed. *Historical Times Illustrated Encyclopedia of the Civil War.* New York: Harper, 1986. Cited as E.

Foley, Capt. James L. "With Fremont in Missouri," Part 1. MOLLUS, 5, 484–521.

Fox, Gustavus Vasa. *Confidential Correspondence.* 2 vols. New York: De Vinne, 1920.

Freeman, Douglas Southall. *Lee's Lieutenants.* 3 vols. N.Y.: Scribner's, 1942. Cited as Lee's.

———. *Robert E. Lee.* 4 vols. New York: Scribner's, 1934–51. Cited as REL.

Friedrich, Otto. "We Will Not Do Duty Any Longer for Seven Dollars Per Month," *American Heritage,* 2/88, 64–70; *Best of American Heritage.* N.Y.: American Heritage, 1991, 186–205.

Goolrick, William M. *Rebels Resurgent.* Alexandria: Time-Life, 1985.

Grant, U. S. *Personal Memoirs.* 2 vols. Charles L. Webster & Co., 1892.

Greeley, Horace. *The American Conflict.* 3 vols. Hartford: O. D. Case, 1865.

Henderson, G. F. R. *Stonewall Jackson.* Reprint, N.Y.: Da Capo, 1988.

Herbert, Capt. George B. *The Popular History of the Civil War.* N.Y.: F. M. Lupton, 1884. (Issued in numerous editions under at least three titles.)

Hoerner, Harlan H. *Lincoln and Greeley.* Urbana: University of Illinois Press, 1953.

Howe, M. A. DeWolfe. *Home Letters of General Sherman.* N.Y.: Charles Scribner & Sons, 1909.

Jones, John B. *A Rebel War Clerk's Diary;* Earl Schenck Miers, ed. Baton Rouge: Louisiana State University Press, 1993.

Jones, J. William, D.D. "Southern Historical Society Papers." Vols. 1–52. Broadfoot Publishing Company, Morningside Bookshop, 1990.

Josephy, Alvin M., Jr. *War on the Frontier.* Alexandria: Time-Life, 1986.

Leech, Margaret. *Reveille in Washington.* New York: Harper, 1941.

Lincoln Lore (magazine). Cited as LL.

Long, E. B., and Barbara. *The Civil War Day by Day.* N.Y.: Doubleday, 1971. Cited as DxD.

Longstreet, James. *From Manassas to Appomattox.* Reprint, N.Y.: Mallard, 1991.

Lord, Francis A. *They Fought for the Union.* New York: Bonanza, 1940.

Lusk, W. C., ed. *War Letters of William Thompson Lusk.* [Commager, *Blue & Gray*, 487–89]

McClellan, George B. *McClellan's Own Story.* New York: Webster, 1887.

McElroy, Robert. *Jefferson Davis.* New York: Smithmark, 1937.

McHenry, Robert, ed. *Webster's American Military Biographies.* New York: Dover, 1978. Cited as AMB.

Miers, Richard S., ed. *Lincoln Day by Day.* 3 vols. Washington: Sesquicentennial Commission, 1960. Cited as LDD.

Military Order of the Loyal Legion of the United States. 67 vols. Reprint, Wilmington, N.C.: Broadfoot Publishing Company, 1991–98. Cited as MOLLUS.

Miller, Francis Trevelyan, ed.-in-chief. *The Photographic History of the Civil War.* 10 vols. N.Y.: Review of Reviews, 1912.

Moore, Frank, ed. *The Rebellion Record.* 10 vols. Reprint, N.Y.: Arno, 1977. Cited as RR.

Neely, Mark E., Jr. *The Abraham Lincoln Encyclopedia.* N.Y.: McGraw-Hill, 1982. Cited as ALE.

———. *The Fate of Liberty.* N.Y.: Oxford, 1991.

Nevin, David. *The Road to Shiloh.* Alexandria: Time-Life, 1983.

Nevins, Allan. *The War for the Union.* 4 vols. N.Y.: Scribner's, 1959–71.

Nicolay, John G., and John Hay. *Abraham Lincoln.* 10 vols. New York: Century, 1886.

Official Records of the Union and Confederate Navies in the War of the Rebellion. 30 vols. Washington, D.C.: U.S. Govt. Printing Office, 1892–1930. Cited as NOR.

O'Flaherty, Daniel. *General Jo Shelby.* Chapel Hill: University of North Carolina Press, 1954.

Priest, John Michael. *Before Antietam.* Shippensburg, Pa.: White Mane, 1992.

Proceedings, General Court-martial, Sgt. William Walker, 3rd South Carolina Regiment. National Archives, Record Group 153.

Robertson, James I. *Soldiers Blue and Gray.* Columbia: University of South Carolina Press, 1988.

———. *Stonewall Jackson.* N.Y.: Macmillan, 1997.

Sears, Stephen W. *George B. McClellan.* New York: Ticknor & Fields, 1988.

Sifakis, Stewart. *Who Was Who in the Civil War.* N.Y.: Facts on File, 1988. Cited as WWW.

Smith, William F. "The Eighteenth Corps at Cold Harbor." *Battles & Leaders* 4, 221-30.

Stevens, Hazard. *The Life of Isaac Ingalls Stevens.* 2 vols. Boston: Houghton Mifflin, 1900.

Todd, William. *The Seventy-ninth Highlanders.* Albany, N.Y.: n.p., 1886.

Tucker, Glenn. *Chickamauga, Bloody Battle in the West.* Indianapolis, Indiana: Bobbs-Merrill, 1961.

Utley, Robert M. *Cavalier in Buckskin.* Norman: University of Oklahoma Press, 1986.

Virginia Cavalcade (magazine), 1969-76.

War of the Rebellion: Official Records of the Union and Confederate Armies. 128 vols. Reprint, Harrisburg: National Historical Society, 1971. Abbreviated as OR; cited by serial numbers.

Warner, Ezra J. *Generals in Blue.* Baton Rouge: Louisiana State University Press, 1964. Cited as GB.

———. *Generals in Gray.* Baton Rouge: Louisiana State University Press, 1959. Cited as GG.

Welles, Gideon. *Diary;* Howard K. Beale, ed. 3 vols. N.Y.: Norton, 1960.

Woodruff, Thomas M. "Early War Days in the Nation's Capital," MOLLUS, 28, 87-105.

Index

Page numbers in *italics* refer to the illustrations.

304   Index

Hagerstown, Md., 38, 155
Hagood, Gen. Johnson, 112, 115
Halleck, Gen. Henry W., 6, 19, 20, 37,
    79, 86, 133, 149, 151, 172, 194,
    200, 212, 221, 225, 227
Hallowell, Col. Edward N., 258, 259
Hamilton, Gen. Charles S., 220
Hampton Roads, Va., 96, 218, 262, 287
Hancock, Gen. Winfield S., 132, 133
Hanover Court House, 159
Hardee, Gen. William, 114, 117, 118, 122
Hardeman, William D., 251
Harding, Col. Chester, 277
Harper's Ferry, Va., 26, 38, 144, 151,
    160, 192, 195, 197, 289
Harriet Lane, USS, 47, 102
Harrisburg, Pa., 37, 38, 39, 88, 100,
    184, 235, 255
Harrison's Landing, Va., 32
Hartford, Conn., 155, 156
Hartford, USS, 47
Hartwell, Col. A. S., 258
Hatteras Inlet, N.C., 32, 184
Hawkins, Col. C., 32, 184, 186, 229
Hawkins, Maj. Henry P., 229
Hawkin's Zouaves, 32
Hebert, Gen. Louis, 251
Henderson, Capt. H. A. M., 281
Henderson, Ky., 37
Herrick, Lt. Col. Thomas P., 219
Herron, Francis J., 80
Higgins, Capt. Edward, 51
Higginson, Col. Thomas Wentworth, 10,
    11
Highlander Regiment, 66, 73
Hildeburn, Samuel, 64
Hill, Gen. A. P., 209
Hill, Gen. Daniel H., 124, 198
Hiller, Lt. Col. Hiram M., 107
Hilton Head, S.C., 3, 4, 6, 7, 9, 10, 226,
    227, 233, 235, 286
Hindman, Gen. Thomas C., 207
Hoffman, Asst. Adj. Gen. Southard, 215
Holt, Joseph, 20, 109, 110
Hood, Gen. John B., 127, 146, 147, 215,
    229, 270
Hooker Brigade, 252, 253, 254
Hooker, Gen. Joseph, 84, 87, 90, 149,
    151, 152, 231, 252
Houston, Tex., 98, 105, 129, 130, 236
Howorth, Master's Mate W. L., 251
Huger, Gen. Benjamin, 198, 200
Huiskamp, Lt. Herman J., 106, 107
Humphreys, Gen. Andrew, 135
Hunter, Gen. David, 17, 19, 226, 227, 257
Hurlbut, Gen. Stephen A., 220, 221

Hurley, William C., 103
Hussar, USS, 212

I

Illinois Military Units
    4th Cavalry, 219
    10th Regiment, 56
    15th, 284
    16th Cavalry, 281
    21st, 179, 180
    87th Regiment, 225
Imboden, Gen. John D., 281
Infield Scott, USS, 235
Iowa Military Units
    1st Cavalry, 265
Ireland, Capt. David, 73
Isaac Smith, USS, 204
Isondiga, CSS, 263, 264
Itasca, USS, 49
Iverson, Col. Alfred, 215
Ivy, CSS, 224

J

Jackman, Pvt. John, 210
Jackson, Thomas J. (Stonewall), 10, 45,
    46, 48, 49, 50, 51, 52, 53, 60, 75,
    76, 78, 79, 80, 81, 83, 143, 144,
    146, 160, 161, 162, 165, 181, 195,
    200, 202, 209, 210, 214, 224, 226,
    229, 243
Jackson, USS, 248
Johnson, Lt. Amos, 238
Johnston, Gen. Joseph E., 114, 122,
    144, 145, 146, 160, 161, 209, 232,
    233, 261, 286
Jones, Ensign J. E., 251
Jones, Capt. O. G., 98
Jones, Gen. Samuel, 112, 117
Jones, Gen. William E., 86, 87

K

Kampmann, Maj. J. H., 98
Kanawha, USS, 80, 192
Kansas Military Units
    6th Cavalry, 219, 280, 281
    7th Cavalry, 219, 220
    9th Militia, 275
    11th Cavalry, 291
    16th Cavalry, 280, 281
Kansas-Nebraska Bill, 115
Kapp, Friedrich, 91
Kauffman, Capt. Albert B., 250
Kaufmann, Sigismund, 91
Kearny, Gen. Stephen W., 15
Kelly, Gen. J. H., 114, 251, 252, 262, 263